W9-CBE-821

Essential Publishing, Inc.
378 Northlake Boulevard, Suite 109
North Palm Beach, FL 33408
www.essentialpublishing.org
(866) 770-1916

Copyright © 2013 Gary Null, Ph.D.

ISBN 978-0-9771309-6-2

Library of Congress Control Number: 2012955555

DISCLAIMER: The nutritional and health information provided in this book is intended for educational purposes only. Nothing listed or mentioned in this book should be considered as medical advice or a substitute for medical advice for dealing with stress or any other medical problem. Consult your health-care professional for individual guidance on specific health issues and before following this or any program. Persons with serious medical conditions should seek professional care. The author and publisher specifically disclaim any liability, loss or risk, personal or otherwise, which is incurred as a consequence, directly or indirectly, of the use and application of the contents of this book.

coolingtheplanet.org

PRINTED IN THE U.S.A.

This publication was printed by a Certified Green Printer in the United States of America, providing jobs for American workers. It was also printed, with the health of the environment in mind, on recycled paper and with vegetable-based inks, and Gary Null and Associates is planting more trees than were required to print this publication through *Cooling the Planet.*

For
Jim and Norma

I chose to dedicate this book to Jim Joseph and Norma Lamb, two of the listeners of my daily internet radio show *The Gary Null Show* on www.prn.fm. Jim and Norma, like hundreds of thousands of my listeners around the world, are the reason why my staff and I work tirelessly, day and night, researching and conveying the best possible information from around the world. Every single day, people around the world use information that we and the guests that we interview provide to improve and enhance their overall experience of living.

Jim and Norma truly exemplify the benefits of *learning* how to live healthfully, and the rewards of helping others do the same. Jim is a successful author, activist, health advocate, and award-winning artist. As a retired combat marine, he has dedicated his life to promoting peace and to helping fellow humans on their journey to health and community participation. Norma, a former Manhattan architect and expediter, now leads weekly dance programs and is an authority in her community on raw and living foods, social issues and local politics. Jim started listening to my radio program in 1977; he also attended many of my seminars, and had been part of my running group in NYC. When I learned of Jim's success in applying the information that he had gleaned from years of listening to *The Gary Null Show* to help his wife Norma heal from cancer, I decided to have them on my show and asked them to appear in some of our videos.

Over 20 years ago, when Norma was diagnosed with an aggressive breast cancer that had metastasized to the lymph nodes, her oncologist recommended a double mastectomy and the removal of two lymph nodes. Even though they were facing extraordinary stress, and under the threat of a surgeon's knife, their cool heads prevailed. They chose, instead, to follow protocols they had heard on my radio program; they also sought out the care of a remarkable doctor I had interviewed several times on my radio program – Emanuel Revici, M.D. Both Jim and Norma followed the protocols precisely – Norma while maintaining her high-pressure job of expediting the building of skyscrapers in NYC – and just three months later she was in complete remission. When Norma showed the results of that test to the oncologist who had just 90 days earlier recommended the invasive, expensive (and extremely painful) surgeries and radiation and chemotherapy treatments, he balked. Not only did he refuse to call Dr. Revici, he dismissed the results as incredible and impractical – an all too common (and unfortunate) response by our modern medical establishment to which I've spoken endlessly about throughout my career.

Ten years later, Norma broke her ankle doing cart wheels at the beach. She was in her 50's at the time, and surgeons, again, recommended invasive surgery; they wanted to insert pins and plates to mend the break. Instead, Jim and Norma insisted that the orthopedics at the hospital simply reset her ankle bone. While stunned by their request, the surgeon complied. After several months of magnet therapy, which they learned about from listening to our radio program, and extensive nutritional therapy, the bone healed. She, once again, made a speedy recovery while avoiding surgery, costly drugs, physical therapy, and the possibility of a lifetime of pain and disability in her ankle.

Since then, Jim and Norma continue to listen to our show on www.prn.fm. They lead a healthy, vital life and are major contributors to their community, enjoying a wonderful, expansive group of friends and fellow contributors. I share Jim and Norma's story with you because they inspire hope for humankind and trust in the reality that a long and vibrant life is not only possible, but probable when following the dietary guidelines outlined in this book. It is with deep gratitude that I thank them for their dedication over the years, and invite you to join us on this essential and fulfilling experience of creating health.

–Gary

This book is dedicated to empowering you to achieve your goal of optimal wellness.

We begin to end our pain and suffering through the realization that we are a miracle; each of us; body, mind and spirit... a miracle worth fighting for. Your deep appreciation of this fact will have you committed, without reservation, to quenching painful inflammation; the flames of arthritis, as well as other debilitating illnesses so that you may fully experience and celebrate your aliveness and well being.

Publisher's Preface

"Education is not the filling of a pail, but the lighting of a fire."
– William Butler Yeats

I am one of the lucky ones, having had the good fortune of being introduced to my vocation at the young age of 13. I recall working on my first magazine into the wee hours of the night with a team of passionate writers, editors, proofreaders and graphic artists. The publication was *Ais Eiri (resurrection) Magazine* – the first magazine of Irish America, published by *An Claidheamh Soluis* The Irish Arts Center. I suppose it was destiny that years later I wound up working full time at *The Chelsea Clinton News* while studying literature at NYU, and that only a few short years after, became a publisher myself – first of magazines, then of books. To me, books are a way of traveling to another reality; they are a glimpse into the world of our fellow humans, and an offering of something (information, insight, motivation, comfort, and even adventure) that stirs the mind and soul to grander explorations and new possibilities. This book and its companion *Reverse Arthritis Naturally: A Proven Approach to a Pain-free Life* by Dr. Gary Null accomplishes just this.

While each book tells a unique story in its own right, and every story is common to the basic challenges that we face as humans, our goal as publishers is to make it easy for you to enjoy it. So, it is the process of *creating* a work of art in form and function, beauty and simplicity that inspires me, and my staff, to the end. It is our sincere hope that you find this here, and more. As you flip through these pages, you will be treating yourself to the delectable world of vegan vegetarian cuisine. Feast your eyes upon it, and then your body by embracing and utilizing the vital information and delicious healing recipes within. Then, you will begin to realize the health and vitality that is your birthright.

I was first introduced to Gary Null in 1988 through James Menzel Joseph, my good friend and co-founder of the 53rd and 54th street block association in Hell's Kitchen New York. (You can find an example of Jim's inspirational painting at the beginning of this book along with a dedication from Gary to Jim and his wife Norma). Jim had already been listening to Gary's daily radio program for 11 years when we met. I remember that day as if it were just yesterday. We were sitting at the Money Tree Diner on the corner of 52nd street and 10th avenue, and I was speaking to Jim about some health issues that I was experiencing. Jim suggested that my diet might have something to do with it. I thought he was crazy...after all, in that very moment I was eating something from each of the four basic groups defined in the food pyramid that we learned about in elementary school. I was consuming a cheeseburger (meat), a chocolate milk shake (dairy), a hamburger bun (for my grain), plus vegetables – French fried potatoes, and the lettuce, onion and tomato that came with the burger! Boy was I in for a wake-up call. It was then that Jim suggested I tune into *The Gary Null Show* internet radio program, and I've been listening since my 20's. Now, 25 years later, I'm serving as the publisher for his books.

As I reflect on the last 25 years, I observe how the human species, defined as a group having the mental capability of abstract reasoning, language, introspection, problem solving and culture through social learning, has somehow diminished these capabilities and strayed far from what is real and true. We have become victims of our own unfounded, untested beliefs, and not just in the area of health and medicine. We have evolved to fight – and to be in continuous conflict with – nature rather than accept its realities, and this is affecting our health in terrible ways. Millions of us in America (and in other Western civilizations) are suffering with chronic diseases, but few have laid down the proverbial sword (synthetic manmade solutions such as pharmaceutical drugs and surgeries, for example) to entertain the logical, harmonious, less invasive approaches that Dr. Null has been recommending for decades.

Because of this, you will never find me too far from people like Gary Null, Ph.D. whose actions are dedicated to elevating human consciousness and founded in a genuine concern for and connection to our Earth and all that is *authentically* natural. Gary's specialty, of course, is inspiration – inspiring others through example, walking his talk. His contributions, quite frankly, are seemingly endless. From numerous award-winning documentaries, dozens of yet to be bested world records in foot races around the globe, and well over 80 books published to date, there are few who have directly impacted the health of others as he has. Not only has he personally raised tens of millions of dollars for public radio and television throughout our nation ($27 million for one not-for-profit commercial-free radio station in New York City alone), he also founded www.prn.fm, which is the top internet radio station (in terms of the number of listeners) out of more than 43,000 internet radio stations on the world wide web.

Gary also contributes to our economy in many other ways including employing dozens of people in his NYC office, health food stores, and nutritional supplement company. He is also in the process of launching his new natural health, vegan-vegetarian retreat center and spa, opening in the spring of this year (2013) and featuring the dishes you will see on these pages. Gary Null is a true testament to the potential of the human spirit. His work has touched millions of people, helping them improve their health and their life dramatically, and in numerous cases, people have saved their own lives after taking and applying his well-founded advice. As the popular phrase goes… *Knowing and not doing is the same as not knowing.* We rejoice in knowing that many of you, like Dr. Null's listeners, are of the "doing" kind. Both of these books, as well as Gary's numerous other offerings – including his internet radio show and those of his 80 other hosts on 24-hour, 7-day a week www.prn.fm – provide you with important knowledge on health, economics, politics and spirituality for practical everyday solutions to the challenges each of us faces.

It seems that in our modern world, we have convinced ourselves that if something is simple it cannot be effective. This could not be farther from the truth. In fact – and to our danger – it is because simplicity is eluding us that we are struggling to find well-being in this ever-increasingly complex and chaotic world that we've built. But we can choose differently. As you page through this book, breathe in the splendor that these photographs represent, and allow the beauty of these natural foods to touch your heart – enough that you want nothing more than to begin now to make inner beauty, balance, and nature the foundation of your world.

I remain hopeful that Dr. Null's messages, and the truth that they offer, resonate as deeply in you as they do in me and so many others today, and encouraged that the lifestyle he and other leaders in the natural health industry have proven to be so effective in preventing and eradicating disease becomes the cornerstone of a beautiful relationship between you, food and life for all of your time on this magnificent planet.

May it be a relationship like that described by the Irish poet and author Thomas Moore – *"A friendship that like love is warm; A love like friendship, steady."* I encourage you to allow the important information in this recipe book and its companion book to influence you and steady your course to optimal health and well-being.

Morgéan Ó Conghalaigh
Publisher

About Gary Null

Time magazine called him "The New Mr. Natural." *My Generation* magazine dubbed him one of the top health gurus in the United States. Through his bestselling books, documentaries, and daily radio show, Gary Null, Ph.D. has been one of the foremost voices of the health movement for over 35 years. An internationally renowned expert in the field of health and nutrition, Gary Null is a *New York Times* bestselling author, producing over 70 books on healthy living, and the director of over 100 critically acclaimed full-feature documentary films on natural health, self-empowerment and the environment. For more than 35 years, Gary has had a weekly program on Pacifica radio stations KPFK and WPFW, and New York City's WBAI; he also had his own very popular weekly program on WABC as well as ABC national radio. Currently, he is the host of *The Gary Null Show,* the country's longest running nationally syndicated health radio talk show, heard daily on The *Progressive Radio Network* (www.prn.fm).

Throughout his career, Dr. Null has continued to be a strong voice for the consumer, standing up against big pharmaceutical corporations, exposing the massive drugging of children in our schools, the medicinal abuse of seniors, and the unnecessary use and overuse of X-Rays. In addition, he has conducted original investigative reports on numerous topics including the suppression of complimentary medical therapies in the U.S. He has also challenged proponents of the Western medical system and others about the diseases produced by an unhealthy diet. In this regard, he has publicly debated spokespersons for the meat, dairy, and sugar industries.

Gary's entire adult life has been spent fighting for a better way for all of us to live. He has made hundreds of radio and television broadcasts throughout the country as an environmentalist, consumer advocate, investigative reporter and nutrition educator. His material has been used by *20/20* and *60 Minutes,* and more than 28 different Gary Null television specials have appeared on PBS stations throughout the nation, inspiring and motivating millions of viewers. Gary Null has channeled his passion for natural health and his extensive knowledge of nutrition to create a truly exceptional line of health products that have helped thousands of people experience optimum health, naturally. *See more at www.GaryNull.com.*

Acknowledgments

I would like to thank a number of individuals who contributed greatly to this project and without whom it would have been impossible. First, our two chefs: Wesley Wobles and William Shear. Wesley is an innovative and accomplished chef whose artistic presentation and unique vision provided a perfect interpretation of my recipes. William, a chef with amazingly diverse worldwide experience, used his natural creativity and passion for excellence to bring my recipes to life. Our expert photographer, Kristin Hess, was able to capture the beauty and healthy essence of these spectacular dishes with great finesse, and her superb use of lighting and style is to be commended. In addition to editing the recipes, Nancy Ashley was a critical element of every aspect of this project, including the directing and coordination of the preparation and photography of every dish. All worked long hours, nights, and weekends, to allow this beautiful cookbook to take shape. Two very talented artists, Mia Rognstad and Melissa Goldman, spent many days working with me on perfecting the recipes and dish presentations. Both were essential to the initial creative process.

Special thanks, also, to Essential Publishing who did an incredible job of creating a gorgeous, tantalizing work of art from these recipes and photographs. This great team, led by insightful publisher, Morgėan Ó Conghalaigh, his talented managing editor, Lynn Komlenic, and their graphics team of Jeri Monastero and Stephanie Haas poured their hearts and souls into this project, assisting me in turning my vision into a reality. They have allowed me to bring you my knowledge of how to eliminate arthritis and inflammation with delicious health-building gourmet vegan dishes in an easy-to-understand and thoroughly delightful presentation. The tools to heal yourself naturally are now at your fingertips in this aesthetically inspiring volume.

And, finally, to James Menzel-Joseph whose superb artistic contribution and the inspiration offered on the aptly named *Riding the Breeze* painting— serve as a beautiful example of the creativity and aliveness that is available when we are truly healthy and well. I am grateful not only for the art Menzel has contributed in this book but also for the art he has shared with me throughout our years of working together, and that is proudly displayed in my home, my office in New York City and throughout "The Villa," my newly opened natural health resort in Texas. As an artist, author, philosopher, activist, and longtime vegan vegetarian, Menzel-Joseph is the embodiment of what is possible when embracing this lifestyle fully.

Foreword

Diet Prevents and Cures Inflammatory Diseases

Dr. Gary Null's exciting new book *Anti-arthritis, Anti-inflammation Cookbook* is an important offering that comes to us at a critical time in our human history. As I have written extensively in my own publications, we as a nation are facing unprecedented, widespread disease that is, quite frankly, shocking for our relative affluence and accomplishment compared to other nations around the globe.

The positive news is that there are *proven* solutions available to anyone not wishing to suffer from inflammatory diseases like arthritis any longer. After starting a low fat, vegan diet as recommended in the *Anti-arthritis, Anti-inflammatory Cookbook* by Dr. Gary Null, relief from arthritis pain and other signs and symptoms of inflammation typically begins as early as four to seven days. Within four months, maximum healing occurs and most patients can claim cure with this cost- and side-effect free approach. I know this to be true; first, because I have successfully treated *over 5,000 patients* at my residential clinic in Northern California applying similar principles and food choice recommendations. Second, because extensive scientific research published in leading medical journals over the past half-century confirms the benefits of a healthy diet free from animal products, including dairy, as well as vegetable oils.

Inflammatory diseases, including many forms of arthritis, are classified medically as *autoimmune diseases.* These are conditions that happen when the body's tissues are attacked by its own immune system. The name for the specific disease that results is based upon the organ or system most affected. For example, inflammatory bowel diseases, like ulcerative colitis and Crohn's disease, are the result of an out of control immune system attacking the bowels. Multiple sclerosis is from assaults on the brain and spinal column. Understanding why the body appears to turn on itself leads to prevention and effective dietary treatments.

COMMON AUTOIMMUNE DISEASES	
Ankylosing spondylitis	Polymyositis
Crohn's disease	Psoriasis
Dermatomyositis	Psoriatic arthritis
Diabetes (type 1)	Rheumatoid arthritis
Glomerulonephritis (kidney)	Scleroderma
Lupus	Thyroiditis (resulting in hypothyroidism)
Multiple sclerosis	Ulcerative colitis
Myasthenia Gravis	Uveitis
Nonspecific inflammatory arthritis	Vitiligo
Pernicious anemia	

The mechanisms by which an unhealthy diet causes autoimmune diseases are complex and involve both our intestine and immune system. When functioning properly, a single layer of cells lining the intestine forms an effective barrier separating the intestinal contents from the interior of the body. In this manner, enormous amounts of foreign proteins from dietary and microbial origin are kept out of the body. The integrity of this barrier can be compromised by an unhealthy diet plentiful in meat, dairy products, and some vegetable-derived oils, by viral infections, and by chemicals, including medications like NSAIDs. In addition, approximately 1% of people suffer gut wall damage from high-gluten foods, like wheat, barley, and rye (this condition called Celiac disease), and I applaud Dr. Null's attention to gluten-free options throughout this volume. The end result of all this bowel injury, for the majority, is what is commonly known as a "leaky gut."

Large food and bacterial proteins from the intestinal contents can now leach into the bloodstream. Confronted with these "foreign" proteins, the immune system makes antibodies against these invaders. As far as the immune system is concerned, protein from a cow deserves the same serious life-saving response, as would protein from an infecting virus. Most people are able to remove the leaked proteins, regardless of origin, from their blood stream with only subtle consequences, some joint stiffness, headaches, and body aches.

For unknown reasons, the immune systems of people with serious autoimmune diseases become confused about which proteins are the real enemies. The antibodies synthesized in response to foreign food proteins are not directed solely to the invaders, but also cross-react with similar looking proteins found in the body's own tissues. (This process is known as molecular mimicry.) Antibodies looking for cow's milk on their journey are known to find and attack the insulin-producing cells of the pancreas and type-1 diabetes follows. Antibodies seeking out pork passed through a leaky gut find the cells of the kidneys, causing life-threatening inflammation (glomerulonephritis).

The correct diet to prevent and treat these autoimmune diseases was discovered first by observing populations of people who eat differently. People following grain and vegetable based diets were found to be free of these diseases; those eating meat, dairy products and common vegetable oils were sick. It is well documented that the autoimmune conditions listed were once rare to nonexistent in rural populations of Asia and Africa. This is primarily because of their rice, sweet potato, corn, millet, and/or bean based, near vegan diets. For example, as recently as 1957, no case of rheumatoid arthritis could be found in Africa. However, with a change in their diet these same racial groups become ill. Although unknown in Africa before 1960, African-Americans lead in the incidence of lupus in the US, when they exchange barley and beans for butter and bacon.

Treatment of arthritis and other autoimmune diseases with diet became fashionable in the 1920s. Positive results led to rigorous scientific studies performed over the past half century which have consistently shown that a low-fat vegan diet, the antithesis of the American Diet, will stop described and demonstrated in this book, will stop the body from attacking itself and cure autoimmune diseases.

I have seen it time and again, which is why I am a great supporter of Dr. Null's work; and here's the great news for you—the benefits begin as soon as you stop eating "foreign" animal proteins and toxic vegetable oils, and replace them with grains, vegetables, and fruits. Complete healing of a "leaky gut" may take as long as four months, at which time full benefits are usually appreciated. In the case of arthritis, this means a reduction in or elimination of joint pain, and increased mobility. Even though new attacks stop, it is important to realize that the previously done damage can be permanent.

This is why I suggest that the sooner one learns about, and more to the point, implements the lessons in Dr. Null's *Anti-arthritis, Anti-inflammatory Cookbook*, the more likely he or she will be in reversing their pain and suffering and preventing future harm. This applies not only for yourself, but potentially others in your circle of influence who may be dealing with the discomfort of arthritis and other diseases of inflammation. I recommend this book wholeheartedly to anyone desiring a healthier, more enjoyable, pain-free life.

John McDougall, MD
Board-certified Internist
National bestselling author
Founder of the McDougall Program
www.drmcdougall.com

Table of Contents

Introduction 1

An Inflammation Nation 4

    The Diseases of Inflammation 5

    Lifestyle Diseases 6

    Are You at Risk for Arthritis and

        other Diseases of Inflammation? 8

Creating a Thriving, Healthy Lifestyle 16

The Anti-Arthritis, Anti-Inflammation Diet 21

    Carbohydrates 21

    Proteins 22

    Fats 24

    Fiber 26

    Antioxidants 26

    Phytonutrients 27

Top Anti-arthritis, Anti-inflammation Supplements 29

Anti-arthritis, Anti-inflammation Herbs and Spices 33

Foods to Avoid 35

    High-Acid Foods 35

    Processed and Artificial Foods 35

Foods to Include 36

    Beans and Legumes 36

    Nuts and Seeds 36

    Whole Grains 36

    Fruits 36

    Food High in Omega-3 Fatty Acids 36

    Antioxidant Rich Foods 37

    Sea Vegetables 37

    Foods Rich in Folic Acid 37

    Vegetables 37

More Healing Foods 39

Oils to Avoid/Oils to Include 40

Nightshade Vegetables – Avoid or Include? 41

The Benefits of Eating More Raw Foods 42

15 Great Anti-inflammatory Snack Ideas 42

Table of Contents

Introduction (cont.)

The Importance of Organics 43

The Benefits of Juicing 44

1, 2 & 3-Day Diet Cleanses for Arthritis, Pain

and Inflammation Flare-ups 46

The Anti-arthritis, Anti-inflammation Pantry 47

Pantry Basics & Specialty Items 47

The Anti-arthritis, Anti-inflammation Refrigerator 48

Equipment for the Vegetarian Lifestyle 49

Substitutions and Variations 52

Suggestions for Meal Planning &

Transitioning to the Vegetarian Lifestyle 53

How to Use This Book 55

The Start of a Healing Journey 59

Breakfast 61

Amaranth Peach Delight 62

Apple Cinnamon French Toast with Bananas and Raspberries 63

Banana Coconut Buckwheat Cereal 64

Blueberry Apricot Oatmeal 65

Blueberry Oatmeal with Soy Yogurt 67

Cinnamon Pear Pancakes 68

Coconut Nut Rice 69

Crunchy Granola 70

Fluffy Raisin Couscous 72

Hawaiian Rice Cereal 73

Nutty Fruit Breakfast 74

Quinoa Breakfast Delight 75

Quinoa Pancakes 77

Raspberry Blueberry Oatmeal 78

Seven Grain Cereal with Peaches and Walnuts 79

Strawberry Blueberry Sunshine 80

Sweet Cinnamon Oatmeal 83

Triple Fruit Oatmeal 84

Two Grain Oatmeal 85

Table of Contents

Appetizers, Side Dishes, Sauces & Dips 87

Barley with Collard Greens and Leeks 89

Bavarian Cabbage 90

Black Bean Sauce 91

Caponata 92

Creamy Tofu Dip 93

Date Spread 94

Exotic Tofu Dip 95

Ginger Black Bean Dip 96

Greek Tomato Sauce 97

Green Plantain Tostones with Garlic Mojo Sauce 99

Guilt-Free Guacamole 100

Heavenly Stuffed Tomatoes 103

Herbed Tofu Croquettes 104

Holiday Stuffed Mushrooms 107

Potato Pancakes 108

Spicy Hummus 109

Spicy Peanut Sauce 110

Spicy Tomato Salsa 111

Sweet Nutty Spread 112

Tahini-Broccoli Cream Dip 112

Tahini Oat Sauce 112

Unfried Zucchini Fritters 113

Vegetarian Chopped Liver 114

Soups 117

Algerian Chili 119

Cashewy Bean Soup 120

Chinese Cabbage Soup 121

Cream of Broccoli Soup 123

Cream of Mushroom Soup 124

Cream of Sweet Potato Soup 126

Cucumber Mint Soup 127

Curried Lentil Soup 128

Delectable Tomato Squash Soup 129

Table of Contents

Soups (cont.)

Favorite Vegetable Soup 130

Gary's Noodle Soup 133

Gazpacho 134

Hearty Winter Soup 135

Hot Spinach and Bean Soup 136

Italian Style Pinto Bean Soup 137

Italian White Bean Soup with Bowtie Pasta 139

Jamaican Pepperpot Soup 140

Jamaican Squash Soup 143

Lemon Tree Soup 144

Mango Squash Soup 145

Miso Tofu Soup 146

New Fangled Old Timey Soup 147

Old Country Potato Soup 148

Onion Soup 149

Papaya Yam Soup 150

Penne Pasta and Kidney Bean Soup 151

Portuguese Kale and Potato Soup 152

Potato Leek Soup 153

Potato Mustard Soup 154

Potato Tomato Soup 157

Pumpkin Cream Soup 158

RAW Cajun Squash Soup 159

RAW Delectable Tomato Squash Soup 160

Sabzi Ka Shorba 161

Savory Cream of Potato Soup 162

Spicy RAW Spinach and Avocado Soup 164

Thick and Hearty Borscht 165

Turnip and Black Bean Soup 167

Venice Noodle Soup 168

Zucchini Soup 169

Table of Contents

Salads 171

    Aduki Bean Salad 172

    Apple, Walnut, and Tofu Salad 173

    Artichoke and Chickpea Salad 175

    Arugula Orange Pepper Salad 176

    Beet Salad 178

    Bitters Sweet 179

    California Marinade 181

    Chopped Veggie Bean Salad 182

    Cold German Leek Salad 183

    Cool Garden Noodles 185

    Eggplant Salad 187

    Enticing Endive with Berries and Seeds 188

    Endive Salad 190

    Fennel and Pecan Salad with Peaches 191

    Forbidden Rice Salad 192

    French Watercress Salad 195

    Fresh Corn Salad 196

    Golden Broccoli Supreme 197

    Grecian Olive and Rice Salad 198

    Indonesian Sprout Salad 199

    Insalata Siciliana 200

    Italian Mushroom and Potato Salad 203

    Japanese Buckwheat Salad 204

    Mellow Rice Salad 205

    Mykonos Bean Salad 206

    Navy Salad 207

    Nice Rice Salad 208

    Quinoa and Edamame Salad 209

    Raisin and Brown Rice Salad 210

    Red Salad 213

    Sassy Bean and Quinoa Salad 214

    Seaweed Salad 215

    Sesame Bean Salad 217

Table of Contents

Salads, cont.

Spicy Bulgur Salad 218

Superior Spinach Salad 219

Steamy Summer Salad 220

Tahini Potato Salad 223

Thai Style Salad 224

Thyme for Salad! 226

Walnut and Black Bean Salad 227

Warm Potato and Dulse Salad 227

Entrees 229

Angel Hair Pasta with Mushrooms and Peas 230

Aromatic Green Casserole 231

Bammie Cakes 233

Broccoli and Cauliflower with Shiitake Mushrooms ... 234

Broccoli au Gratin 237

Broccoli Tortellini Salad 238

Brown Rice with Peppers and Herbs 240

Brussels Sprout Creole 241

Butternut Squash with Toasted Sesame Sauce 242

Butternut Tofu 245

Cajun Tofu 247

Carrot Kidney Bean Loaf with Mushroom Gravy 248

Cauliflower with Garlic Hummus Sauce 250

Chickpea and Zucchini Curry 253

Coconut Chickpea Burgers 254

Crunchy Herbed Green Beans 255

Curried Barley with Avocado 256

Curried Potato Masal 259

Dalsaag 260

Divine Potato Casserole 261

Eggless Zucchini Pesto Quiche 262

Eggplant Parmesan Sesame 264

Eggplant Wraps with Roasted Red Pepper Tomato Sauce ... 266

Fettuccine with Creamy Asparagus Sauce 269

Table of Contents

Entrees, cont.

Galuska 271

Gary's Fat Free Sweet Potato and Chickpea Stew 272

Gary's Favorite Casserole 275

Goulash 276

Green Pea and Millet Couscous 277

Hawaiian Tempeh Kebabs 278

Hot and Spicy Bean Wraps 279

Indian Ratatouille 280

Indonesian Kale 282

Jamaican Vegetable Root Stew 283

Khaloda Algerian Eggplant 284

Lemon Tofu 287

Lentil Burgers 289

Linguini with Garden Vegetables 290

Millet Coriander Stir-Fry 291

Mushroom Bean Curry with Butternut Squash 292

Mushroom-Stuffed Tomatoes 295

Noodles Deluxe 296

Okra Curry 297

Peppery Pasta Salad 299

Purple Cabbage and Spaghetti Squash Stir-Fry 300

Red Brazilian Rice 303

Rice and Lentils 304

Risotto with Tomatoes and Peas 305

Saffron Rice 306

Sautéed Dandelion Greens with Corn and Red Peppers 308

Sautéed Kale with Fava Beans 309

Shiitake-Stuffed Eggplants 310

Sicilian Green Beans 311

Sliced Tofu with Garlic Sauce 313

Spaghetti Squash Italiano 314

Spaghetti with Eggplant Marinara 315

Spaghetti with Garlic Tomato Vegetable Sauce 316

Table of Contents

Entrees, cont.

Spring Scalloped Vegetables 318

Sweet and Sour Bean Stew 319

Sweet and Sour Tempeh 320

Sweet Cabbage and Apple Casserole 321

Sweet Loaf 323

Swiss Chard with Red Lentils and Carrots 324

Tempeh and Green Bean Ragout 325

Tempeh Marinara with Rice Penne 326

Tempeh with Cacciatore Sauce 329

Tempeh with Noodles and Vegetables 330

Tofu Orleans 333

Tomato Chutney with Quinoa Flatbread 334

Vegan Chili Deluxe 336

Vegetarian Lasagna 337

Yukon Mashed Potatoes with Mushroom Gravy 339

Desserts 341

Angelica Rice Lady Fingers 343

Anise Raisin Bread 344

Apple Banana Turnovers 347

Banana Caramel Custard 348

Bananas Flambé 351

Cantaloupe with Cherry Cream 352

Chilled Cherry Dessert Soup 353

Chocolate Pudding 354

Coconut Cherry Ice Cream 355

Coconut Custard Pie 356

Golden Strawberry Blueberry Crumble 357

Holiday Gingerbread 359

Lemon Cherry Cake 360

Orange Glazed Apples 362

Peach Walnut Crisp 363

Pear Hazelnut Crisp 365

Pears with Raisin Stuffing 366

Table of Contents

Desserts, cont.

Pecan-Maple Chia Custard 367

Plantain Dessert Tamale 368

Poached Peaches with Raspberry Sauce 371

Pretty Parfait 372

Raspberry Custard 374

RAW Banana and Pineapple Dessert Soup 375

RAW Blueberry Jello 376

RAW Cinnamon Papaya Pudding 377

RAW Strawberry Dessert Soup 378

Simple Carob Cake 379

Southern-Baked Pumpkin Surprise 380

Stewed Plums 381

Sticky Sweet Rice with Papaya 382

Sweet Cassava Pudding 383

Sweet Potato Pie 384

Toasted Nut Brittle 385

Truly Trifle 386

Vegan Apple Cake 388

Resources 390

Conversion Table & Lists 396

Index 399

Introduction

More than ever, Americans are becoming aware of the profound connection that exists between the foods we eat and our health. Thankfully, a growing number of consumers are demanding that their food be produced organically without the use of genetic engineering or chemical pesticides. Many are choosing to take charge of their health by turning away from conventional treatments and pharmaceuticals and embracing the old adage of "let thy food be thy medicine."

As individuals become increasingly mindful of their dietary choices, I'm frequently asked by them to share some of my favorite recipes for health. For years, I've worked with some of America's finest chefs to create an outstanding collection of delicious and wholesome vegan recipes. My goal in writing the *Anti-arthritis, Anti-inflammation Cookbook* is to share with you the very best creations from my kitchen, which will not only dazzle your taste buds, but also enhance your health in powerful ways. From comforting savory soups and inventive salads to mouth-watering entrees and decadent yet guilt-free desserts, the recipes in this book will surely cause family and friends to tell you that "health food never tasted so good." This cookbook is a wonderful guide for anyone looking to transition from the unhealthy staples that define the Standard American Diet (S.A.D.) to foods that truly satisfy and energize the body. It's also a fantastic resource for longtime vegetarians and vegans who are seeking creative and appetizing new recipes to add to their repertoire.

Accompanying our recipes are over 300 beautiful photographs to show you that natural healing foods have a certain place in the world of aesthetics and artistic presentation. In order to maximize nutritional benefit and accommodate individuals with food sensitivities, all of the recipes included in this book are dairy-free while a high percentage are raw (uncooked) and gluten-free. Although these original recipes were developed by gourmet chefs, each of them has been tested to make sure that anyone – even those without professional training – can prepare these meals at home.

Before you begin cooking your way to optimum health, it is important that we examine the connection between diet and good health. Here we will discover what inflammation is, where it comes from and how it affects our well-being. We also speak about one of the most notable of all diseases of inflammation, *arthritis.* Because arthritis is a multi-factorial disease, I have written the companion book *Reverse Arthritis and Pain Naturally: A proven approach to an anti-inflammatory, pain-free life* to explore the many causes of arthritis and to present a protocol for prevention and healing that includes the wonderful foods you will find in this book. As we'll see, choosing to follow an anti-inflammatory diet may well be one of the most important decisions you could ever make.

An Inflammation Nation

Today, in America, we are confronted with alarmingly high rates of chronic disease. Millions of people across the country struggle each day with degenerative ailments including diabetes, cancer, heart disease, Alzheimer's disease, lupus and arthritis. Although the symptoms associated with these illnesses can vary greatly, all of these conditions share one root cause: *inflammation.*

Inflammation is a naturally occurring process of the immune system that protects us against infection, wounds, and other trauma. Under normal conditions, any time that your cells are damaged the body immediately creates a pro-inflammatory response, which, in turn, signals the body's healing mechanisms to repair the damage. For example, when you get a cut on your hand, your blood vessels swell (pro-inflammatory response) allowing healing to occur through clotting and the creation of new tissue below a scab.

Certain triggers, however, may cause the inflammatory process to become chronic or excessive, resulting in serious damage to the body including, in the case of arthritis, the breakdown of joints and tissues and its associated pains and disabilities. The scientific literature demonstrates that such ongoing inflammation leads to a wide range of degenerative diseases.

Chronic inflammation is directly linked to our dietary choices, as well as other critical lifestyle factors. Given the high incidence of chronic disease in this country, it's no surprise that the Standard American Diet consists mostly of pro-inflammatory foods. The worst offenders are highly processed foods such as refined carbohydrates, sugars, salts and unhealthy fats. These foods, which are low in nutrients and high in calories, *make up nearly two-thirds of what we consume.* Meat, seafood, eggs and dairy products, which promote inflammation and lack life-sustaining ingredients such as fiber, antioxidants and phytonutrients, account for another quarter of the Standard American Diet. Our overconsumption of these pro-inflammatory foods is not only a major factor in the development of many illnesses, including diabetes, heart disease and arthritis, but is also a key contributor to the weakening and suppression of our immune system, and to unhealthy weight gain and obesity.

The Diseases of Inflammation

While inflammation is a key factor in all diseases, the most well-known disease of inflammation is arthritis. There are three primary types of arthritis: Rheumatoid arthritis, osteoarthritis and gout; in actuality, however, the family of arthritis includes more than 100 conditions that affect the joints, causing stiffness, pain, and restriction of movement. In the U.S. alone, arthritis currently affects an astonishing 50 million adults, and is the leading cause of disability. While many groups in the U.S. (including the current medical community) believe and promote arthritis as a natural part of aging, the fact is that we are not all destined to become arthritic with advancing age. In truth, most of us can reverse and even avoid arthritis and other diseases of inflammation by embracing a healthy lifestyle that includes an anti-inflammatory diet.

Lifestyle Diseases

The term "lifestyle disease" refers to diseases related to how a person, or group of people, lives. In large part, the chronic diseases that plague us today are predominantly lifestyle related, and therefore avoidable. Even when a genetic predisposition is present, in most cases a person can prevent or overcome that disease with the proper lifestyle choices. Factors such as the quality of our food, air and water, the quality of our sleep, our environmental conditions, and our support networks, as well as our ability to handle stress all determine our level of health. As you can see, lifestyle diseases like arthritis are "multi-factorial," and therefore require a multi-faceted, integrative approach for prevention and healing. While there are many things in life that we cannot control, we can regulate most of what we put into our bodies and allow into our experience. Good health, then, begins with an understanding of what our body, mind and spirit require daily – and on an on-going basis – to become and remain healthy. Then, as we take actions that are in alignment with what we learn and come to know through honest inquiry, we become engaged in the activity of creating health as a way of living – and our lives will reflect this.

Are You at Risk for Arthritis and other Diseases of Inflammation?

There are many risk factors for chronic inflammation and, hence, diseases of inflammation like arthritis; the primary factor is the Standard American Diet, which this book addresses directly through the offering of more than 270 delicious anti-inflammation recipes. Changing how and what we eat is possibly the most important and immediate way we can effect a change in our health. The companion for this cookbook, titled *Reverse Arthritis & Pain Naturally* offers a complete protocol for reversing and preventing arthritis and other diseases of inflammation. In it, you can read first-hand testimonials from people currently afflicted with arthritis who benefited directly from this protocol simply through changing eating and exercise habits, and in only three weeks!

When reading through this list of factors, however, consider that it is not only the number of risks that may be affecting you, but the *degree* to which you are affected by these risks that determines your overall exposure and therefore chance of developing chronic disease. If you are experiencing any of these risks and are determined to resolve them, I encourage you to get the support that you need from qualified professionals. Experts can be extremely helpful for addressing issues adequately and completely on your journey of health and well-being.

Straight Talk from Gary

Since we know that inflammation is at the root of all chronic disease, it follows that if you aspire to be free from disease then you will be actively cultivating an anti-inflammatory lifestyle, which includes – among other things – shifting from the Standard American Diet to an alkalinizing vegan vegetarian diet. What you may not comprehend are all the forces that are working against your health in our present society. As I discuss in *Reverse Arthritis & Pain Naturally: A proven approach to an anti-inflammatory, pain-free life*, our current medical treatment paradigm, which includes the powerful influence of pharmaceutical concerns, is deeply wedded to symptomatology, and, therefore, treatment protocols focused on managing *symptoms* rather than addressing the *root causes* of disease as in the case of integrative medicine. This is especially egregious when it comes to the handling of lifestyle diseases like arthritis, because these modern-day treatment protocols – largely pharmaceutical- and surgical-based – are not, on the whole, able to reverse or even stop the progression of the condition. On the contrary, and in most cases, they are causing only further inflammation and tissue degeneration. Moreover, we cannot rely on the Federal Drug Administration (FDA) – the branch of the government tasked with protecting the American public from harmful substances – to oversee the drug industry with any kind of vigor. The relationship between the two groups has become so incestuous that the pharmaceutical industry now regards the FDA as a client rather than a strong and potent regulating body. Sadly, it is the American people who are paying the price. But you can change this! Arm yourself with the correct information on how to create health, such as what I'm presenting in the next section, and take positive actions daily. This is all you need to do to create your new and healthy way of living.

1 The Standard American Diet (S.A.D.) – The S.A.D., which is at the heart of our fast-food nation, is perhaps the leading cause of inflammation today in Western cultures; it is also a *direct* cause of diabetes and obesity. This high calorie, high refined-carbohydrate diet full of chemicals, sugars, salts and unhealthy fats is not only low in nutritional value but is an unequivocal source of chronic inflammation. Meat, seafood, eggs and dairy products are all foods that promote inflammation, and must be eliminated – or severely curtailed – in order to reduce inflammation and one's risk for all diseases, including arthritis.

2 Overweight Conditions Including Obesity – While overweight and obese conditions are indeed a *result* of consuming the unhealthy foods of the Standard American Diet, they are also an added and on-going cause of inflammation in the body, and therefore a *cause of all* disease. Make no mistake about it; you are substantially increasing your risk of developing chronic diseases if you are overweight or obese. Shifting to a vegan, or predominantly vegetarian, diet is *essential* for minimizing inflammation and disease, maintaining proper weight, and ensuring healthful longevity.

3 Smoking – Studies abound of the deleterious effects of smoking on one's body; in fact, scientific data is now linking smoking with the progression of arthritis. Smoking is not only aggravating to the delicate tissues of our lungs and breathing passageways and our heart, it also results in extensive free-radical damage, which is directly linked to inflammation and tissue degeneration. Releasing this habit is essential for an anti-inflammatory lifestyle, and for creating health.

4 Alcohol & Recreational Drug Use – Alcohol is highly acid forming, and therefore, not at all recommended if you suffer from any chronic disease whatsoever, including arthritis. Recreational drugs, especially synthetic, are the same; they create inflammation throughout the system by way of the immune response. Both should be avoided in the anti-inflammation lifestyle.

5 Pharmaceutical Drug & Over-the-Counter (OTC) Drug Consumption – While arthritis and other pharmaceutical medications including OTC drugs such as non-steroidal anti-inflammatory drugs (NSAIDs), may appear helpful initially, in the long term they are damaging to the tissues and to overall health. See my book *Reverse Arthritis & Pain Naturally* for research related to the ineffectiveness of pharmaceuticals in preventing and eradicating inflammatory conditions.

6 Allergies & Food Sensitivities – Allergies (both airborne and food related) create an immune (and therefore inflammatory) response in the body through the secretion of histamines. Because many of our key crops have experienced genetic manipulation over the years, a greater number of people have developed sensitivities to foods such as wheat, corn and soy. Additionally, most people have some degree of lactose intolerance because we as humans to do not possess the full set of enzymes for digesting dairy products sufficiently. If you suffer from chronic allergies or any of these food sensitivities, then you are experiencing ongoing inflammation in the body. To minimize inflammation due to allergies, it is recommended that you adopt a vegan diet while securing the appropriate testing to help you determine which foods – and other triggers – to eliminate.

7 Chemical Toxicity – Because we often cannot see the pollutants in our air, our water, or in our foods, we underestimate their negative effect on our overall health. The truth is that our planet has become increasingly polluted through the actions of humans in relationship to our highly industrialized, chemical-infiltrated lives. From heavy metals – such as mercury in our dental carries and lead in our water, paints, pottery, costume jewelry and children's play toys – to toxins such as PCBs from plastics, and PAHs from petroleum products, chemicals have infiltrated every one of us, increasing our risk of disease. If you consume non-organic foods, you are ingesting higher amounts of pesticides, herbicides and fungicides than if you were consuming organic foods. The same goes for cosmetics, skin-care products, other health and beauty aids, and cleaning products. (See more in "Why Organic?" in this book.) Furthermore, exposure to molds and radiation, as well as Electromagnetic Frequencies (EMFs) creates an inflammation response in the body, and we have all seen the reports of the deleterious effects of prolonged and chronic exposure to these and other pollutants. If you suspect that you are suffering from heavy metal or other chemical toxicity, have a sample of your tissue tested by a reputable source to determine if additional detoxification actions are required.

8 Illness & Disease – If you suffer from chronic, regular acute illnesses, such as colds, flu, and other maladies, it is a sure sign that your body's immune system is compromised, and is experiencing higher levels of inflammation. The lifestyle changes outlined in my anti-arthritis, anti-inflammation book *Reverse Arthritis & Pain Naturally* – including the shift to a predominantly vegan diet – will not only boost and strengthen your immune system, they will minimize the damaging effects of ongoing inflammation.

9

Stress – As science has now proven, stress is a major contributor to disease. The physiological response of stress, which includes the secretion of adrenaline and cortisol, is a natural and important part of our body's ability to react and respond to life-threatening dangers. While this response is important and helpful, it is not without side-effects. When stress becomes chronic, through our continuous process of perceiving situations and events in our lives as life-threatening when they are not, it affects nearly every system in your body, and is potentially lethal. In order to minimize the inflammatory effects of stress and to lead a healthy life, it is critical to adopt lifestyle habits that support a calming of mind – and its fear-based responses – through practices like yoga, meditation, tai chi, chi gong and others. See the next section for more insights on the importance of mind/body practices for healthful living.

10

Improper Body Mechanics & Physiological Stress – This issue is of particular importance to those suffering from or concerned about preventing arthritis, as joint and spine weaknesses tend to follow muscle weakness, which naturally occurs when body misalignment issues aren't properly addressed. Whether from birth, as in the case of a shorter limb and some cases of scoliosis; by accident, as in broken bones; or repetitive overuse, as in the case of laborers and professional athletes, structural misaligment predisposes people to the tissue degeneration innate to arthritic conditions. Additionally, when our bodies are subjected to repetitive physical movements over time – as simple as carrying a heavy bag on one shoulder or crossing our legs, extra pressure is placed on the joints, and chronic inflammation from rubbing and tearing of tissues occurs. If you recognize that you have structural challenges and wish to avoid arthritis, it is important to convert to the anti-inflammatory diet that we are presenting in this book, and seek the support of professionals who can assist you in either correcting the imbalances, or minimizing their effects.

Creating a Thriving,
Healthy Lifestyle

There are several key aspects to a thriving and healthy lifestyle. I have spent my life sharing these concepts with health-seekers from across the globe. Trust me when I tell you this: you can have the healthy life that you want. It is simply a matter of shifting your focus, and getting started. This recipe book, along with these suggestions will get you oriented in the right direction. So let's get going!

1 **Think positively and focus on what you want.** The first step in creating a healthy, long life is deciding now to focus on health as *your way of living* – as opposed to it being some thing that you think about or do only when you're sick, ill or overweight. In addition to the items listed below, a positive mental framework anchored in health, rather than *disease or fear of disease*, is essential. Let me illustrate. Many say that "dieting," for example, does not work, and in fact this is proven to be true for the majority of the population. Why is this? When we think about dieting, we think of lack, deprivation, and scarcity, which is highly unappealing and very uncomfortable to us pleasure-seeking humans. Our inherent drive to avoid pain then makes it extremely difficult to follow through with something that we associate so much pain with – like dieting. So we set ourselves up for failure simply because of how we perceive the situation. If you really want to enjoy a healthy weight level, do everything you can to imagine how you will feel, and all the wonderful things that will occur when you are living your healthy life. This will keep you committed and moving in the right direction.

2 Adopt a vegan vegetarian diet. While we have spoken about this throughout the book already, it bears repeating. Studies show that the cultures that consume a predominantly plant-based diet live longer, healthier lives, and are less prone to developing lifestyle diseases. The vegan vegetarian diet will not only strengthen your immune system, it will: assist you in dropping excess weight and in maintaining a healthy weight; aid in improving your sleep; reduce pain in your joints while increasing joint mobility if you are already affected by arthritis; and elevate your energy and mood.

3 Consume fresh vegetable and fruit juices. Fresh juices are a powerhouse of nutrition, providing important vitamins, minerals, antioxidants and phytonutrients that assist in nourishing the body's tissues while reducing inflammation. They can also be powerful detoxifiers that can help the body release toxic residue.

4 Drink purified water, and lots of it! With the number of chemicals and toxins in our water supply today, it is essential to drink purified water. Our bodies are approximately 80% water, which is why it is essential to stay well hydrated with water that is NOT adding to our toxic load. Regular hydration helps to lubricate the muscles around and tissues of the joints so that movement becomes easier for those affected by arthritis.

5

Exercise regularly. It is very unlikely that I need to mention the value of regular, consistent exercise; however, I will for the reason that one of the biggest problems related to the advancement of arthritis – osteoarthritis in particular – *is lack of movement and exercise!* This may come as a surprise, especially because we are conditioned by today's medical community that the joint degeneration of arthritis is caused by overuse of the joints. This couldn't be farther from the truth. We need to move our bodies to keep them healthy. If you are suffering from symptoms of arthritis now and want to regain strength and mobility, see trained professionals to determine how you can start moving your muscles and joints safely again. It will help you immensely in your healing process.

6

Get enough high-quality sleep. Not enough can be said about the benefits of high-quality sleep, as it is during sleep that our bodies go about the business of repairing and restoring function. Unfortunately, few of us get the amount of sleep (on average eight hours) that is necessary for keeping lifestyle diseases at bay. There is an old adage in Chinese medicine that every hour of sleep before midnight is like two after, and, in general, our circadian rhythms are more in alignment with earlier than later sleep times. So if you want a healthier life, get to bed earlier and get your eight hours.

7

Become a master at handling stress. As I mentioned before, stress is one of the main causes of disease. Much of the stress that we deal with on a daily basis is related to the fears, either real or imagined, that we have about life. Mindfulness practices including yoga, meditation, Tai chi, Chi gong, guided relaxation, and other techniques are incredibly helpful for minimizing stress and therefore reducing the damaging effects of a frequently engaged stress response.

8 Minimize exposure to environmental toxins. In addition to drinking purified water, consuming organic foods, using organic personal care and household products whenever possible, and replacing silver dental carries (which contain mercury) with composite fillings, there are numerous other things that you can do to both avoid taking in more toxins, but to also significantly decrease your personal use of products and services that contribute to our already toxic landscape. By focusing on creating a healthier environment without, you are also creating within.

9 Learn about natural health therapies, and include them as a part of your health program. Natural health therapies can aid in the prevention & alleviation of inflammation and pain, as well as disease. Acupuncture, physical therapy, chiropractic treatment and massage all aid in improving circulation and body function. The added benefit is that they help to decrease stress and promote a sense of well-being.

10 Create a health support network. Transitioning to a healthy, vegetarian-based lifestyle takes some effort, but support from health-oriented family and friends can be extremely beneficial. Ask for specific help when you need it, including from experts. Nutritional coaches, physical trainers, naturopathic physicians, and other trustworthy health care providers are invaluable assets on this journey. Consider starting or joining a support group for healthy eating and living, and stay informed: read books, go to lectures, talk to others who are learning about health, and find reputable resources online. All of this will help you be successful in your quest for healthy living.

The Anti-arthritis, Anti-Inflammation Diet

When we choose to consume a plant-based diet rich in unprocessed fruits, vegetables, beans, legumes and whole grains, we can fight the onset and progression of arthritis and inflammatory diseases and greatly increase our health and vitality. Let's take a closer look at the building blocks of the foods we eat and what role they play in our health.

Carbohydrates

Carbohydrates come in two forms: complex and refined, or simple. While all carbohydrates supply energy, only complex carbohydrates supply fiber, phytonutrients and the vitamins and minerals that are necessary for health. Eating this type of carbohydrate also helps control inflammation levels in the body. Examples of complex carbohydrates include: fruits, vegetables, whole-grain brown rice, quinoa and organic whole-wheat flour as well as sorghum and the amaranth grain. Complex carbohydrates are broken down slowly by the body and therefore have a minimal effect on blood sugar. Maintaining a normal blood sugar level is key to avoiding all sorts of ailments (particularly diabetes), and living a healthful life. Complex carbohydrates should account for approximately 65% of your daily caloric intake.

Simple carbohydrates on the other hand do not contain vital nutrients and are broken down quickly by the body, leading to spikes in blood sugar and fluctuation of energy levels. The regular consumption of simple carbohydrates is a huge factor in the development of inflammatory disease. Examples of refined or simple carbohydrates are conventional flour, white rice, sugar and high fructose corn syrup. Unfortunately, many of the foods that fill the shelves of America's grocery stores are made up in part or entirely of these sources of carbohydrates.

Proteins

When many of us think of protein we immediately imagine animal proteins –
a steak, a pork chop, a grilled chicken cutlet, or a tall glass of milk, but are
these the only sources of protein? More importantly, are they the best sources
of protein? The answer in one word is "No." Protein is made up of amino
acids, which are the building blocks of life. Amino acids fall into two distinct
categories and understanding the difference is important. Nonessential
amino acids are ones that the body can produce on its own from other
nutrients that are present in our diet. Essential amino acids – of which
there are eight – are nutrients that need to be present in our food in order
for our bodies to manufacture a whole protein molecule. Without them we
would starve. Meat, dairy, fish, eggs, nuts, seeds, legumes, fruits, grains and
vegetables all contain a variety of the eight essential amino acids and some
are considered complete proteins. All protein sources are not created equal,
however. Protein from animal sources is difficult for humans to digest, since
we do not possess within our bodies the full array of enzymes required for
this task. Undigested food particles, therefore, tend to accumulate in our
intestinal tract and in our blood stream, wreaking havoc on our system
by way of ailments such as irritable bowel syndrome (IBS), diverticulosis,
atherosclerosis, and heart disease.

To get all eight essential amino acids from a vegetarian diet, it is best to
combine food from many different sources. Vegetarian sources of protein such
as nuts, seeds, legumes, fruits, grains and vegetables are much easier to digest,
making them a far better source of protein for the human body. Furthermore,
most vegetarian sources of protein have significantly better "bioavailability,"
meaning the body recognizes and utilizes these protein sources more rapidly
and efficiently, and with limited metabolic stress and waste. This is further
evident in those who consume a large portion of raw and living sources of
protein such as sprouted legumes, nuts and seeds, and micro-greens.

Since protein is not stored in our body and is constantly being replaced, it is important to get all eight essential amino acids into your diet throughout the day. Protein is present in the cells of our body and performs many different functions, from maintaining healthy hair, skin and nails to allowing muscles to repair and grow from exercise and everyday stresses. A good method of calculating the right amount of protein for you is by taking 9/10 of a gram of protein per kilogram of body weight a day. For most of us, this equates to between 40 and 60 grams of protein (around 12-20% of one's diet), but extenuating circumstances such as pregnancy, high fever, and engaging in consistent rigorous exercise can increase the amount needed.

More importantly, do not be fooled by myths and marketing agendas perpetuated by proponents of high protein diets that they are healthy. High protein diets cause numerous maladies and can lead to serious health conditions, including heart and kidney disease. You can read more about this in my book titled *Reverse Arthritis and Pain Naturally.* What is most important for you to know about protein is to consume a wide variety of the highest quality sources available, which are all vegetarian.

Fats

Americans get an enormous amount of calories by consuming fats, and unfortunately they are the harmful kinds. Like carbohydrates and proteins, fats come in different forms and some are better than others. Fats have a strong connection to inflammation as well as heart health and cholesterol levels. Fats also help improve skin quality and protect our organs and blood vessels, all while providing a vital source of energy.

The so-called "bad" fats are saturated fats and hydrogenated or trans-fats. These pro-inflammatory fats come from animal and dairy sources such as meats, cheese and butter, as well as coconut and palm oil. One way to identify a saturated fat is to bring it to room temperature: if it's solid, limit your consumption. The one exception to the above is coconut oil, which is rich in MCT's (medium chain triglycerides) and has a positive impact on the heart, and in overall health.

Healthier fats are the unsaturated fats, which fall into two categories: monounsaturated and polyunsaturated. Polyunsaturated fats supply what are called Essential Fatty Acids (EFA's), including omega-6 and omega-3. Like the essential amino acids, essential fatty acids cannot be manufactured by the body, so they must be obtained through the diet. Omega-6 fatty acids can be found in corn, soy and sunflower (or safflower) oil. Leading sources of omega-3 fatty acids are fish, walnuts, flax seeds, chia seeds and hemp seeds, as well as their oils. The importance of polyunsaturated fats and the EFA's they contain cannot be overstated. Many different body systems including cellular and hormonal function are affected by the presence of polyunsaturated fats. Additionally, omega-3 fatty acids are known to possess strong anti-inflammatory properties. Since omega-6 is much more prevalent in the American diet, a good rule of thumb is to reduce omega-6 consumption while increasing the sources of omega-3. A healthy ratio of omega-6 to omega-3 is around 3:1 (hemp oil has a natural 3:1 ratio). Monounsaturated fats help promote healthy cholesterol levels and decrease inflammation. It is important to incorporate foods that are high in monounsaturated fats into your diet. Great sources include nuts, seeds, olive oil and avocados.

Try to limit the heat applied to the fats you use, as this destroys the EFA's and makes the oils much harder for the stomach to digest. To be safe, you should limit your fat intake to about 10-15% of total caloric consumption per day. Of this, only about 20% should be from saturated fat (or about 5% of total calories per day); for a person on a 2000Kcal/day diet that's only 100 calories!

Fiber

Fiber is a critically important facet of our diets. Dietary fiber comes almost exclusively from complex carbohydrate sources with none being found in meats or cheeses. Fiber comes in two different forms: soluble and insoluble. Soluble fiber readily absorbs water. This helps aid in digestion and also fills you up so you're hungry less often. Insoluble fiber does not absorb water but is also important in your diet because it helps with elimination and the removal of toxins from the colon. Many studies link a high fiber diet with reduced inflammation. Excellent sources of fiber include: lettuce, spinach, beans and legumes, lentils, vegetables, fruits and grains. In addition, tubers and root vegetables such as yams and rutabagas offer great sources of fiber. Not all fibers are the same, however, so it is important to include a variety from different sources for maximum benefit.

Antioxidants

Found in abundance in fruits and vegetables, antioxidants are essential to fighting inflammatory disease. Antioxidants work to neutralize free radicals, or potentially harmful molecules that have become unstable after losing one of their orbiting electrons. In an attempt to restore balance, free radicals steal electrons from other molecules, causing damage to the body that frequently leads to inflammation. By scavenging free radicals, antioxidants help boost the immune system and protect against inflammatory conditions. Free radicals are a result of the body's normal metabolic processes, but increase with the ingestion of animal products, cooked fats (including oils), processed foods, alcohol, cigarettes, and radiation, as well as chemical pollutants found in water, air and food. Given the pervasive environmental contaminants many of us are exposed to on a daily basis, it is critically important to consume antioxidant-rich foods such as fruits, berries, vegetables, herbs and spices. Examples of antioxidants are vitamin C, vitamin E, beta-carotene, zinc and selenium.

Phytonutrients

Modern research has discovered a huge group of beneficial compounds in plants known as phytonutrients or phytochemicals. Phytonutrients are chemicals produced by plants to help them withstand the damaging effects of ultraviolet light, freezing, drought, parasites and other dangers. A single fruit or vegetable may contain up to several hundred phytochemicals, many of which have been proven to promote health.

Phytonutrients express themselves as rainbow colors, and we get the most benefit from eating a variety of these pigments. For example, studies have shown that lycopene, the red phytochemical found in tomatoes, beets, and watermelon contributes to heart health; and indoles, found in broccoli, kale, Brussels sprouts and other cruciferous vegetables, possess anti-cancer properties. Many phytonutrients such as curcumin in turmeric and anthocyanins in tart cherries have been shown to exhibit powerful anti-inflammatory properties.

Top Anti-arthritis, Anti-inflammation Supplements

*Note: please refer to my book **Reverse Arthritis & Pain Naturally** for further instructions on proper dosages, and scientific references.*

Antioxidant Vitamins – Supplementation with antioxidant vitamins directly targets the inflammation and free radical damage that leads to chronic diseases such as arthritis. As a general rule, antioxidant vitamins are extremely helpful in creating health, and are recommended for everyone regardless of current medical conditions. For arthritis, vitamin C is essential for maintaining and repairing bones and cartilage, and its beneficial effects are amplified when it is taken with glucosamine. Additionally, vitamin E and vitamin A or beta-carotene daily may help to prevent and reduce arthritic pain.

Bromelain – Bromelain is an enzyme derived from pineapple, which studies have found to ameliorate pain and improve physical mobility in arthritis sufferers.

Chondroitin Sulfate – This substance works to hold cartilage together at a molecular level, allowing collagen proteins to form tissue. It stimulates repair and helps to limit damage from arthritis.

Decursinol – Belonging to the class of chemical compounds known as coumarins, this pain-relieving supplement is derived from a type of root native to Asia. Studies have observed that decursinol protects against oxidative stress and reduces pain and inflammation.

Gamma Linolenic Acid (GLA) – GLA is high in prostaglandins that turn off inflammation and reduce pain. This compound is found in borage, evening primrose and black currant oils.

Glucosamine – Glucosamine is a primary nutrient for repairing joint cartilage and tissue damage. Since glucosamine is naturally manufactured by each cell in the body, it is a perfectly safe supplement.

Grape Seed Extract – Grape seed extract contains pycnogenol, an antioxidant known to strengthen collagen. Other inflammation-fighting antioxidants found in grape seed extract are proanthocyanidins, which research suggests benefit arthritis sufferers.

Hyaluronic Acid (HA) – Hyaluronic Acid is a naturally occurring substance found in abundance in joint tissues, and acts as an important mediator of inflammation and proper tissue formation.

Methylsulfonylmethane (MSM) – After water and sodium, MSM – a natural sulfur – is one of the most significant components in the body. Taking MSM daily helps suppress inflammation.

Minerals – Minerals play an essential role in joint health. Since the Standard American Diet does not contain adequate quantities of these nutrients, it is no surprise that arthritis and other inflammatory conditions are so pervasive. Adequate supply and absorption of calcium, phosphorus, boron and magnesium are essential for the formation of healthy bones, while zinc and selenium are important for the immune system. Other vital minerals are potassium, copper and manganese.

Niacinamide – This form of vitamin B3 helps both osteoarthritis and rheumatoid arthritis. Effects are not immediate, but result in a gradual reduction of symptoms and improved range of motion over time. Niacinamide should not to be confused with niacin.

Omega-3 Fatty Acids – The regular intake of these anti-inflammatory fats is important for everyone. Good sources of omega-3s include fish oil, walnut oil, krill oil and flaxseed oil, as well as chia seeds, salmon and sardines. Research has established the ability of these fats to relieve pain from arthritis.

Probiotics – Probiotics refers to the beneficial intestinal bacteria that play a key role in digestion and immunity, and in safeguarding health. Excellent food sources of probiotics are sauerkraut, kimchi, miso, and sour pickles.

Quercetin – Quercetin is a naturally occurring flavonoid found in various foods such as apples, onions and tea. Studies have observed this compound to exhibit immune-boosting, antioxidant activity.

S-Adenosylmethionine (SAMe) – This is an activated form of methionine that seems to restore white blood cell activity in joint fluid by reversing glutathione depletion. SAMe also serves to protect and rebuild cartilage.

Superoxide Dismutase (SOD) – This enzyme should be taken with water on an empty stomach, about a half hour before meals. Supplementation with SOD suppresses pain and inflammation, and the benefits are compounded when it is taken with vitamin E.

Vitamin B Complex – A vitamin B complex contains B1, B2, B5 and B6. These vitamins regulate the nervous system health and enhance the utilization of other nutrients. They also play a key role in the activities of enzymes – proteins that are responsible for the chemical reactions in the body.

Vitamin K – Research implicates this vitamin as a potent anti-inflammatory that helps in the prevention and treatment of arthritis.

Anti-arthritis, Anti-inflammation Herbs and Spices

If you are struggling with pain and inflammation, there are a number of herbs and spices that can be incorporated into your regimen to support your anti-inflammatory health program. Refer to my book *Reverse Arthritis & Pain Naturally* for specific recommendations on dosages and usage, and scientific attributions.

Aloe Vera – Aloe Vera is a strong detoxifier of the intestines, and the juice helps to cleanse the body of toxins that can cause inflammation and arthritis.

Boswellia – The healing properties of the boswellia herb have been recorded in Ayurvedic medical literature for thousands of years. Boswellia works similar to nonsteroidal anti-inflammatory compounds but without the toxic side effects.

Cat's Claw – A plant native to the Amazon, cat's claw stands out as an anti-inflammation, anti-arthritis superstar. Studies document the power of this herb to aid healing in patients suffering from osteoarthritis.

Cayenne – Capsaicin, the active component of cayenne peppers, alleviates arthritis pain and inflammation when applied topically. Research has shown capsaicin cream helps to manage the pain related to both rheumatoid arthritis and osteoarthritis.

Comfrey – Research shows the success of comfrey in reducing pain and improving mobility in patients suffering from arthritis and pain.

Devil's Claw – A shrub native to southern Africa, devil's claw has been used for centuries as a natural pain-relieving remedy. Today, a wealth of scientific evidence demonstrates the amazing anti-arthritis and analgesic properties of devil's claw.

Ginseng – A popular root utilized in Traditional Chinese Medicine, ginseng is increasingly seen in Western medicine as a viable complementary treatment for arthritis and other conditions. In addition to acting as an anti-inflammatory, Siberian ginseng has been observed to stimulate the immune system and combat cancer.

Nettles – Nettle leaves display notable arthritis-fighting properties in individuals with osteoarthritis; the leaves can also be crushed and made into a poultice to decrease rheumatic pain. Stinging nettle extract has also been shown to inhibit pro-inflammatory factors associated with rheumatoid arthritis.

Turmeric – The powerful health-boosting properties of turmeric, and its main constituent, curcumin, have been the focus of recent scientific research. Studies conclude that curcumin is an outstanding natural anti-inflammatory that reduces joint pain and stiffness and increases mobility.

White Willow Bark – Sometimes referred to as "nature's aspirin," white willow bark exerts powerful analgesic effects in people suffering from joint pain.

Foods to Avoid on the Anti-arthritis, Anti-inflammation health program

Foods to Avoid – High Acid and Processed Foods

The Standard American Diet includes an excess of acid-forming foods such as meat, dairy, refined sugar and flour. Consuming these foods causes the blood pH levels to drop below its ideal range of 7.2 —7.4, and results in an overly acidic state. To compensate for the acid environment, vital alkaline minerals such as calcium and magnesium are leeched from bones and deposited into the bloodstream in a process that weakens bones and joints and promotes arthritis. Research shows a strong connection between an acid pH and poor bone health. Furthermore, lower than normal pH levels suppress the immune system and contribute to the development of many other chronic illnesses.

High-Acid Foods

Refined sugar
(basically all conventionally prepared baked goods)

Refined flour

Dairy
(milk, egg & cheese products)

Meats of all kind
especially ham, bacon and foods cooked with lard

Seafood

Soft drinks

Alcohol

Coffee

Processed and Artificial Foods

Deep-fried foods

Overcooked foods

Processed foods

Trans fats
(partially hydrogenated oils)

Synthetic sweeteners
(Splenda, NutraSweet and Equal)

Artificial colors

Food additives

Food preservatives

Genetically Modified (GM) foods

Foods to Include on the Anti-arthritis, Anti-inflammation health program

Foods to Include – Alkaline-Forming Foods

To optimize prevention and healing of chronic diseases such as arthritis, the diet should consist of 80% alkaline-forming foods. Some common alkaline-forming foods are:

Beans/Legumes

green beans
lima beans
peas
soybeans
sprouted beans
tempeh (fermented)
tofu (fermented)

Nuts and Seeds

alfalfa
almonds
Brazil nuts
chestnuts
chia
coconuts
radish
sesame

Whole Grains

amaranth
buckwheat
millet
quinoa
teff

Fruits

apples
apricots
avocados
bananas
berries
currants
dates
figs
grapefruit
grapes
kiwis
lemons
limes
mangoes
melons
nectarines
olives
oranges
papayas
peaches
pears
persimmons
pineapple
quince
raisins
raspberries
strawberries
tangerines
watermelon

The most alkaline-forming foods are lemons and melons.

Foods High in Omega-3 Fatty Acids

fruit
most green leafy vegetables
non-green leafy vegetables
grains
legumes
chia seeds
flax seeds
hemp seeds
walnuts

The best animal sources of omega-3s are wild-caught salmon and cold water oily fish; these have been shown effective in the reduction of inflammation; however, care must be taken to obtain the highest quality sources. Avoid farm-raised fish altogether.

Antioxidant Rich Foods

acai berry
acerola
Red Delicious
Granny Smith and
Gala apples
artichoke hearts
bilberry
black beans
blackberries
blueberries
camu camu
cherries
collard greens
cranberries
goji berry
guava
kiwi
mango
maqui berry
noni
pecans
pinto beans
plums
Russet potato
prunes
pumpkin
raspberries
red beans
red kidney beans
spinach
strawberries

Sea Vegetables

arame
bladderwrack
dulse
hijiki
kelp
kombu
nori
sea palm
wakame

Foods Rich in Folic Acid

alfalfa
asparagus
avocado
banana
Brussels sprouts
broccoli
cantaloupe
carrots
cauliflower
celery
corn
dark leafy greens
garbanzo beans
grapes
grapefruit
lentils
oats, okra
papaya, peas
seeds and nuts
soy
squash
strawberries

Vegetables*

Artichoke
asparagus
beets and beet greens
bell peppers
broccoli
Brussels sprouts
cabbage
carrots
cauliflower
celery
chard greens
collards
corn
cucumbers
dandelions
eggplant
endive
garlic
ginger
horseradish
kale
lettuce
mushrooms
mustard greens
okra
onions
parsley
potatoes
pumpkin
radishes
spinach
sprouts
squash
tomatoes
watercress
wheatgrass
wild greens
yams

*Note: Eliminate nightshade vegetables if you are sensitive to them.

More Healing Foods*

Chlorella – Chlorella is a type of algae packed with a diverse set of detoxifying agents, vitamins, minerals and amino acids. It has been observed in studies to reduce oxidative DNA damage and various forms of inflammation.

Garlic – Garlic offers many health benefits, and individuals looking to prevent and treat chronic diseases are advised to incorporate this superfood into their diet; consuming garlic raw is best. Garlic is also abundant in anti-inflammatory sulfur compounds such as diallyl sulfide (DAS) and thiacremonone, which have been shown to fight arthritis as well as other conditions of inflammation.

Ginger Root – The benefits of ginger on patients suffering from arthritis and other conditions of inflammation have been well documented for decades. A group of powerful antioxidants unique to ginger, called gingerols, are a relative of capsaicin and piperine, well-known anti-inflammatory compounds.

Green Tea – Widely hailed for its medicinal qualities, green tea possesses numerous compounds that promote joint health and mitigate the impact of various types of arthritis.

Spirulina – Also known as blue-green algae, spirulina holds great promise as a natural means of curbing arthritis and other inflammatory conditions while promoting healing throughout the body.

*See my book *Reverse Arthritis & Pain Naturally* for a complete list of beneficial foods in fighting arthritis and inflammation.

Oils to Avoid/Oils to Include

Over-consumption of fats, including oils, is one of the key factors driving obesity today. The best rule for oils, when it comes to health, is using them in moderation. As you will see below, there are very few oils with an omega-6/omega-3 ratio (at most 4:1) that make it an anti-inflammatory condiment. Even olive oil, at a ratio of 12:1, which is preferred for use in the Mediterranean Diet is not considered anti-inflammatory. Although, it is far healthier than corn oil, for example, which has a ratio of 46:1.

Oils with best omega-3/omega-6 ratio (best for the anti-inflammatory diet)

flax seed oil

hemp oil

walnut oil

Use in Moderation

avocado oil

coconut oil

grape seed oil

Macadamia nut oil

extra virgin olive oil

pumpkin seed oil

Limit or avoid these Oils

canola oil (non-GMO)

corn oil

cottonseed oil

peanut oil

safflower oil

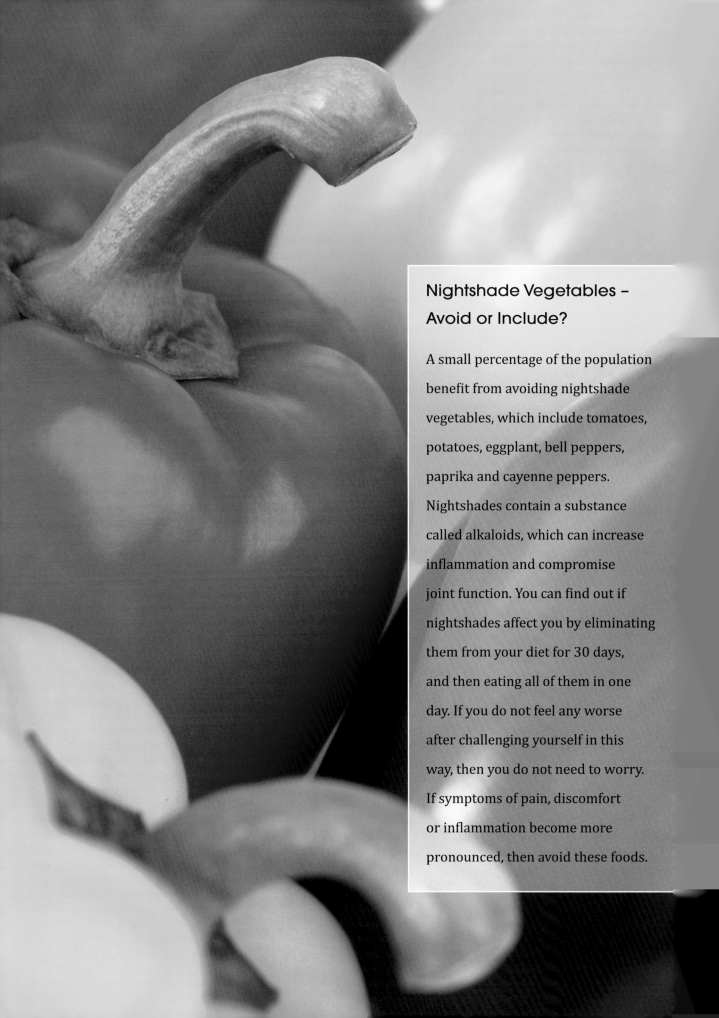

Nightshade Vegetables – Avoid or Include?

A small percentage of the population benefit from avoiding nightshade vegetables, which include tomatoes, potatoes, eggplant, bell peppers, paprika and cayenne peppers. Nightshades contain a substance called alkaloids, which can increase inflammation and compromise joint function. You can find out if nightshades affect you by eliminating them from your diet for 30 days, and then eating all of them in one day. If you do not feel any worse after challenging yourself in this way, then you do not need to worry. If symptoms of pain, discomfort or inflammation become more pronounced, then avoid these foods.

The Benefits of Eating More Raw Foods

Not enough can be said about eating foods as close to how Mother Nature intended, *and uncooked.* The raw foods movement is gaining tremendous momentum in our country because of the ability of raw foods, and fresh raw juices to thwart disease and literally turn back the hands of time. Consuming raw foods has many benefits including strengthening the immune system, purifying the blood, detoxifying our cells, improving digestion (since raw foods are some of the easiest to digest), clearing up skin issues, reversing the effects of oxidative stress, elevating mood, regulating hormone balance and weight, and, of course, reducing pain and inflammation. I have provided several raw food recipes herein for you to try out. If you enjoy them – as I do – I encourage you to learn more about raw foods, and how they can help you on your journey to health.

15 Great Anti-inflammatory Snack Ideas

Ginger Black Bean Dip and Veggies – page 96

Exotic Tofu Dip with cucumber slices wrapped in nori – page 95

Spicy Hummus with alfalfa sprouts in a sprouted wheat wrap – page 109

Crunchy Granola over non-dairy yogurt – page 70

Guilt-free Guacamole with Baked Corn Chips – page 100

Date spread on Manna Bread, Anise Raisin Bread, or fresh cut raw apples – page 94, 344

Spring Roll Wraps with avocado, shredded veggies and basil with Spicy Peanut Sauce – page 110

Fresh fruit with Sweet Nutty Spread – page 112

Tahini-Broccoli Cream Dip on tomatoes – page 112

Creamy Tofu Dip with celery and raw fennel sticks – page 93

Toasted Nut Brittle – page 385

Golden Strawberry Blueberry Crumble over non-dairy yogurt – page 357

Sweet Nutty Spread on Anise Raisin Bread – page 112, 344

The Importance of Organics

Because organic foods contain a significantly lower amount of pesticides and chemicals than conventional produce, eating organic foods automatically decreases inflammation in our body, and therefore our risk of disease. While it is commonly believed that "organic" automatically means "pesticide-free" or "chemical-free," this is not true. However, organic farmers are obligated to use pesticides that are derived from natural sources rather than synthetically manufactured compounds. They also employ creative mechanical and cultural tools to help control pests without chemicals, such as insect traps, careful crop selection, and biological controls like predator insects and beneficial microorganisms. Moreover, scientific studies consistently show higher levels of nutrients in organic over conventional produce.

While organic products can be expensive, it is often useful to participate in co-op buying, as well as other group buying clubs to reduce costs. It is also helpful, whenever possible, to buy directly from organic farmers, which results in a lower price altogether. Lastly, in weighing the pros and cons of utilizing organics, we must consider the costs of ill-health that could occur from a lifetime of exposure to the dangerous synthetic chemical toxins in conventional produce. All in all, organic foods are far healthier than conventional produce. Choose them as often as possible to increase your chances of preventing disease.

Below is a list of the most highly sprayed fruits and vegetables. In these cases, it is absolutely essential to purchase organic if you wish to limit your exposure to poisonous chemicals.

1. Apples
2. Celery
3. Strawberries
4. Peaches
5. Spinach
6. Imported nectarines
7. Imported grapes
8. Sweet bell peppers
9. Potatoes
10. Domestic blueberries
11. Lettuce
12. Kale/collard greens

The Benefits of Juicing

Juicing is one of the best ways to prevent and reverse inflammatory disease. When we juice, the health-boosting antioxidants, vitamins, minerals, enzymes, phytonutrients and chlorophyll found in fruits and vegetables are much more easily absorbed by the body than if we were to eat these foods whole. These beneficial constituents work synergistically to promote and maintain healthy cells and reduce chronic inflammation that results in degenerative diseases.

The juices you drink should always come from fresh organic produce; you can make them at home with your own juicer, or order at your favorite juice bar. Begin the first week with one 16 oz. glass of per day, 8 oz. in the morning and 8 oz. in the afternoon; try a nice cleansing detoxification juice such as cucumber, celery, apple and lemon. The second week, add a 16 oz. cabbage and apple juice to your regimen and for the third week, incorporate another juice consisting of grapefruit, kiwi, pear and lemon. By having three 16 oz. glasses of juice a day, you are flooding your body with essential nutrients that promote your health in powerful ways. For example, the chlorophyll in these juices acts as a natural chelator, removing toxic heavy metals from the body, while the sulfur compounds found in cabbage juice help guard against cancer. If you don't mind the taste of garlic, push a few cloves through your juicer to create a potent antiviral, antibacterial blend. To help stimulate healing in the gastrointestinal system and stomach, add a teaspoon of probiotic powder along with 1000 mg of buffered vitamin C and 2 oz. of aloe vera juice. You can also mix in different supplements like green tea extract, curcumin or astragalus to further enhance its functional food healing value. One day a week, it's a good idea to add a scoop of non-GMO brown rice, pea or hemp protein powder into your juices and use that as your fasting day. By restricting calories in this way, you are detoxifying the body and contributing to the health of your cells.

For many years I've incorporated juicing in my protocols for health. In my new book, *Reverse Arthritis & Pain Naturally,* we document the dramatic progress realized by dozens of arthritis patients who followed a lifestyle modification protocol that featured juicing as a key component. The extraordinary healing power of juicing is discussed in great detail in my latest edition of *The Joy of Juicing* (Avery, 2013).

1, 2 & 3-Day Diet Cleanses for Arthritis, Pain and Inflammation Flare-ups

On occasion you will find yourself sick, low on energy, or feeling the effects of an inflammatory diet and lifestyle, which occurs frequently around the holidays when we may not be as wise in our choices. When this happens, the absolute best thing to do is to give your body a break by consuming alkalizing fresh juices, smoothies with greens and protein powders, and some of the lighter soups (***Cucumber Mint Soup*** (p. 127), ***Curried Lentil Soup*** (p. 128), ***Miso Tofu Soup*** (p. 146), or ***Onion Soup*** (p. 149), along with plenty of purified water and as much rest as you can get, for one to three days. You will notice a remarkable difference in a very short amount of time.

The Anti-arthritis, Anti-inflammation Pantry

Herbs & Spices

allspice
almond extract
basil
bay leaf
black pepper
Cajun seasoning
cardamom
cayenne pepper

chili powder
cinnamon
cloves
coriander
cumin
curry
dill
dry mustard

garlic
ginger
marjoram
nutmeg
oregano
paprika
parsley
red pepper flakes

rosemary
sage
sea salt
tarragon
thyme
turmeric
vanilla extract

Pantry Basics

Beans & Legumes
- aduki, dried and/or canned black beans, dried and/or canned
- Chickpeas, dried and/or canned
- kidney beans, dried and/or canned
- lentils, red and green, dried and/or canned
- pinto beans, dried and/or canned
- white beans, (Northern, Navy or Cannellini) dried and/or canned

Condiments
- apple cider vinegar
- balsamic vinegar
- tamari or Nama Shoyu (raw version)

Grains & Flours
- barley
- bulgur wheat
- couscous
- millet
- gluten-free oat flour
- pasta, rice and buckwheat
- quinoa
- quinoa flour
- rice, brown & brown basmati
- steel cut oats
- wheat flour

Nuts
- almonds
- coconut flakes, unsweetened
- pecans
- pistachio
- walnuts

Oils
- extra virgin olive
- sesame
- walnut

Seeds
- caraway
- chia
- fennel
- flax
- pumpkin
- sesame, black & white
- sunflower

Sweets
- coconut milk (canned)
- date sugar
- dried fruits (currants, cherries, cranberries, goji berries, dates, raisins, apricots, mangoes, peaches, sultanas)
- maple syrup, Grade B

Miscellaneous
- almond butter
- artichoke hearts (jar)
- natural peanut butter
- non-dairy milk (almond, rice, soy), powdered or Tetra-pak sea vegetables of choice (arame, wakame, hijiki, dulse, nori, kombu)
- tahini (ground sesame paste)
- vegan bread crumbs
- vegan spaghetti sauce (jar)
- vegetable broth (powdered or Tetra-pak)

Pantry Specialty

Beans & Legumes
- fava bean, dried and/or canned mung bean, dried

Condiments
- Bragg's Liquid Aminos
- chili sauce
- gomasio
- Tabasco

Grains & Flours
- amaranth
- barley flour
- bran
- rice flour
- wheat germ

Nuts
- cashew
- hazelnuts
- macadamia
- pine nuts

Oils
- avocado
- hot chili oil
- pumpkin seed

Seeds (Additional for Sprouting)
- alfalfa, dried
- clover, dried
- fenugreek, dried

Sweets
- brown rice syrup
- molasses
- organic apple juice (Tetra-pak)

Miscellaneous
- anise powder
- arrowroot powder
- capers
- kelp flakes (for sprinkling on salads)
- kelp powder (optional for adding to sauces & dressings)
- vegan egg replacer

The Anti-arthritis, Anti-inflammation Refrigerator

Fresh Foods

dark leafy greens (kale, collards, Swiss chard, dandelion, etc.)

flaxseed meal (ground flaxseeds)

flaxseed oil

fresh ginger

fresh herbs (variety)

juices (freshly squeezed, or bottled (no sugar added))

lettuces (variety: consider arugula, romaine, radicchio, red and green leaf, baby lettuces, spring mix)

miso, brown or golden

non-dairy milk (almond, rice, and soy)

olives, black and green (pitted and un-pitted)

prepared mustard

soy yogurt, plain

tofu or tempeh

vegan cheese

vegetables (variety of the rainbow)

Frozen Foods

corn

edamame

fruits (variety)

Equipment for the Vegetarian Lifestyle

There are a few pieces of kitchen equipment worth singling out that will be helpful for you on your journey of healthy living.

Food Processor – A food processor allows you to do everything from gently combining and mixing foods to puréeing them. There are numerous sizes available; however, a medium-sized 11-cup processor is sufficient for most vegetarian kitchens.

Juicer – With the increase in popularity of juicing, there are numerous juicers on the market today. There are typically three key types of juicers – centrifugal juicers, auger juicers, and juice presses. Centrifugal juicers spin the produce through a blade to extract the juice, and are almost always faster than single or double auger juicers, and definitely faster than juice presses. Juice presses (Norwalk, for example) are slow, and very expensive but result in the highest, most nutritious yields – all other things being equal. Faster is not always better, however, as heat tends to destroy the delicate enzymes, and faster processing can leave a good amount of juice behind in the pulp. A good middle ground in terms of price and speed is a single or double auger type (Check out Green Power, Green Star, Omega, Sampson, Super Angel); but if time is of the essence, then centrifugal is fine (try the Breville in this case).

Good Quality Blender – Not all blenders are alike! There are several stand-out blenders (Vita Mix, Blendtec's K-Tec), which are kitchen workhorses and actually do far more than blend; they can make fruit smoothies in seconds, and convert dried grain into flour. These are not cheap machines, but if you spend a lot of time in the kitchen, they may be worth the investment. Others (KitchenAid, Breville and Cuisinart) have less horsepower, are less expensive, and perfectly adequate for what you will encounter in this recipe book.

Equipment for the
Vegetarian Lifestyle cont.

Vegetable Spiralizer – This fun, little, inexpensive manual machine makes raw "spaghetti" and "noodles" in minutes with your favorite vegetables (zucchini, squash, beets, etc.). Topped with one of my delicious raw or cooked sauces and you have a power-packed, highly conversational meal! There are a few brands to choose from (Saladacco, Benriner, World Cuisine, Spirooli); just look online.

Sprout Bags – Sprouting is an easy, fun and extremely cost effective way to achieve highly nutritious foods. Most people are unaware that sprouts are some of the most nutritious foods on the planet, packed with easily digestible vitamins, minerals and phytonutrients. You can sprout beans, seeds and legumes in a matter of 1-3 days and add to soups, salads, or use on your favorite veggie wrap. Sprout bags are readily available at your local health food store, and most stores offer classes for beginners.

Food Savers – Foods savers, which extract air from and seal heavy duty plastic bags are wonderful for freezing foods, and storing them for longer periods of time. While it's ideal to consume foods when they are as fresh as possible, saving food properly can also save you lots of time. Consider doubling your batches of granola (p. 70), nut brittle (p. 385) and other easily storable snacks, or freezing individual sizes of your favorite entrées for quick and easy meals.

Most Important Equipment Consideration

Get Rid of Your Microwave! We advise never using a microwave oven for the heating and cooking of foods. Among other hazards, microwaves alter the chemical and molecular structure of your food, and zap the nutrition right out of them.

Substitutions and Variations

While the recipes that follow contain specific recommendations for nuts, seeds, yogurts, non-dairy milks, veggies, fruits, beans, greens and grains, feel free, when you are out of the specific type recommended in the recipe, to substitute something similar. Substitutions out of necessity can lead to some of the most wonderful culinary surprises!

Almost all beans can be substituted for one another, as can grains and dark leafy greens. When substituting vegetables consider type, where grown (above or below ground), and predominant taste (sweet, sour, bitter or salty) and substitute within the same general family, e.g. pumpkin for squash, bok choy for Chinese cabbage. Nuts are very different in their fat content, with almonds containing the least amount of fat; it is best, therefore, to minimize swapping these out for higher fat-content nuts like cashew or Macadamia nuts. There are three primary categories for fruits (acid, sub-acid and sweet), and it is recommended to substitute within the same category or an adjoining category. (Consult a food-combining chart (available at most health food stores) for more information on this.) In the case of non-dairy milks and yogurts, these typically have foundations in one of the following: soy, rice, almond or coconut milk. While there are different consistencies and tastes in these offerings (especially in the case of coconut milk, which is extremely rich and dense), they are generally suitable as exchanges for one another. Note that Greek-style yogurt tends to be lower in sugar than others.

Substituting dried herbs for fresh
While fresh are always more flavorful and ideal, substituting dried herbs for fresh is perfectly acceptable. When the need arises, use this general rule of thumb:
1 teaspoon of the dried herb = 1 tablespoon of the fresh.
However, it is best to go by taste, so allow the dried herbs to settle into the mix and reconstitute for a minimum of five minutes before tasting.

Suggestions for Meal Planning & Transitioning to the Vegetarian Lifestyle

There are some keys to being successful at a vegetarian lifestyle; below are some tips to help with your success. If you are transitioning – especially from the Standard American Diet – remember that the key is to focus on *adding...* more healthy meals, juices, snacks, and green salads while reducing your intake and portions of unhelpful foods. As you do this, your palate will change and become more open to the vegetarian lifestyle. In terms of elimination, start with the mind to substitute healthier options for the high fat, high calorie items that you may be currently consuming, e.g. granola with yogurt for donuts, cookies and muffins; nut brittle for candy bars; rice crackers and baked corn chips for potato chips, etc. This, combined with increasing your intake of pure water will aid in automatically reducing your inflammation.

Note: if you are currently facing a serious debilitating illness, it is recommended that you move immediately to the healthy, anti-inflammatory protocol outlined in my book *Reverse Arthritis & Pain Naturally* after consulting with a naturopathic physician. Life-threatening challenges require immediate mobilization and reinforcement to assist with recovery.

- Eat as much of the rainbow as possible in a given week. There are vegetables and fruits across the spectrum of color with different and wonderful nutritional profiles. Nature intended it this way, and you will feel more vibrant when you eat a wide variety of fruits and vegetables.
- Consider how to incorporate more raw foods in your diet.

Suggestions for Meal Planning & Transitioning to the Vegetarian Lifestyle cont.

- Consume at least one good-sized salad per day. You can prepare a large base salad one day in the week and store in air-tight containers for easy consumption throughout the week. Simply add different toppings to create variety.

- Consider eating more calories at lunch time, when our digestive powers are the highest, and eating lighter fare, including salads, for dinner.

- Plan your meals for the week in advance if possible, and create a shopping list to simplify your efforts.

- When juicing, make extra, and store in stainless-steel containers for ongoing consumption. (While it's ideal to consume juices within ½ hour, if you top off a container and then screw on the lid so some juice overflows, you are minimizing the amount of oxygen in the container and the juice will stay fresher.)

- Have at least one healthy dip on hand regularly, and cut up raw veggies and store in an air-tight container for easy snacking. Consider unusual veggies for variety (all raw): fennel, rutabaga, jicama, sweet potato, purple cabbage, snow peas, snap peas, green beans, okra, and bok choy stems (very crispy and delicious).

- Have fun! The vegetarian world is full of delicious surprises: talk to people, visit your local health food store and look around – you will find some amazing things to help you on your journey to wellness.

How to Use This Book

With the popularity of today's cooking shows, including those dedicated to competitions between chefs for the purposes of separating the wheat from the chaff so to speak, you may be thinking that it's nice to watch someone else make a gourmet meal, but that you probably would not do as well yourself. This would be especially true if you viewed television programs in the past featuring such famously sophisticated chefs as Julia Child or James Beard. Until recently, the emphasis in American cuisine has been placed on meat, fat, dairy, sugar, and flour: in effect, the most unhealthy, immune-suppressing, pro-inflammatory, disease-causing recipes imaginable. Even today, the vast majority of cookbooks on the market cater to the highly conditioned American appetite for salty and crunchy, sweet and soft foods that lead to inflammation, free radicals and disease. Even some of the vegetarian recipe books use ingredients that I would never select because they are heavily processed. For example, there are numerous popular vegan restaurants in the United States that serve dishes made with seitan, a highly processed gluten, which is often deep fried – a double negative.

I was inspired to write this book to offer something that is refreshingly different from the typical vegetarian cookbook. It is my belief that most people choose a cookbook because they want to be more creative with their cooking and have a greater variety of dishes in their diet. This book not only has some of the healthiest and most delicious anti-inflammatory recipes that I have used regularly over the years in my own home and health centers, but it is bursting with beautiful photographs that are intended to stir your inner "top chef," and health nut (pun intended).

Next we bring you our dishes, each one created with the idea that it should contain nutrients that help the body heal, turn off inflammation, repair DNA, enhance detoxification and provide maximal nutritional benefits. We have selected foods that are known to be rich in phytonutrients, chlorophyll, and high quality diverse fibers in addition to being low glycemic and easy to digest. Many of the recipes are naturally gluten free and free from added sugar (except the desserts), and nearly all contain at least one ingredient touted for its anti-inflammatory properties. We have also noted recipes that contain at least one ingredient with recommended sources of omega-3 fats. We've chosen a unique way of marking each recipe with the following symbols to help you quickly understand the dense nutritional value of these meals. The recipes can be made even more interesting by changing them to meet your own preferences. For example, if we feature basil in a particular recipe but you prefer tarragon, then use tarragon, and if we suggest rice milk but you most enjoy almond milk, then by all means make the change. One of the key ingredients of a healthy life is enjoying what we are doing, and this means in the kitchen too! Have fun and experiment, and don't despair. If you really want to make one of these recipes and you are missing one or two ingredients, take a culinary risk by making a substitution or two – you may just end up with a gastronomic delight. As you will find, it is hard to go wrong with vegetables and fruits.

YOUR GUIDE TO HEALTHFUL SYMBOLS

Gluten Free

Sugar Free

Contains foods with
healthy omega-3s

Contains herbs & foods
that are known to
fight inflammation

Lastly, hundreds of studies in the peer-reviewed literature have shown the health benefits of eating more fresh fruits and vegetables, and realigning to a Mediterranean-style program. This means reducing caloric intake (which naturally occurs when you increase the percentage of fruits and vegetables in your diet), and including seeds, nuts, legumes and herbs that aren't normally in the Standard American Diet. We have provided a lengthy list of foods as well as superfoods and other health nutrients in the earlier sections of this book. Please refer to my *Reverse Arthritis & Pain Naturally* book for a complete list of foods accompanied by scientific literature in support of them. *Reverse Arthritis & Pain Naturally* provides a much more in-depth look at these healthful foods, and how to combine them in ways that benefit you even more. For example, if a smoothie recipe calls for strawberries, you will know how to enhance its benefits further by adding some superfoods such as acai, black currant, mangosteen, or noni berry. As you learn, you will grow in your ability to become your own best health advisor, while taking important steps to eradicate – and even prevent – the chronic illnesses that are plaguing most Americans today. You can do it; you can create unparalleled health in your life. Many people are, and they are reaping the rewards of a vital and fulfilling existence free from disease.

The Start of a Healing Journey

It's clear that our physical well-being is intimately linked to our dietary choices. By taking responsibility for what foods we eat and adopting a diet rich in anti-inflammatory foods, we set ourselves on the path to vibrant health and happiness. The recipes in this cookbook were designed to support and inspire you on your path to wellness. I invite you to come along on this joyful, exciting and absolutely delicious journey of healing. Now let's get cooking!

–Gary Null

> "Within just a few weeks, I can feel a great, great improvement – at least 50 percent. I am much more alert; I'm feeling really good."
>
> – Robert, 53-year-old arthritis sufferer

BREAKFAST

There is hardly anything more important in maintaining proper weight and good health than enjoying a healthy morning workout and a delicious breakfast daily. Seems we have forgotten the importance of fueling up with healthy foods in the morning (when we most need the calories) for the long day ahead. Instead, we are opting for high-calorie "breakfasts" that are also high in fat and low in nutritional value, such as muffins or egg and sausage sandwiches; or, we are skimping on breakfast altogether, shifting calorie intake to large dinners and late-night snacking, which is seriously deleterious to longevity and health. I know you will agree with me after reviewing the recipes within this chapter that a healthy "break-the-fast" revolution is underway – one that will have you falling in love with this most glorious time of the day over and over again!

– Gary

Amaranth Peach Delight

Yield: 2 servings

Amaranth is a highly nutritious gluten-free "grain" that is actually not a grain but a seed from a tall flowering plant. This relative of beets, Swiss chard, spinach, and quinoa is unusually rich in the essential amino acid lysine, and a good source of minerals including iron, magnesium, phosphorus, and manganese.

2 cups water
1 cup amaranth
1 teaspoon chia seeds
½ cup dried peaches, chopped
¼ cup raisins
½ cup pecans, chopped
½ teaspoon ground cinnamon
¼ teaspoon ground cloves
¼ teaspoon ground nutmeg

Combine water, amaranth, and chia seeds in a medium-size saucepan and bring to a slow boil over medium heat.

After 15 minutes, add the dried peaches, raisins, pecans, cinnamon, cloves and nutmeg, and cook to desired consistency

Garnish with pecans.

Apple Cinnamon French Toast with Bananas and Raspberries

Yield: 2 servings

½ cup applesauce
1 cup almond milk
1 teaspoon ground cinnamon
1 teaspoon vanilla extract
1 tablespoon flaxseed meal
2 tablespoons sunflower oil
4 slices of whole grain, spelt or gluten-free bread
1 banana, sliced
½ cup raspberries
Maple syrup

Combine the applesauce, almond milk, cinnamon, vanilla extract, and flaxseed meal in a large bowl and mix well.

Heat the oil in a skillet over medium heat, soak the bread on both sides in the mixture, and then fry until light brown.

Serve with sliced banana, raspberries, and maple syrup.

Spelt is a form of wheat and should be avoided by those on a gluten-free diet. Note that this recipe becomes gluten-free with a choice of bread that fits into this category.

Cinnamon is a warming spice that tastes incredible and is surprisingly healthy for you. Not only is cinnamon anti-inflammatory, but it has antifungal, anti-bacterial and antiparasitic properties, and has been shown effective in helping to control blood sugar levels.

Banana Coconut Buckwheat Cereal

Yield: 2 servings

½ cup uncooked Cream of Buckwheat cereal
¼ cup flaxseed meal
2½ cups water
1 tablespoon dried apricot
1 tablespoon dried currants
1 tablespoon raisins
1½ teaspoons ground cinnamon
½ cup banana, sliced
¼ cup toasted coconut flakes, for garnish

Combine Cream of Buckwheat, flaxseed meal, and water in a medium saucepan and bring to a slow boil over medium heat.

Add the apricots, currants, raisins, and cinnamon, and cook 5 to 8 minutes to desired consistency, stirring frequently.

Garnish with sliced banana and coconut.

Blueberry Apricot Oatmeal

Yield: 2 servings

1 cup water
¾ cup gluten-free steel cut oats
1 tablespoon chia seeds
1 teaspoon ground cinnamon
½ teaspoon ground ginger
½ cup fresh blueberries; reserve a few for garnish
½ cup sliced apricot
½ banana, sliced, for garnish

Bring water to a boil in a medium saucepan; add the steel cut oats, chia seeds, cinnamon, ginger, blueberries, and apricot slices. Reduce heat.

Simmer 5 to 8 minutes to desired consistency, stirring frequently.

Garnish with sliced banana and berries.

Not all oats are gluten-free! Many oats are contaminated by gluten-containing grains – like wheat and barley – during the growing and harvesting process. Check your health food store for gluten-free varieties, as they lessen inflammation.

Blueberry Oatmeal with Soy Yogurt

Yield: 2 servings

1 cup water
½ cup gluten-free steel cut or rolled oats
1 teaspoon chia seeds
1 teaspoon ground cinnamon
½ teaspoon ground ginger
¼ cup fresh or frozen blueberries
¼ cup plain soy yogurt
1 sprig mint, for garnish

Bring water to a boil in a medium saucepan; add the steel cut oats, chia seeds, cinnamon, ginger, and blueberries. Reduce heat.

Simmer 5 to 8 minutes to desired consistency, stirring frequently.

Top with soy yogurt, and garnish with mint.

Chia seeds are one of the best sources of vegetarian omega-3s that you can consume. Use them as often as you can in salads, cereals, desserts and more!

Cinnamon Pear Pancakes

Yield: 4 servings

½ cup barley or gluten-free oat flour
1 tablespoon flaxseed meal
1 ½ teaspoons baking powder
1 teaspoon ground cinnamon
½ teaspoon ground nutmeg
½ cup almond milk

½ cup pear, peeled and chopped
1 teaspoon vanilla extract
1 teaspoon almond extract
2 tablespoons walnut oil
Maple syrup
Few sprigs of mint, for garnish
⅛ cup pear, for garnish

Combine flour, flaxseed meal, baking powder, cinnamon, and nutmeg in a large bowl.

Add the almond milk and mix thoroughly, then add the pear, vanilla extract, and almond extract and stir until smooth.

Heat the oil in a large skillet over medium heat. Add pancake batter to the hot oil and create the desired pancake size.

Cook each pancake for approximately 3 minutes or until the top of the pancake starts to bubble and the underside starts to brown.

Flip the pancake and cook for an additional 2 minutes or until brown. Garnish with chopped pear and mint.

Serve with maple syrup or fresh fruit and nuts.

Tip! If you don't have flaxseed meal, but have a coffee grinder, you can make instant, fresh flaxseed meal by grinding the flaxseeds yourself. Just make sure to clean out and dry your grinder well before grinding, as these seeds are mucilaginous and need to be handled carefully around water to make usage and clean-up easier.

Coconut Nut Rice

Yield: 2 servings

1 cup brown rice, cooked
½ cup toasted coconut flakes; reserve half for garnish
½ cup cashews, chopped
½ cup dried apricots, chopped
1 teaspoon chia seeds
1 teaspoon ground cinnamon
½ teaspoon ground nutmeg
¼ cup all natural apple juice
¼ cup sunflower seeds, for garnish

Combine brown rice with coconut, cashews, apricots, chia seeds, cinnamon, and nutmeg in a medium bowl.

Place half the mixture and the apple juice in a food processor and pulse until coarsely ground.

Add back to the rest of the rice and mix well.

Garnish with apricot pieces, sunflower seeds and coconut.

When using fruit juices in recipes, it is best to use fresh-squeezed juices, or juices with "No Added Sugar." This will lower the calories and increase the health value of your meal.

Crunchy Granola

Yield: 6 servings

5 cups uncooked gluten-free
   rolled oats
½ cup flax seeds
2 cups unsweetened coconut
½ cup walnuts
½ cup cashews
½ cup almonds
¼ cup bran
½ cup sunflower seeds
2 tablespoons ground cinnamon

1 teaspoon ground nutmeg
1 teaspoon ground ginger
½ cup apple juice
½ cup date sugar
1 teaspoon vanilla extract
2 tablespoons walnut oil
½ cup maple syrup, grade B
½ cup dried cranberries
½ cup raisins
½ cup goji berries, for garnish

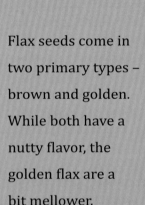

Flax seeds come in two primary types – brown and golden. While both have a nutty flavor, the golden flax are a bit mellower.

Try both to see what you prefer!

Preheat oven to 275°.

Mix together in a large bowl the oats, flax seeds, coconut, walnuts, cashews, almonds, bran, sunflower seeds, cinnamon, nutmeg, and ginger.

In a small bowl combine the apple juice, date sugar, vanilla extract, walnut oil, and maple syrup and mix well until the sugar is fully dissolved.

Add this mixture to the oats and stir until they are well-coated.

Spray a large baking pan with non-stick cooking oil. Transfer the granola to the baking pan and spread evenly.

Bake for 1 hour or so until toasted and crispy, stirring at least every 5 minutes to prevent burning. Turn off the oven and, while the granola is still warm, stir in the cranberries and raisins.

Garnish with goji berries. Store extra in an air-tight container.

Serving Tip: sprinkle over vegan yogurt for a wonderful mid-day snack.

Fluffy Raisin Couscous

Yield: 2 servings

Goji berries – the little-known super-fruit from Asia – are packed with antioxidants, and contain high amounts of beta carotene and vitamin C. They also contain essential fatty acids, which is what makes them a super food for the anti-inflammatory diet.

1½ cups couscous, cooked
1 tablespoon maple syrup
½ cup raisins
½ cup cranberries
½ cup dried currants
¼ cup sultanas
1 teaspoon ground cinnamon
¼ teaspoon ground cloves
¼ cup goji berries
¼ cup slivered almonds

Combine the couscous, maple syrup, raisins, cranberries, currants, sultanas, cinnamon, and cloves in a medium bowl and mix well.

Top with goji berries and almonds.

Hawaiian Rice Cereal

Yield: 2 servings

¼ cup shredded unsweetened coconut, for garnish
½ cup chopped macadamia nuts, for garnish
½ cup apple or other fresh juice
1 banana, sliced
½ cup pitted fresh cherries, chopped
½ cup fresh pineapple, chopped
2 cups cooked brown rice
1 teaspoon flax seeds, raw or toasted

Preheat oven to 375°

Place unsweetened coconut and macadamia nuts on an ungreased baking pan and bake for 3-5 minutes, or until light brown.

In a medium saucepan combine the apple juice, banana, cherries, and pineapple and cook over low heat for 3–5 minutes.

Stir in the brown rice, flax seeds and macadamia nuts and cook for an additional 2 minutes.

Garnish with toasted coconut.

Pineapple is one of the best anti-inflammatory fruits on the market today; it is a natural source of bromelain – an enzyme that has been shown to protect against a variety of chronic diseases.

Nutty Fruit Breakfast

Yield: 2 servings

Organic red raspberries have been shown to have a much higher levels of antioxidants than conventional berries. Plus, some new research is linking raspberries to improved metabolism, and therefore effective in weight management.

1 cup barley, cooked
2 tablespoons barley malt
1 teaspoon ground cinnamon
1 teaspoon chia seeds
1 banana, mashed
¼ cup dried figs, chopped
½ cup red raspberries
½ cup blueberries
½ cup walnuts, chopped

Combine barley, barley malt, cinnamon, chia seeds, and mashed banana in a large bowl.

Add the figs, raspberries, blueberries, and walnuts and mix well.

Garnish with fresh fruit.

Quinoa Breakfast Delight

Yield: 2 servings

1 cup red or white quinoa, cooked
1 tablespoon chia seeds
1 teaspoon ground cinnamon
½ teaspoon ground ginger
1 tablespoon maple syrup, grade B
½ cup walnuts, chopped
½ cup Brazil nuts, chopped
¼ cup chopped dried figs
1 package fresh blackberries
¼ cup pumpkin seeds, for garnish

Combine quinoa, chia seeds, cinnamon, ginger and maple syrup in a large bowl.

Add the walnuts, Brazil nuts, figs, and blackberries and mix well.

Garnish with fresh fruit and pumpkin seeds.

Quinoa, pronounced (KEEN-wah), is another one of the "pseudograins" (like amaranth, it is actually a seed, even though it is called a grain), and very high in protein.

Quinoa Pancakes

Yield: 4 servings

¾ cup quinoa flour
¼ cup gluten-free rolled oats
1 tablespoon flaxseed meal, golden or brown
½ teaspoon baking soda
1 teaspoon baking powder
½ cup apple juice
½ cup almond milk
2 tablespoons sunflower oil
Maple syrup
½ cup raspberries

In a large bowl, mix together quinoa flour, oats, flaxseed meal, baking soda, and baking powder.

Add apple juice and almond milk and stir until smooth.

Heat the oil in a large skillet, and add pancake batter to the hot oil, creating the desired pancake size.

Cook each pancake for approximately 3 minutes or until top starts to bubble and the underside starts to brown.

Flip the pancake and cook for an additional 2 minutes or until brown.

Serve with maple syrup and raspberries.

Maple syrup is known to contain over 50 antioxidants. We prefer Grade B Maple syrup because it is darker and has a more complex flavor.

Raspberry Blueberry Oatmeal

Yield: 2 servings

Ground ginger – another warming spice – like cinnamon is also anti-inflammatory, and is a very good source of vitamin E, as well as minerals.

1 cup water
¾ cup gluten-free steel cut oats
1 tablespoon chia seeds
1 teaspoon ground cinnamon
½ teaspoon ground ginger
½ cup blueberries, for garnish
½ cup raspberries, for garnish
½ banana, sliced, for garnish

Bring water to a boil in a medium saucepan; add the steel cut oats, chia seeds, cinnamon, and ginger, and reduce heat.

Simmer 5 to 8 minutes to desired consistency, stirring frequently.

Garnish with blueberries, raspberries, and banana.

Seven Grain Cereal with Peaches and Walnuts

Yield: 2 servings

2½ cups water
1 cup multigrain cereal (pre-packaged)
1 tablespoon chia seeds
1 large peach, peeled, pitted and sliced; reserve half for garnish
½ cup walnuts
1 tablespoon maple syrup, grade B
1 tablespoon ground cinnamon
½ teaspoon ground ginger

Combine water, cereal, and chia seeds in a saucepan and bring to a slow boil over medium heat.

Add the peach slices, walnuts, maple syrup, cinnamon, and ginger and cook 10 to 15 minutes to desired consistency, stirring frequently.

Garnish with sliced peaches.

It is important when buying peaches that you select organic vs. conventional, as peaches are one of the most highly sprayed fruit crops in America.

Strawberry Blueberry Sunshine

Yield: 2 servings

1 cup brown rice, cooked
1 tablespoon flax seeds
1 teaspoon ground cinnamon
½ teaspoon ground ginger
½ cup strawberries, halved
½ cup blueberries
¼ cup sunflower seeds
½ cup cashews, chopped
2 tablespoons shredded unsweetened coconut, for garnish (can be toasted for extra flavor)

Combine brown rice, flax seeds, cinnamon, ginger, strawberries, blueberries, sunflower seeds, and cashews in a bowl and mix well.

Garnish with shredded coconut.

Sunflower seeds are naturally rich in omega-3 fatty acids, and are an excellent source of vitamin E.

Sweet Cinnamon Oatmeal

Yield: 2 servings

2 cups water
1 cup gluten-free steel cut or rolled oats
1 teaspoon chia seeds
1 teaspoon ground cinnamon
½ teaspoon ground ginger
½ cup dried apricots
¼ cup dried currants
¼ cup goji berries, for garnish
½ cup almonds, chopped, for garnish

Bring water to a boil in a medium saucepan; add the steel cut oats, chia seeds, cinnamon, ginger, apricots and currants and reduce heat.

Simmer 5 to 8 minutes to desired consistency, stirring frequently.

Garnish with goji berries and almonds.

Apricots are an excellent source of vitamin A and carotenes, which possess antioxidant properties that are essential for vision.

Triple Fruit Oatmeal Delight

Yield: 2 servings

2 cups water
1 cup gluten-free steel cut oats
1 teaspoon chia seeds
1 pear, peeled and diced; reserve a slice for garnish
1 banana, peeled and sliced; reserve a few slices for garnish
1 apple, peeled and diced: reserve a slice for garnish
1 teaspoon ground cinnamon
½ teaspoon ground nutmeg

Bring water to a boil in a medium saucepan; add the steel cut oats, chia seeds, pear, banana, apple, cinnamon, and nutmeg and reduce heat.

Simmer 5 to 8 minutes to desired consistency, stirring frequently.

Place in individual dessert dishes and garnish with sliced fruit.

Pears are loaded with health benefits: they are high in dietary fiber, antioxidants, minerals and vitamins, and one of the very low calorie fruits!

Two Grain Breakfast

Yield: 2 servings

2 cups water
¾ cup brown rice
¼ cup barley, cooked
1 teaspoon ground cinnamon
1 teaspoon ground nutmeg
½ teaspoon ground cloves
1 banana, sliced; reserve some of the slices for garnish
½ cup dried cranberries
¼ cup dried mango
1 tablespoon coconut flakes, for garnish

Bring water to a boil in a medium saucepan; add brown rice, barley, cinnamon, nutmeg, and cloves and simmer over low heat for 15 minutes.

Add the banana, cranberries, and mango and cook until the rice and barley are done, approximately 30 minutes.

Garnish with coconut and sliced banana.

Cranberries are full of powerful phytonutrients, and are believed to offer protection from inflammatory diseases.

APPETIZERS, SIDE DISHES, SAUCES & DIPS

Part of what makes a vegetarian diet so appetizing are the wonderful accompaniments for the variety of fruits and vegetables that you will come to love. Re-training the palate only takes a little bit of time, but when it happens, and you begin to have a diet rich with the bounties of the earth you will cherish every meal. Small plates are truly special because they can be combined for a fantastic meal with friends and family, and are perfect for parties. Or use them every day as a delectable snack or healthy addition to big green salad. Either way, have fun, experiment, and enjoy!

- Gary

Barley with Collard Greens and Leeks

Yield: 2 servings

1 cup collard greens, sliced thin
¼ cup vegetable broth
½ cup leeks, sliced
2 cloves garlic, minced
1 cup fresh tomatoes, chopped
¾ cup mushrooms, sliced; reserve a few slices for garnish
½ cup red bell peppers, sliced
¼ cup fresh parsley, chopped
½ teaspoon dried oregano
Sea salt to taste
½ teaspoon freshly ground black pepper
3 cups barley, cooked

Place the collard greens in a steamer and steam over boiling water for 20 minutes.

Heat the vegetable broth in a skillet over medium heat and sauté the leeks and garlic for about 3 minutes until tender.

Add the tomatoes, mushrooms, bell pepper, parsley, oregano, salt, and black pepper and sauté for about 10 minutes, stirring frequently.

Add the steamed collard greens and sauté for an additional 5 minutes.

Garnish with sliced mushrooms and serve with cooked barley.

Green leafy vegetables, like collards, are extremely good vegetarian sources of omega-3 fatty acids. Plus, collards are a very good source of dietary fiber, and high in vitamins A, C, E, K and – believe it or not – protein.

Bavarian Cabbage

Yield: 2 servings

¼ cup vegetable broth
1 small yellow onion, diced
1 clove garlic, chopped
1 oz. kombu or arame seaweed, soaked in water for about
    10 minutes to reconstitute
1 cup green cabbage, shredded
½ cup red cabbage, shredded
1 Granny Smith apple, diced
1 teaspoon maple syrup
Sea salt to taste
½ teaspoon freshly ground black pepper
1 tablespoon apple cider vinegar

Heat the vegetable broth in a large pan over medium heat and sauté onion, garlic, and seaweed until tender, about 3 minutes.

Add green and red cabbage, apple, maple syrup, salt, pepper, and vinegar, and cook covered over low heat for approximately 20 minutes.

Garnish with fresh fruit.

Did you know that cabbage contains a surprising amount of one particular omega-3 fatty acid called alpha-linolenic acid, or ALA? There is actually much more ALA in 100 calories of cabbage than there is in 100 calories of salmon...and so much less overall fat!

Black Bean Sauce

Yield: 4 servings

1 cup black beans, cooked
2 tablespoons water
1 tablespoon extra virgin olive oil
1 small yellow onion, diced
1 clove garlic, minced
1 tomato, chopped
2 tablespoons fresh basil, chopped
2 tablespoons fresh parsley, chopped
1 bay leaf
Sea salt to taste
½ teaspoon freshly ground black pepper
¼ teaspoon crushed red pepper

Place the beans and water in a blender or food processor and pulse until coarsely chopped; set aside.

Heat the oil in a medium saucepan over medium heat and sauté the onion and garlic until the onion is translucent.

Add the tomato, chopped beans, basil, parsley, bay leaf, salt, black pepper, and crushed red pepper and sauté for 10–15 minutes.

Serve over brown rice or quinoa.

Black beans are super high in dietary fiber and protein, and a good source of omega-3 fatty acids. They are also rich in folate (naturally occurring B9), a very important nutrient that aids the body in cell reproduction.

Caponata

Yield: 4 servings

½ cup vegetable broth
1 large yellow onion, diced
2 cloves garlic, minced
2 stalks celery, sliced
4 tomatoes, chopped
½ cup fresh basil, chopped
2 small eggplants, diced

4 tablespoons pine nuts
2 tablespoons capers, drained
2 tablespoons apple cider
   vinegar
Sea salt to taste
½ teaspoon freshly ground
   black pepper

Heat the vegetable broth in a skillet over medium heat and sauté the onion, garlic, and celery until the onion is translucent.

Add the tomatoes and basil and simmer covered for 10 minutes, stirring frequently.

Add the eggplant, pine nuts, capers, vinegar, salt, and pepper and simmer for 15 minutes.

Serve with toasted bread.

Pine nuts contain a whopping amount of the mineral copper, which helps to keep the bones strong.

Creamy Tofu Dip

Yield: 6 servings

2 cups silken tofu
2 tablespoons chopped fresh parsley
2 tablespoons prepared mustard
2 tablespoons apple cider vinegar
2 tablespoons chopped fresh dill; reserve some for garnish
Sea salt to taste
½ teaspoon freshly ground black pepper
¼ cup chives

Place the tofu, parsley, mustard, vinegar, dill, salt, pepper and half the chives in a food processor or blender and purée until smooth.

Place in a serving dish and garnish with dill.

Serve chilled with raw vegetables; we love sliced celery, raw fennel and bok choy stems! Also, try this with lightly steamed asparagus.

Tofu contains omega-3 fatty acids, and is extremely high in tryptophan – an essential amino acid that aids in the production of protein in the body. This is what makes tofu an excellent source of protein in the vegetarian diet.

Date Spread

Yield: 5 servings

1 cup cooked red kidney beans
2 tablespoons dates, chopped
1 tablespoon fresh mint, chopped
½ cup cashews, chopped
1 tablespoon chia seeds
2 tablespoons grade B maple syrup
1 teaspoon almond extract
1 teaspoon vanilla extract
Sea salt to taste

Purée the beans, dates, and mint in a food processor until smooth.

Add the cashews, chia seeds, maple syrup, almond extract, vanilla extract, and salt, and pulse until well mixed.

Serve with crackers or raw vegetables.

Snack Suggestion: Try this yummy spread with Manna bread (from the frozen foods section at the health food store), fresh cut apples, or Anise Raisin Bread, p. 344.

Red kidney beans are actually one of the highest sources of antioxidants of all foods that we consume. Plus, they are a very good source of dietary fiber, which means they prevent blood sugar from rising too much after a meal, so they are great for people challenged by diabetes.

Exotic Tofu Dip

Yield: 6 servings

2 cups silken tofu
2 tablespoons fresh chives, chopped
1 clove garlic
4 tablespoons prepared mustard
3 tablespoons balsamic vinegar
2 tablespoons chopped fresh dill
Sea salt to taste
1 teaspoon freshly ground black pepper
1 tablespoon paprika, for garnish
1 small bunch chives, for garnish

Place the tofu, chives, garlic, mustard, vinegar, dill, salt, and pepper in a food processor or blender and purée until smooth.

Place in a serving dish and garnish with paprika and chives.

Serve chilled with assorted raw vegetables.

Snack Suggestion: For a great snack, make thin slices of cucumber and carrot or fresh raw red pepper and roll with tofu dip and alfalfa sprouts in a sheet of raw or toasted nori.

Paprika contains high levels of vitamin C, antioxidants and phytonutrients. In addition to being used as an antibacterial agent, it is known to aid in digestion.

Ginger Black Bean Dip

Yield: 6 servings

1 cup black beans, cooked
2 cloves garlic, minced
1 teaspoon ginger, minced
1 tablespoon tamari
½ chili pepper, minced
1 tablespoon cilantro, chopped
1 teaspoon toasted sesame oil
Sea salt to taste
½ teaspoon freshly ground black pepper

Place beans, garlic, and ginger in a food processor and purée until smooth.

Add tamari, chili, cilantro, sesame oil, salt, and pepper and pulse until well mixed.

Garnish with goji berries.

Serve with sesame bread sticks, vegetable chips, dried fruit, or fresh cut vegetables.

Capsaicin, the substance that gives chili peppers their characteristic hotness, is a known anti-inflammatory agent. Plus, the heat in chili peppers tends to curb one's appetite, so that you consume less food.

Greek Tomato Sauce

Yield: 4 servings

2 tablespoons extra virgin olive oil
1 yellow onion, diced
2 cloves garlic, minced
½ green bell pepper, chopped
One 16-ounce can whole tomatoes, chopped
2 tablespoons fresh parsley, chopped
2 tablespoons fresh basil, chopped
Sea salt to taste
½ teaspoon freshly ground black pepper

Heat the oil in a large saucepan over medium heat and sauté the onion, garlic, and bell pepper until the onion is translucent.

Add the tomatoes, parsley, basil, salt, and black pepper and simmer over medium heat for 25 minutes.

Serve hot over rice pasta, lightly steamed greens (kale, Swiss chard, or broccoli rabe) or vegetables.

Parsley is rated as one of the best plant sources of anti-inflammatory compounds and vitamin K, which has been found to promote bone health and be helpful in the prevention of osteoporosis, a disease of inflammation.

Green Plantain Tostones with Garlic Mojo Sauce

Yield: 5 servings

1 green plantain, left in its peel
2 tablespoons walnut oil

Place the plantain in a pot of water and boil until tender, about 15 minutes. Remove and let cool.

When cool enough to touch, remove the peel and discard.

Slice the plantain into 1½ inch pieces.

Flatten the pieces with a small plate into round patties.

Place in a skillet with heated walnut oil and sauté on both sides until golden brown.

Garlic Mojo Sauce:
6 cloves garlic, smashed
4 limes, juiced
Pinch cayenne
¼ cup fresh oregano leaves, chopped
Sea salt to taste
½ teaspoon freshly ground black pepper
1 tablespoon parsley, chopped, for garnish

Add the garlic to a food processor and purée.

Add the lime juice, cayenne, oregano, salt, and pepper and pulse until well mixed.

Place the sauce on the tostones and garnish with parsley.

Walnut oil is high in omega-3 fatty acids, and antioxidants, and is known to enhance the quality and texture of skin. Use it externally for help with eczema.

Guilt-Free Guacamole

Yield: 6 servings

2 packages frozen green peas, thawed
1 clove garlic, minced
1 tablespoon fresh parsley, chopped
¼ cup fresh lime juice
4 scallions, chopped; reserve half for garnish
½ cup fresh cilantro, chopped
½ teaspoon jalapeno, chopped
Sea salt to taste
½ teaspoon freshly ground black pepper

Place the peas, garlic, parsley, lime juice, half the scallions, cilantro, jalapeno, salt, and pepper in a food processor and purée until smooth.

Cover and refrigerate for 30 minutes to an hour.

Garnish with scallions.

Serve with vegetable chips, baked corn chips or fresh vegetables cut into pieces.

Bright-colored citrus fruits, including limes, lemons, oranges, grapefruits and tangerines are not only high in anti-oxidants, but contain important omega-3 fatty acids.

Heavenly Stuffed Tomatoes

Yield: 4 servings

1 tablespoon olive oil
2 scallions, chopped
1 clove garlic, minced
½ red bell pepper, chopped
6 medium tomatoes
1 bag of fresh spinach (about 10 ounces) washed, drained
 and chopped
½ cup walnuts, chopped
½ package silken tofu, crumbled
1 teaspoon fresh rosemary, chopped
½ teaspoon ground ginger
½ teaspoon fresh thyme, chopped
Sea salt to taste
Freshly ground pepper to taste
½ cup vegan Parmesan cheese, grated
1 bunch scallion greens, sliced 2 inches long, for garnish

Preheat oven to 375°.

Heat the oil in a skillet over medium heat and sauté the scallions, garlic and red bell pepper for 2 minutes.

Cut a ½-inch slice from the stem end of each tomato; scoop out the pulp and seeds.

Place the scallion-garlic-red bell pepper mixture, tomato pulp, spinach, walnuts, tofu, rosemary, ginger, thyme, salt, and pepper in a mixing bowl and mix well.

Stuff the tomatoes with the mixture, top with vegan parmesan and place in a greased baking dish.

Bake for 15 minutes or until the cheese is lightly brown.

Garnish with scallion greens.

Rich in vitamins and minerals, spinach is a powerhouse of health-promoting phytonutrients such as carotenoids like beta-carotene, and flavonoids that provide outstanding antioxidant protection. Spinach is also extremely high in vitamin K, vitamin A, and folate – all extremely important for bone and tissue health.

Herbed Tofu Croquettes

Yield: 6 servings

2 tablespoons olive oil
1 medium yellow onion, diced
2 cloves garlic, minced
1 green bell pepper, diced
3 stalks celery, diced
¼ pound mushrooms, minced
1 package firm tofu, drained
3 tablespoons flaxseed meal
¼ cup sunflower seeds
½ cup cashews, chopped
1 tablespoon tamari (soy sauce)
1 teaspoon fresh thyme, chopped
1 teaspoon fresh oregano, chopped
Sea salt to taste
½ teaspoon black pepper
½ cup wheat germ
2 tablespoons parsley, for garnish, chopped

Preheat oven to 350°.

Heat the oil in a skillet over medium-high heat and sauté onion, garlic, green pepper, and celery until the onion is translucent.

Add mushrooms and sauté for 5 minutes.

Place the tofu, sautéed vegetables, flaxseed meal, sunflower seeds, cashews, tamari, thyme, oregano, salt, and pepper in a food processor and purée until smooth.

Form the mixture into croquettes about 2 inches wide.

Place the wheat germ in a shallow bowl. Roll the croquettes in the wheat germ until well-coated and chill for 30 minutes.

Spray a baking sheet with non-stick olive oil spray, place croquettes evenly on the sheet, and bake for 10 minutes or until lightly brown.

Garnish with parsley.

Wheat germ is another nutritional powerhouse very high in vitamin E, minerals, omega-3 fatty acid, and folate to name a few. People who have included this wonderful anti-inflammatory food in their health diet have reported an increase in energy, stamina and overall well-being.

Holiday Stuffed Mushrooms

Yield: 6 servings

6 large mushrooms, de-stemmed (mince stems & set aside)
2 tablespoons extra virgin olive oil
1 medium yellow onion, diced
2 cloves garlic, minced
1 red bell pepper, chopped
2 tablespoons flax seed, ground
2 teaspoons fresh parsley, chopped
½ teaspoon fresh sage, chopped
½ teaspoon fresh rosemary, chopped
½ teaspoon fresh thyme
Sea salt to taste
½ teaspoon freshly ground black pepper
1 tablespoon fresh chives, chopped, for garnish

Preheat oven to 350°.

Place mushroom caps on a baking sheet sprayed with non-stick olive oil and bake for 15 minutes, or until brown.

Heat olive oil in a skillet over medium-high heat and sauté onion, garlic, and red bell pepper until the onion is translucent.

Place the minced mushroom stems, onion-garlic-red pepper mixture, ground flax seeds, parsley, sage, rosemary, thyme, salt, and pepper in a food processor and pulse until coarsely chopped.

Stuff mushroom caps with filling and garnish with chives.

While mushrooms are considered a vegetable by many, they are really a fungus. Mushrooms pack proteins, vitamins and minerals, amino acids, antibiotic and antioxidant appeal, and certain varieties have been used for centuries for their medicinal properties.

Potato Pancakes

Yield: 4 servings

For centuries, raw potato juice has been considered one of the most successful home remedies for conditions of arthritis and inflammation. To make: cut a medium-sized, organic potato into thin slices, without peeling the skin. Place slices in a large glass filled with cold filtered water overnight. Strain and drink the water in the morning on an empty stomach for the best results.

3 Yukon gold potatoes, grated
1 yellow onion, grated
1 clove garlic, minced
1 tablespoon flaxseed meal
2 tablespoons gluten-free oat flour
1 tablespoon parsley, chopped
Sea salt to taste
½ teaspoon freshly ground black pepper
Pinch cayenne
¼ cup olive oil
Shredded apple, chives, and bean sprouts for garnish

Place the grated potato, grated onion, garlic, flaxseed meal, flour, parsley, salt, pepper, and cayenne in a large bowl and mix well.

Form the mixture into patties and set aside.

Heat the oil in a large skillet over medium heat and sauté the potato pancakes until golden brown, about 5 minutes on each side.

Garnish with apple, chives, and bean sprouts.

Spicy Hummus

Yield: 6 servings

2 cups chickpeas, cooked
1 red bell pepper, roasted
½ medium yellow onion, chopped
1 jalapeño, seeded and minced
3 cloves garlic, minced
2 tablespoons fresh cilantro, chopped

1 tablespoon chipotle pepper in adobo sauce
Pinch cayenne
Sea salt to taste
½ teaspoon freshly ground black pepper
1 tablespoon water
1 teaspoon paprika, for garnish
¼ cup parsley leaves, for garnish

Place all the ingredients in a food processor and purée until smooth. Add water if necessary to achieve desired consistency.

Garnish with paprika and parsley.

Serve with sliced fresh vegetables or vegetable chips.

Snack Suggestion: Place a dollop of hummus on a sprouted wheat wrap along with some thinly sliced raw fresh veggies and sprouts. Roll up and eat!

Chickpeas (Garbanzo beans) are a good source of antioxidants, and contain important omega-3 fatty acids. They are also very high in dietary fiber, and as such are a wonderfully satisfying food and snack.

Spicy Peanut Sauce

Yield: 2 servings

¼ cup all natural peanut butter
1 tablespoon tahini
1 clove garlic
1 tablespoon fresh lime juice
2 drops hot chili oil
2 tablespoons apple cider vinegar
⅓ cup hot water as needed
1 tablespoon chives, minced, for garnish

Combine peanut butter, tahini, garlic, lime juice, chili oil, and apple cider vinegar in a blender or food processor and purée until smooth.

Add hot water as necessary to achieve desired consistency.

Garnish with chives.

Serve over cooked noodles or with assorted raw vegetables.

Snack Suggestion: Make spring roll wraps by reconstituting wrap in a bit of warm water for 20-30 seconds, adding avocado, shredded cabbage and carrot, basil and chopped peanuts. Roll and dip in sauce.

Tahini is high in fat, but it does not contain cholesterol. It is also high in manganese, which is helpful in nerve and brain health. Most importantly, tahini is a solid source of copper – a mineral that has anti-inflammatory properties.

Spicy Tomato Salsa

Yield: 6 servings

1 cup fresh tomatoes, chopped
¼ cup red onion, chopped
1 tablespoon fresh parsley, chopped
4 tablespoons fresh basil, chopped
1 teaspoon ginger, chopped
1 teaspoon extra virgin olive oil
2 tablespoons fresh hot peppers, minced
Sea salt to taste
½ teaspoon freshly ground black pepper

Combine all the ingredients in a medium bowl and mix until well-blended.

Serve with vegetable chips or raw vegetables.

While tomatoes and other nightshade vegetables are typically not recommended to people suffering from inflammatory conditions, we suggest that they are fine to include moderately as long as you don't suffer from nightshade sensitivity. (See p. 41 for a simple test to determine your sensitivity.)

Nuts are high in calories but pack a powerful punch in a healthful diet. Brazil nuts in particular are very high in vitamins, antioxidants and minerals; they are also an excellent source of selenium, which is very important to heart and liver health, and in the avoidance of cancer.

Broccoli is an amazing vegetable – low in calories, but very high in antioxidants, vitamins and minerals. It is a naturally anti-inflammatory food, and packed with phytonutrients that have been shown to be helpful in minimizing certain types of cancer. And if that weren't enough, broccoli contains small amounts of omega-3 fatty acids too! Let's hear it for broccoli.

Gomasio is a dry condiment typically used in Japanese cuisine. It is made from un-hulled sesame seeds and salt, and therefore contains helpful essential fatty acids.

Sweet Nutty Spread

Yield: 4 servings

¼ cup tahini
¼ cup agave nectar or rice syrup
2 tablespoons chopped almonds

2 tablespoons chopped Brazil nuts

Combine all the ingredients in a food processor and purée until smooth. Serve with vegetable chips or assorted raw vegetables.

Snack Suggestion: Try this great snack on fresh apple or pear slices, or on a piece of Anise Raisin Bread, p. 344.

Tahini-Broccoli Cream Dip

Yield: 4 servings

1 cup (approx. 8 oz.) silken tofu
½ cup tahini
2 tablespoons tamari
½ cup broccoli, chopped and steamed

1 tablespoon scallions, chopped
½ teaspoon freshly ground black pepper

Combine all the ingredients in a food processor and purée until smooth. Serve with vegetable chips or assorted raw vegetables.

Snack Suggestion: Try this great spread on sliced heirloom tomatoes topped with some chopped chives for a wonderful treat or appetizer!

Tahini Oat Sauce

Yield: 2 servings

½ cup tahini
½ cup gluten-free oat flour
1 tablespoon flaxseed meal
1 clove garlic, minced
1 scallion, chopped

1 tablespoon tamari
½ teaspoon freshly ground black pepper
1 cup water
1 tablespoon gomasio

Combine all the ingredients in a medium-size bowl and mix well. Serve at room temperature over brown rice or steamed squash.

Unfried Zucchini Fritters

Yield: 4 servings

Batter:

½ cup plain seltzer
½ cup rice flour
½ teaspoon oregano, chopped
½ tablespoon basil, chopped
¼ teaspoon cumin
Pinch of cayenne

1 clove garlic, minced
1 teaspoon egg replacer
Sea salt to taste
Freshly ground black pepper
  to taste

Combine all ingredients in a bowl and mix well with a whisk until smooth.

Zucchini:

2 medium zucchini, each
  sliced lengthwise into
  4 pieces

1 cup of panko (Japanese
  bread crumbs), or similar
2 tablespoons olive oil

Preheat oven to 350°.

Dip zucchini into batter then roll in breadcrumbs. Place on a nonstick baking sheet and drizzle with olive oil. Bake for 15 minutes, or until golden brown.

Remove from oven and place on paper towel to absorb excess oil.

Serve with a salad or Exotic Tofu Dip (see page 95)

Visit your local health food store for powdered vegan, gluten-free egg replacers. They are perfect for this recipe, and as substitutes for eggs in baking.

Vegetarian Chopped Liver

Yield: 4 servings

¼ cup vegetable broth
1 large yellow onion, diced
2 cloves garlic, minced
½ green bell pepper, chopped; reserve some for garnish
½ red bell pepper, chopped; reserve some for garnish
1 pound green beans, steamed and chopped
1 tablespoon flaxseed meal
½ cup walnuts
2 tablespoons fresh basil, chopped
1 tablespoon fresh thyme, chopped
1 tablespoon fresh parsley, chopped
Sea salt to taste
½ teaspoon freshly ground black pepper
Pinch cayenne

Heat the vegetable broth in a medium skillet over medium-high heat and sauté the onion, garlic, and green and red bell pepper until the onion is translucent.

Place the steamed green beans and flaxseed meal in a food processor and purée. Add the sautéed vegetables, walnuts, basil, thyme, parsley, salt, pepper, and cayenne and pulse until well mixed.

Garnish with green and red bell pepper.

Serve on toasted whole wheat bread.

In spite of their green color, *green* beans contain a wide variety of carotenoids (which are phytonutrients known for their pigment producing qualities) and flavonoids, both of which have been shown to be rich in antioxidant properties.

SOUPS

When it comes to food, there is hardly anything more comforting than a bowl of soup. It hardly matters what time of year, especially because I've included some wonderful cold soups here too. The great thing about soup is that it can be both a meal and a snack. When paired with a green salad, and a piece of wholesome bread with a delicious spread of spicy hummus (p. 109), creamy tofu dip (p. 93), or Caponata (p. 92), you have a healthy and completely satisfying offering on every level. The soup pot is where souls and bodies are nourished, so let these tasty and pleasing recipes soothe all that hungers and ails you; I promise you that they will do this and more.

Note: All of the following soup recipes can be prepared without oil for a healthier meal. While using oil enhances the soup's flavor, it diminishes its health benefits. If you choose to omit the oil, simply sauté onion in purified water.

– Gary

Algerian Chili

Yield: 4 servings

1 tablespoon olive oil
1 medium yellow onion, diced
4 cloves garlic, minced
2 scallions, chopped; reserve 1 tablespoon for garnish
1 stalk celery, chopped
4 cups water or vegetable broth
1 tomato, coarsely chopped
1 small dried red chili
1 red bell pepper, chopped
½ tablespoon sweet paprika
1 tablespoon curry powder
½ cup tomato paste
2 teaspoons ground cumin
3 cups navy beans, cooked
1 bay leaf
Pinch of cayenne
3 tablespoons fresh parsley, chopped; reserve 1 tablespoon
  for garnish
Sea salt to taste
½ teaspoon freshly ground black pepper

Heat the oil in a large saucepan over medium-high heat and sauté the onion, garlic, scallions, and celery until the onion is translucent.

Add the water, tomato, chili pepper, red bell pepper, paprika, curry powder, tomato paste, and cumin, and simmer until the mixture thickens, stirring frequently.

Add the beans, bay leaf, cayenne, parsley, salt, and pepper, and simmer for 15 minutes.

Garnish with parsley and scallion.

Navy beans contain important omega-3 fatty acids, and are an excellent source of dietary fiber, folate and manganese, all of which are very important in heart health.

Cashewy Bean Soup

Yield: 4-5 servings

Cashews are a very rich source of phytochemicals, which aid in the prevention of disease and cancer. Cashews are also an excellent source of minerals, including copper, which has numerous anti-inflammatory properties.

1 tablespoon walnut oil
1 medium yellow onion
2 cloves garlic, minced
1 stalk celery, chopped
1 Carmen pepper, chopped
4 cups water or vegetable broth
2 cups kidney beans, cooked
1 cup brown rice, cooked
½ cup cashews, chopped
¼ teaspoon chili powder
Sea salt to taste
½ teaspoon freshly ground black pepper
1 tablespoon fresh parsley, chopped, for garnish

Heat the oil over medium heat in a large saucepan and sauté onion, garlic, celery, and Carmen pepper until onion is translucent.

Add water or vegetable broth, kidney beans, brown rice, cashews, chili powder, salt, and pepper and simmer over medium heat for 20 minutes.

Garnish with parsley.

Chinese Cabbage Soup

Yield: 2 servings

1 tablespoon olive oil
1 yellow onion, diced
2 cloves garlic, minced
1 stalk celery, diced
3 cups water
2 cups Chinese cabbage, shredded
1 teaspoon freshly grated ginger
Sea salt to taste
½ teaspoon freshly ground black pepper
2 drops hot chili oil
1 teaspoon tamari
½ package extra-firm tofu, diced
1 tablespoon grated lemon zest, for garnish
1 tablespoon chia seeds, for garnish

Heat the oil in a large saucepan over medium heat and sauté onion, garlic, and celery until onion is translucent.

Add water and bring to a boil.

Add cabbage, ginger, salt, and pepper and simmer for 15 minutes.

Add chili oil, tamari, and tofu and stir well.

Garnish with lemon zest and chia seeds.

Chinese cabbage is one of the best utilized cabbages in mainland China, where residents consume up to a pound of fresh leafy vegetables per day. It is incredibly low in calories and packed with antioxidants, making it a natural disease fighter.

Cream of Broccoli Soup

Yield: 2 servings

1 tablespoon olive oil
1 yellow onion, diced
2 cloves garlic, minced
1 cup water
2 cups unsweetened almond milk
¼ cup cubed potatoes
½ cup broccoli florets
2 tablespoons fresh dill, chopped
1 teaspoon tamari
Sea salt to taste
½ teaspoon freshly ground black pepper
1 teaspoon paprika, for garnish
¼ cup bean sprouts, for garnish

Heat the oil in a large saucepan over medium heat and sauté onion and garlic until onion is translucent.

Add water, almond milk, potatoes, broccoli, dill, tamari, salt, and pepper and simmer over low heat for 15 minutes.

Remove the potatoes and broccoli from the soup, place in a food processor with some of the cooking liquid and purée until smooth.

Return to saucepan and stir until well blended.

Garnish with paprika and bean sprouts.

Broccoli is part of the cabbage family, and as such is a powerful food for fighting the inflammation that causes arthritis, heart disease and cancer.

Cream of Mushroom Soup

Yield: 4 servings

Though sometimes overlooked as "just a garnish," parsley is an amazingly powerful herb that is high in antioxidants, and has anti-cancer and anti-inflammatory benefits. Plus! Try chewing on some parsley leaves to freshen your breath.

2 tablespoons walnut oil
1 yellow onion, chopped
2 cloves garlic, minced
1 stalk celery, chopped
1 pound mushrooms, sliced
1 cup vegetable broth
2 cups unsweetened almond milk
1 teaspoon fresh thyme, chopped
Sea salt to taste
½ teaspoon freshly ground black pepper
1 tablespoon fresh parsley, chopped, for garnish

Heat the oil in a large saucepan over medium heat and sauté onion, garlic, and celery until the onion is translucent.

Add sliced mushrooms and sauté until browned. Reserve 1 tablespoon for garnish.

Place the sautéed vegetables in a food processor with ½ cup vegetable broth; purée until smooth and return to the soup pot.

Add remaining vegetable broth, almond milk, thyme, salt, and pepper and simmer for 15 minutes.

Garnish with parsley and chopped mushrooms.

Cream of Sweet Potato Soup

Sweet potatoes are very high in vitamin C, and also contain high amounts of calcium, folate, potassium and beta-carotene. They are a low-glycemic food, so are great for people with diabetes or who want to manage cravings.

Yield: 4 servings

1 tablespoon olive oil
1 large yellow onion, diced
3 cloves garlic, minced
2 sweet potatoes, cubed
2 cups vegetable stock
1 bunch watercress, washed well; reserve ½ cup of leaves, for garnish

2 tablespoons minced fresh parsley
2 cups unsweetened almond milk
Sea salt to taste
Freshly ground black pepper to taste
½ cup sunflower seeds, for garnish

Heat the oil in a large saucepan over medium heat and sauté the onion and garlic over medium heat until the onion is translucent.

Add the sweet potatoes and stock, and simmer for 15 minutes, until tender.

Add the watercress, parsley, almond milk, salt, and pepper and simmer for about 10 minutes.

Remove from heat. Purée in a blender or food processor and return to the saucepan.

Garnish with watercress and sunflower seeds.

Cucumber Mint Soup

Yield: 2 servings

2 cucumbers, peeled and chopped
4 stalks celery
1 cup plain soy yogurt
2 teaspoons fresh mint, chopped
2-3 cups water to desired consistency
¼ cup diced red bell pepper, for garnish
½ cup cucumber zest, for garnish

In a food processor, purée the cucumbers, celery, yogurt, and mint.

Place the purée and water in a medium bowl and blend well.

Garnish with the diced red pepper and cucumber zest.

Cucumbers have a very favorable omega-6/omega-3 ratio, making them a wonderful vegetarian source of these essential fatty acids. Plus, they are great for the skin and complexion.

Curried Lentil Soup

Yield: 6 servings

1 tablespoon olive oil
1 large yellow onion, diced
2 scallions, sliced
4 cloves garlic, minced
1 celery stalk, sliced
4 cups water
1 cup dried green lentils
1 carrot, sliced
1 teaspoon ground coriander

1 teaspoon turmeric
½ teaspoon ground cumin
1 teaspoon paprika
¼ teaspoon cayenne pepper
½ teaspoon ground ginger
Sea salt to taste
½ teaspoon freshly ground
black pepper
¼ cup chopped parsley,
for garnish

Heat the oil in a large saucepan over medium heat and sauté the onion, scallions, garlic, and celery until the onion is translucent.

Add water, lentils, carrot, coriander, turmeric, cumin, paprika, cayenne, ginger, salt, and pepper and simmer for 20 minutes, or until the lentils are soft.

Garnish with parsley.

Curry is another warming spice that is excellent for reducing inflammation and is high in antioxidants.

Delectable Tomato Squash Soup

Yield: 2 servings

1 butternut squash, cut in half, pulp and seeds removed
2 large tomatoes, chopped; reserve some for garnish
3 cups water
2 teaspoons fresh dill, chopped
Pinch cayenne

Sea salt to taste
Freshly ground black pepper to taste
2 tablespoons plain soy yogurt, for garnish
2 sprigs fresh dill, for garnish

Preheat oven to 350°.

Place the butternut squash halves on a baking sheet sprayed with non-stick olive oil and bake for 20 minutes. Peel when cool enough to handle.

Cut the cooked squash into one-inch pieces, place in a food processor with the chopped tomatoes and purée until smooth.

Combine the purée with the water, dill, cayenne, salt, and pepper in a large saucepan and simmer over medium heat for 10 minutes.

Serve hot or cold, garnished with chopped tomatoes, soy yogurt and dill.

The antioxidant lycopene, found in abundance in tomatoes, has been shown to reduce the risk of diseases of inflammation, and prevent cell damage caused by free radicals. Because it is fat soluble, it is especially beneficial for tissues with a high lipid content, like the skin.

Favorite Vegetable Soup

Yield: 4 servings

2 tablespoons walnut oil
1 yellow onion, diced
2 cloves garlic, diced
1 stalk celery, sliced; reserve a few slices for garnish
4 cups vegetable stock
1 cup mung beans, cooked
½ red cabbage, sliced
1 tablespoon chopped fresh parsley
½ teaspoon ground oregano
2 tablespoons fresh basil, chopped
1 tablespoon fresh thyme, chopped
Sea salt to taste
½ teaspoon freshly ground black pepper
1 sprig thyme, for garnish
1 cup basmati or brown rice, cooked

Heat the oil in a large saucepan over medium heat and sauté onion, garlic, and celery until onion is translucent.

Add vegetable broth, mung beans, cabbage, parsley, oregano, basil, thyme, salt, and pepper and cook over medium heat for 15 minutes.

Place soup contents in a blender or food processor and purée. Return purée to saucepan and cook until thoroughly heated.

Garnish with celery, rice, and thyme.

Serving Tip: Many soups can be served over brown rice, millet or quinoa to increase the heartiness and nutritional value of a meal. It's always a great idea to have a small side-salad, or fresh raw veggies with your cooked soups to increase the meal's nutritional value.

Mung beans are an excellent vegetarian source of protein. Plus, they are high in fiber and a low-glycemic food, making them exceptionally good for managing blood sugar and weight. Sprout them for added nutritional benefit.

Gary's Noodle Soup

Yield: 4 servings

1 tablespoon olive oil
1 yellow onion, diced
3 cloves garlic, minced
1 stalk celery, chopped
4 cups vegetable stock
1 package fresh spinach (10 oz.), coarsely chopped
6 stalks asparagus, cut into 1 inch pieces
½ teaspoon cumin
3 tablespoons fresh basil, chopped
Sea salt to taste
¼ teaspoon freshly ground black pepper
Pinch cayenne
8-oz. package buckwheat noodles
½ cup cherry tomatoes, sliced, for garnish

Heat the oil in a large saucepan over medium heat and sauté the onion, garlic, and celery until the onions are translucent.

Add vegetable stock, spinach, asparagus, cumin, basil, salt, pepper, and cayenne and simmer for 10 minutes.

Add noodles and cook for an additional 10 minutes.

Garnish with cherry tomato.

If having a gluten-free meal is important to you, check ingredients of buckwheat noodles to make sure that they do not contain wheat, as some brands do.

Gazpacho

Yield: 4-5 servings

While this cold soup is a great meal and snack in the summertime, I find it appealing as a starter anytime of the year.

6 medium tomatoes, chopped
2 green bell peppers, chopped
2 large yellow onions, coarsely chopped
2 large cucumbers, coarsely chopped
2 canned pimientos, drained
4 cloves garlic, minced
1 large can (16 oz.) tomato juice

Sea salt to taste
½ teaspoon freshly ground black pepper
1 tablespoon olive oil
½ teaspoon Tabasco sauce
⅓ cup red wine vinegar
½ cup fresh parsley leaves, for garnish

Place the tomatoes, green bell peppers, onions, cucumber, pimientos, and garlic in a food processor or blender with ½ cup tomato juice and purée.

Place the puréed vegetables in a large mixing bowl and add the remaining tomato juice, salt, pepper, olive oil, Tabasco, and vinegar.

Cover and place in a refrigerator for at least 3 hours.

Garnish with fresh parsley.

Hearty Winter Soup

Yield: 4 servings

2 tablespoons olive oil
1 leek, chopped
2 cloves garlic, minced
1 stalk celery, chopped
6 cups vegetable broth or water
2 cups red lentils, cooked
½ cup kidney beans, cooked
½ butternut squash, peeled and cubed
2 carrots, sliced
2 tablespoons fresh cilantro, chopped
½ teaspoon cumin
1 teaspoon curry powder
½ teaspoon turmeric
1 teaspoon tamari
½ teaspoon freshly ground black pepper

Heat the oil in a large saucepan over medium heat and sauté the leek, garlic, and celery until the leek is translucent.

Add the vegetable broth or water, lentils, beans, squash, carrots, cilantro, cumin, curry powder, turmeric, tamari, and black pepper and simmer for 30 minutes over medium heat.

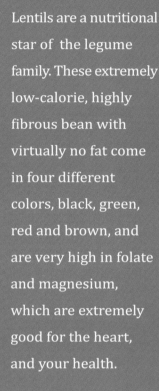

Lentils are a nutritional star of the legume family. These extremely low-calorie, highly fibrous bean with virtually no fat come in four different colors, black, green, red and brown, and are very high in folate and magnesium, which are extremely good for the heart, and your health.

Hot Spinach and Bean Soup

Yield: 4 servings

The combination of kidney beans, spinach and basil make this an anti-inflammatory powerhouse that is also high in omega-3s.

2 tablespoons walnut oil
1 yellow onion, diced
2 cloves garlic, diced
¼ jalapeño pepper, minced
4 cups water
2 cups kidney beans, cooked
½ head cauliflower, cut into florets
1 cup spinach, coarsely chopped
2 tablespoons fresh basil, chopped
Sea salt to taste
½ teaspoon freshly ground black pepper
Pinch of cayenne

Heat the oil in a large saucepan over medium heat and sauté the onion, garlic, and jalapeño until the onion is translucent.

Add water, kidney beans, cauliflower, spinach, basil, salt, pepper, and cayenne and cook over medium heat for 15 minutes.

Italian Style Pinto Bean Soup

Yield: 4 servings

2 tablespoons olive oil
1 yellow onion, diced
2 cloves garlic, minced
1 stalk celery, chopped
1 red bell pepper, chopped
4 cups water
2 cups pinto beans, cooked
2 carrots, sliced
1 cup mushrooms, sliced
½ cup arugula, chopped
½ teaspoon cumin
Sea salt to taste
½ teaspoon freshly ground black pepper

Heat the oil in a large saucepan over medium heat and sauté the onion, garlic, celery, and red pepper until the onion is translucent.

Add water, beans, carrots, mushrooms, arugula, cumin, salt, and pepper and simmer over medium heat for 20 minutes.

Pinto beans are terrifically high in omega-3s and a great source of cholesterol-lowering fiber. They are also high in protein and important minerals like molybdenum – a very good source of folate, which is critical for heart health.

Italian White Bean Soup with Bowtie Pasta

Yield: 4 servings

2 tablespoons extra virgin olive oil
1 yellow onion, chopped
2 cloves garlic, chopped
3 fresh tomatoes, chopped
4 cups water
1 cup kale, chopped
1 cup white beans, cooked
2 tablespoons fresh parsley, chopped
2 tablespoons fresh basil, chopped
Sea salt to taste
½ teaspoon freshly ground black pepper
½ cup small bow-tie pasta

Heat the oil in a large saucepan over medium heat and sauté the onion and garlic until the onion is translucent.

Add the tomatoes and sauté for 10 minutes.

Add the water, kale, beans, parsley, basil, salt, and pepper and bring to a boil.

Add the pasta and cook until done.

Preparation Tip: Make this a gluten-free meal by using noodles made from rice or quinoa.

We love kale! It is one of the most nutritious dark leafy green that you can eat. Try it in your soups and salads (baby kale is now available in health food stores), in your smoothies, or just lightly steamed with a healthy sauce.

Jamaican Pepperpot Soup

Yield: 2 servings

This soup, rich with anti-inflammatory peppers and spices and full of dark leafy greens, is a dynamite soup for those wishing to avoid and prevent inflammatory conditions.

1 tablespoon olive oil
1 yellow onion, diced
3 cloves garlic, minced
2 scallions, chopped
½ jalapeño or habanero pepper, diced
3 cups water
1 pound collard greens, chopped
2 medium bok choy, chopped
1 small yam, peeled and diced
1 teaspoon fresh thyme
½ teaspoon ground ginger
Sea salt to taste
½ teaspoon freshly ground black pepper
Pinch of cayenne
1 cup coconut milk
1 teaspoon bacon-flavored tofu crumbles, for garnish
1 sweet green chili pepper, sliced, for garnish

Heat the oil in a large saucepan over medium heat and sauté the onion, garlic, scallions, and jalapeño until the onion is translucent.

Add water, collard greens, bok choy, yam, thyme, ginger, salt, pepper and cayenne and simmer for 20 minutes.

Place the soup ingredients in a food processor and purée until smooth. Return purée to the soup pot.

Add the coconut milk and simmer on medium heat for 5 minutes.

Garnish with tofu crumbles and green chili pepper.

Jamaican Squash Soup

Yield: 4 servings

1 butternut squash, cut in half, seeds and pulp removed
1 tablespoon walnut oil
2 shallots, minced
1 clove garlic, minced
1 stalk celery, chopped
4 cups vegetable broth
½ cup sunflower seeds
1 teaspoon curry powder
½ teaspoon ground cinnamon
Sea salt to taste
½ teaspoon freshly ground black pepper
1 pinch cayenne

Preheat oven to 350°.

Place the squash on a baking sheet sprayed with non-stick olive oil and bake for 20 minutes.

When cool enough to handle, peel the squash, chop into 1 inch pieces and purée in a blender or food processor with ½ cup of vegetable broth.

In a large saucepan, heat the oil over medium heat and sauté the shallots, garlic, and celery until tender.

Add the puréed squash, vegetable broth, sunflower seeds. curry powder, cinnamon, salt, pepper, and cayenne and simmer for 10 minutes.

Butternut squash is the most popular squash in America, and wonderfully rich with nutrition. It is extremely high in vitamin A and B-complex. Hint: lightly salt and toast up the seeds for a wonderfully tasty, high-protein snack!

Lemon Tree Soup

The lemon in this soup makes it a zesty and tasty dish. Lemons are very nutritious, and are incredibly alkalizing to the body, making them a perfect addition to the anti-inflammatory diet. Try some fresh-squeezed lemon in room-temperature water upon rising for a quick and healthy pick-me-up.

Yield: 2 servings

1 tablespoon extra virgin olive oil
2 large shallots, diced
1 scallion, chopped
2 cloves garlic, minced
1 stalk celery, chopped
3 cups vegetable broth
½ cup brown rice
2 tablespoons flaxseed meal

1 teaspoon turmeric
Sea salt to taste
½ teaspoon freshly ground black pepper
1 tablespoon miso
1 tablespoon tahini
Juice of 2 large lemons
2 tablespoons scallions, chopped, for garnish

Heat the oil in a large saucepan over medium heat and sauté shallots, scallion, garlic, and celery until onion is translucent.

Add the vegetable broth, rice, flaxseed meal, turmeric, salt, and pepper. Cover and simmer 20 minutes until rice is tender.

Whisk together in a small bowl the miso, tahini, and lemon juice; add to soup and stir until well-blended.

Garnish with chopped scallions.

Mango Squash Soup

Yield: 2 servings

2 acorn squash, cut in half, pulp and seeds removed
2 mangoes peeled and sliced; reserve ½ cup slices, for garnish
3 cups water
1 teaspoon ground cinnamon
½ teaspoon ground nutmeg
½ cup halved seedless red grapes, for garnish
¼ cup pomegranate seeds, for garnish

Preheat oven to 350°.

Place the acorn squash halves on a baking sheet sprayed with non-stick olive oil and bake for 20 minutes.

Cut the cooked squash into one inch pieces, place in a food processor with the sliced mango and purée until smooth.

Combine the purée, water, cinnamon, and nutmeg in a mixing bowl and blend well.

Serve hot or cold, garnished with the mango slices, red grapes, and pomegranate seeds.

Mangoes are naturally anti-inflammatory; and did you know that one serving of only 100 calories provides 100% of the Recommended Daily Allowance of vitamin C?

Miso Tofu Soup

Yield: 2 servings

Miso is fermented bean paste, which means it is very helpful in providing healthy bacteria to our digestive systems. It is available in four types (brown, yellow, white and red). The lighter the color, the more mellow the taste.

1 tablespoon walnut oil
4 scallions, sliced
2 cloves garlic, minced
1 large celery stalk, sliced
4 cups water
1 package firm tofu, diced
½ red bell pepper, chopped
½ yellow bell pepper, chopped

3 tablespoons fresh parsley;
   reserve ½ for garnish
½ teaspoon oregano
Sea salt to taste
½ teaspoon freshly ground
   black pepper
4 tablespoons brown rice miso

Heat the oil in a large saucepan over medium-high heat and sauté the scallions, garlic, and celery until tender, about 2 minutes.

Add the water, tofu, red and yellow bell pepper, parsley, oregano, salt, and pepper and simmer for 10 minutes.

Remove 1 cup of hot liquid; dissolve the miso in it and return to the saucepan and blend well.

Garnish with parsley.

New Fangled Old Timey Soup

Yield: 4 servings

3 tablespoons hijiki, dry
1 tablespoon walnut oil
1 yellow onion, diced
2 garlic cloves, minced
1 stalk celery, sliced
4 cups water
1 cup brown rice, cooked
1 cup black-eyed peas, cooked
½ cup watercress, chopped

1 parsnip, sliced
1 carrot, sliced
1 teaspoon tamari
3 tablespoons fresh cilantro, chopped
1 bay leaf
Sea salt to taste
½ teaspoon freshly ground black pepper
¼ cup mint, for garnish

Soak hijiki in 8 oz. of water for 20 minutes and rinse twice.

In a large saucepan, heat the oil over medium heat and sauté the onion, garlic, and celery until the onion is translucent.

Add the water, cooked rice, black-eyes peas, watercress, parsnip, carrot, tamari, cilantro, bay leaf, salt, and pepper and simmer for 15 minutes.

Garnish with mint leaves.

Black-eyed peas are one of my favorites because they have such an appealing presentation. Black-eyed peas are especially rich sources of potassium, which is important for the proper function of all cells, tissues and organs in the body.

Old Country Potato Soup

Yield: 4 servings

1 tablespoon olive oil
1 yellow onion, diced
3 cloves garlic, minced
4 cups of water
4 medium potatoes, cubed
1 tomato, chopped
1 yellow or red bell pepper, diced
1 small head broccoli, cut into
  florets

2 carrots, sliced
½ teaspoon cumin
2 tablespoons fresh basil,
  chopped
1 teaspoon chia seeds
Sea salt to taste
½ teaspoon freshly ground
  black pepper
2 scallions, chopped, for garnish

Heat the oil in a large saucepan over medium heat and sauté the onion and garlic until the onion is translucent.

Add water and potatoes and boil for approximately 15 minutes, or until potatoes are tender.

Transfer potatoes, onions, and garlic to a blender or food processor with ½ cup of the cooking water and purée until smooth.

Return mixture to saucepan; add the remaining ingredients and simmer for an additional 10 minutes until the broccoli is done.

Garnish with scallions.

The word "soup" comes from the Latin word "suppa" meaning bread soaked in broth, and I cannot think of a heartier meal than this soup with a piece of multi-grain bread.

Onion Soup

Yield: 2 servings

2-3 tablespoons extra virgin olive oil
4 large yellow onions, sliced
4 cups vegetable broth
3 cloves garlic, minced
¼ cup chopped fresh parsley
3 tablespoons fresh basil, chopped
1 bay leaf
1 teaspoon fresh thyme
Sea salt to taste
Freshly ground black pepper to taste

Heat the oil in a large pot over medium heat and sauté the onions until caramelized, about 30 minutes.

Add the remaining ingredients; reduce heat and cook, covered, for 20 minutes.

Onions are wonderfully healthful, and rich in polyphenols – one of the largest categories of phytonutrients in foods. Their unique combination of sulfur-containing nutrients and flavonoids makes them a beneficial daily ingredient in the anti-inflammatory diet.

Papaya Yam Soup

Yield: 4 servings

2 yams or sweet potatoes, peeled and diced
2 papayas, peeled and de-seeded
1 tablespoon walnut oil
1 small yellow onion, diced
2 cloves garlic, minced
4 cups water
½ teaspoon ground cinnamon
½ teaspoon ground nutmeg
½ teaspoon ground cardamom
½ teaspoon turmeric
1 tablespoon chia seeds
Sea salt to taste
½ teaspoon freshly ground black pepper

Place the yams and papayas in a food processor or blender and puree until smooth; set aside.

Heat the oil in a large saucepan over medium heat and sauté the onion and garlic until the onion is translucent.

Add the water, yam-papaya purée, cinnamon, nutmeg, cardamom, turmeric, chia seeds, salt, and pepper and simmer over medium heat for 15-20 minutes.

Papayas are a wonderful fruit whose seeds are eatable and wonderfully cleansing to the intestinal tract, and their peppery taste makes them great for salad dressings. The fruit itself is an incredible source of whole-foods nutrition, and contains the digestive enzyme, papain, which is used like bromelain (a similar enzyme found in pineapple) to aid in healing by reducing inflammation.

Penne Pasta and Kidney Bean Soup

Yield: 4 servings

2 tablespoons extra virgin
   olive oil
1 large yellow onion, diced
2 cloves garlic, minced
1 stalk celery, chopped
4 cups vegetable broth
2 tomatoes, chopped
¾ cup kidney beans, cooked
1 carrot, sliced
½ cup kale, chopped

2 teaspoons fresh parsley,
   chopped
2 teaspoons fresh basil, chopped
Sea salt to taste
Freshly ground black pepper
   to taste
½ head cauliflower, cut into
   florets
¼ cup uncooked whole grain
   penne pasta

Heat the oil in a large saucepan over medium heat and sauté the onion, garlic, and celery until the onion is translucent.

Add the vegetable broth, tomatoes, kidney beans, carrot, kale, parsley, basil, salt, and pepper and simmer uncovered for 15 minutes.

Add cauliflower and pasta and simmer for 10 minutes, or until the pasta is tender.

Serve with bread.

There is a wonderful supply of wheat-free and organic pastas available today at your local health food store. It is always possible to substitute gluten-free pasta for the wheat-based pasta to increase the health value.

Portuguese Kale and Potato Soup

Yield: 2 servings

This traditional soup of Portugal features Spanish chorizo. We've whipped up a delicious vegan version that is sure to please the palate, and grandmother!

1 tablespoon olive oil
1 yellow onion, diced
3 cloves garlic, minced
4 cups water or vegetable broth
2 cups fresh kale, chopped; reserve 1 tablespoon, for garnish

1 large Yukon gold potato, peeled and cut into cubes
Sea salt to taste
Freshly ground black pepper to taste
Pinch of nutmeg
3 teaspoons spearmint leaves
1 teaspoon paprika, for garnish

Heat the oil in a large saucepan on medium heat and sauté the onion and garlic until the onion is translucent.

Add the water or vegetable broth, kale, potato, salt, pepper, nutmeg, and spearmint and cook for 15 minutes.

Remove the potato from the soup; place in a blender or food processor with some of the cooking liquid and purée until smooth.

Return to the soup and stir until well blended.

Garnish with chopped kale and paprika.

Potato Leek Soup

Yield: 4 servings

2 tablespoons olive oil
6-8 leeks, sliced
3 cloves garlic, minced
1 stalk celery, sliced
4 cups water
4 potatoes, sliced thin
1 tablespoon fresh parsley, chopped
2 tablespoons fresh basil, chopped
1 teaspoon fresh thyme, chopped
½ teaspoon ground marjoram
Sea salt to taste
½ teaspoon freshly ground black pepper

Heat the oil in a large saucepan over medium heat and sauté the leeks, garlic, and celery until the leeks are translucent.

Add the water, potatoes, parsley, basil, thyme, marjoram, salt, and pepper and cook over low heat until the potatoes are tender, about 20 minutes.

Remove half the potatoes and leeks; purée in a blender or food processor with 1 cup of the soup, and return to pot.

Stir well and serve.

It may surprise you to learn that leeks contain a good amount of omega-3 fatty acids. Paired with the powerful anti-inflammatory herb thyme, which is known to safeguard and increase the amount of healthy omega-3 fats in cell membranes and other cell structures, you have a powerful inflammation fighting meal.

Potato Mustard Soup

Yield: 2 servings

1 tablespoon olive oil
1 yellow onion, diced
2 cloves garlic, minced
4 cups vegetable stock
3 Yukon gold potatoes, cubed
2 tablespoons fresh parsley
1 sprig thyme
Sea salt to taste
½ teaspoon freshly ground pepper
1 pinch cayenne
3 tablespoons grained Dijon mustard
2 tablespoons soy yogurt, for garnish
1 scallion, chopped, for garnish

Heat the oil in a large saucepan over medium heat and sauté onion and garlic until the onion is translucent.

Add the vegetable stock, potatoes, parsley, thyme, salt, pepper, and cayenne and simmer 20 minutes, or until potatoes are cooked.

Place the soup ingredients in a blender or food processor; add the mustard and purée until smooth.

Return to the saucepan and stir well.

Garnish with soy yogurt and scallion.

Mustard seeds are a good source of omega-3s, and – as part of the *brassica* (cruciferous) family – are an excellent anti-inflammatory, anti-cancer food.

Potato Tomato Soup

Yield: 4-5 servings

1 tablespoon olive oil
2 scallions, chopped
2 cloves garlic, minced
4 cups water
4 medium potatoes, peeled and quartered
¼ teaspoon cumin
¼ cup fresh basil, chopped
1 tomato, chopped; reserve 1 tablespoon for garnish
1 red bell pepper, chopped, reserve a few slices for garnish
Sea salt to taste
½ teaspoon freshly ground black pepper
1 tablespoon fresh dill, for garnish

Heat the oil in a large saucepan over medium heat and sauté the scallions and garlic for 2 minutes.

Add water, potatoes, cumin, basil, tomato, red pepper, salt, and pepper and boil for approximately 20 minutes, or until potatoes are tender.

Transfer the soup to a blender or food processor with ½ cup of the cooking water and purée until smooth.

Return mixture to saucepan and stir well.

Garnish with sliced red pepper, tomato and dill.

Even though tomatoes are a nightshade, they are a wonderful source of nutrients, including antioxidants such as lycopene, which have proven valuable in bone health. They are also an incredibly rich source of phytonutrients. Organically grown heirloom varieties are the best – if you can find them – and only if you are not sensitive to nightshades.
See p. 41 for more information on night-shade sensitivities.

Pumpkin Cream Soup

Yield: 4 servings

Pumpkin is such a wonderful vegetable. Rich in antioxidant vitamins such as vitamin-A, vitamin-C and vitamin-E, pumpkin also contains Zeaxanthin, an anti-oxidant known to protect against Age Related Macular Degeneration (ARMD). So this fall, eat your pumpkins!

1 cup silken tofu
1 cup pumpkin, puréed
1 Golden Delicious apple, peeled, cored and chopped
2 tablespoons walnut oil
1 small yellow onion, diced
1 scallion, chopped
1 clove garlic, minced
1 stalk celery, chopped
4 cups vegetable broth
1 teaspoon curry powder
¼ teaspoon ground turmeric
¼ teaspoon ground cumin
1 tablespoon fresh basil, chopped
1 tablespoon flaxseed meal
Sea salt to taste
Freshly ground black pepper, optional

Place the tofu, pumpkin, and apple in a food processor or blender and puree until smooth; set aside.

Heat the oil in a large saucepan over medium heat and sauté onion, scallion, garlic, and celery until the onion is translucent.

Add the vegetable broth, purée, curry powder, turmeric, cumin, basil, flaxseed meal, salt, and pepper and simmer for 15 minutes.

RAW Cajun Squash Soup

Yield: 2 servings

1 butternut squash, peeled and chopped into pieces
1 red bell pepper, chopped
2 tablespoons cilantro, chopped
¼ chipotle pepper (de-seed to desired heat), chopped
1 teaspoon basil, chopped
⅓ teaspoon Cajun seasoning
Sea salt to taste
Freshly ground black pepper to taste
½ – 2 cups water
½ cup watercress, for garnish

Place all ingredients except water in a food processor and purée until smooth.

Add enough water to achieve desired consistency and stir well.

Serve chilled, garnished with watercress.

Eating our veggies and fruits raw gives us access to not only the full-spectrum of nutrients available in the food, but also to enzymes, which are utilized to assist in the digestion of the food. Eating more raw foods will improve your energy, your mood, and your overall health markedly.

Garlic is a powerhouse of an herb with anti-microbial, antibacterial and antiviral properties, which is what makes it so effective in the prevention and elimination of chronic disease. Garlic can do everything from lowering blood pressure, to preventing clots, to preventing infections. Oh, and did we mention it's an anti-inflammatory as well? Go garlic!

RAW Delectable Tomato Squash Soup

Yield: 2 servings

4 large tomatoes, chopped
½ butternut squash, peeled and chopped
2 cloves garlic, minced
1 teaspoon dill
½ cup fresh corn kernels
Sea salt to taste
Freshly ground black pepper to taste
Pinch cayenne
½ – 2 cups water
½ cup fresh basil, chopped, for garnish

Place tomatoes, squash, and garlic in a food processor and purée.

Add dill, corn, salt, black pepper and cayenne and mix well.

Add enough water to achieve desired consistency and stir well.

Serve chilled, garnished with fresh basil.

Sabzi Ka Shorba

Yield: 4 servings

1 tablespoon walnut oil
1 yellow onion, diced
1 teaspoon black mustard seeds
2 to 3 cups water (depending on desired consistency)
1 cup dried yellow lentils
1½ cups sliced carrots
1½ cups cauliflower florets
1½ cups broccoli florets
½ teaspoon ground cumin
¼ teaspoon chat masala
1 tablespoon chopped fresh cilantro
¼ teaspoon sea salt
½ teaspoon freshly ground black pepper

Heat the oil in a large saucepan over medium-high heat and sauté the onion until translucent.

Add the mustard seeds and cook until they start to pop.

Add the water, lentils, carrots, cauliflower, broccoli, cumin, chat masala, cilantro, salt, and pepper and simmer over medium heat for 25-35 minutes.

This traditional Indian soup full of garden-fresh vegetables and flavorful spices make it a highly tasty, healthful, anti-inflammatory dish. Pair it with a salad with ginger dressing, and a nice piece of whole-grain bread for a hearty and delicious meal.

Savory Cream of Potato Soup

Yield: 4 servings

2 tablespoons olive oil
1 yellow onion, sliced
2 cloves garlic, minced
1 stalk celery, sliced
1 cup peeled and cubed potatoes
2 cups water
2 cups unsweetened almond milk
¼ teaspoon cayenne
Sea salt to taste
½ teaspoon freshly ground black pepper
1 scallion, chopped, for garnish
Alfalfa sprouts, for garnish

Heat the oil in a large saucepan over medium heat and sauté the onion, garlic, and celery until the onion is translucent.

Add the potatoes and water and cook over medium heat for 15 minutes.

Remove potatoes and sautéed vegetables from the soup and place in a blender or food processor; purée until smooth.

Place the purée back in the soup pot; add the remaining ingredients and cook for 10 more minutes, stirring frequently.

Garnish with sliced scallions and alfalfa sprouts.

Almond milk is wonderfully rich and highly digestible. Reports indicate it is more nutritious than other non-dairy alternatives and extremely beneficial for our bones because it contains very good levels of calcium and vitamin D.

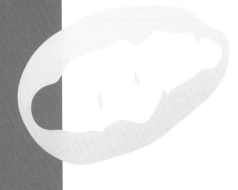

This is an extremely nutritious mixture of highly beneficial nutrients and healthy fats. Avocados – one of Mother Nature's finest foods – are the fruit of an evergreen tree that can grow 65-feet tall. It is a highly anti-inflammatory food that in spite of its high fat content is beneficial in weight loss and weight management when consumed in moderation.

Spicy RAW Spinach and Avocado Soup

Yield: 3 servings

1 cucumber, peeled and chopped
½ – 2 cups vegetable broth
2 cups spinach, washed and chopped
2 cups tomatoes, cubed
½ ripe avocado, diced
1 teaspoon fresh ginger, minced
1 tablespoon flaxseed oil
1 clove garlic, minced

1 tablespoon lemon juice
1 tablespoon apple cider vinegar
½ teaspoon light miso
½ teaspoon salt
½ teaspoon freshly ground black pepper
½ teaspoon cayenne
1 teaspoon chia, for garnish
1 teaspoon flax seeds, for garnish

Combine all ingredients in a food processor or blender and blend until smooth.

Chill for 1-2 hours.

Garnish with chia or flax seeds.

Thick and Hearty Borscht

Yield: 4 servings

1 tablespoon olive oil
2 yellow onions, diced
2 cloves garlic, minced
6 cups vegetable stock
5 beets, chopped; reserve
   ½ cup for garnish
1 large carrot, sliced
2 leeks, chopped
2 potatoes, diced
2 cups red cabbage, shredded

2 cups green cabbage,
   shredded
2 teaspoons caraway seeds
Sea salt to taste
½ teaspoon freshly ground
   black pepper
2 tablespoons apple cider
   vinegar
1 bay leaf

Heat the oil in a large saucepan over medium heat and sauté the onions and garlic until the onions are translucent.

Add the vegetable stock, beets, carrot, leeks, potatoes, red and green cabbage, caraway seeds, salt, pepper, vinegar, and bay leaf, and simmer for 30-40 minutes.

Garnish with chopped beets.

Beets are an extremely nutritious food, offering tremendous benefit through their unique mix of anti-oxidants proven helpful in eye health and overall nerve tissue health. They are a good source of omega-3 fatty acids, and are becoming known as a powerful anti-inflammatory food.

Turnip and Black Bean Soup

Yield: 4 servings

1 tablespoon olive oil
1 yellow onion, diced
2 cloves garlic, minced
2 cups black beans, cooked
4 cups water
1 large turnip, diced
Kernels from 1 ear of fresh corn
1 teaspoon fresh thyme, chopped
½ teaspoon cumin
1 bay leaf
Sea salt to taste
½ teaspoon freshly ground black pepper
¼ teaspoon cayenne
Garnish with 2 tablespoons chives, minced, for garnish

Heat the oil in a large saucepan over medium heat and sauté the onion and garlic until onion is translucent.

Add remaining ingredients and simmer over low heat for 20 minutes.

Garnish with chives.

Turnips are a nutritious root vegetable used widely across Eastern Europe, Asia and other parts of the world. They are high in antioxidants like others – cabbage, kale and Brussels sprouts – in the Brassicaceae family, and their tops (turnip greens) are a store-house of incredibly vital nutrients. Use the tops in soups or juices, or sauté lightly with garlic in olive oil for a delicious side.

Venice Noodle Soup

Yield: 4 servings

This recipe is only gluten-free if you use gluten-free noodles, and there are many tasty options available at your health food store these days.

2 tablespoons extra virgin olive oil
1 yellow onion, diced
4 cloves garlic, minced
1 stalk celery, sliced
6 cups water
1 potato, sliced
¼ cup fresh parsley, chopped
Sea salt to taste

½ teaspoon freshly ground black pepper
2 bay leaves
¼ cup fresh dill, chopped
1 zucchini, sliced
¼ cup sliced button mushrooms
½ cup broccoli florets
2 cups uncooked noodles

Heat the oil in a large saucepan over medium heat and sauté the onion, garlic, and celery until the onion is translucent.

Add the water, potato, parsley, salt, pepper, bay leaves, and dill, and simmer over medium heat for 20 minutes.

Add the zucchini, mushrooms, broccoli, and noodles and simmer for about 10 minutes until the noodles are cooked.

Zucchini Soup

Yield: 4 servings

1 tablespoon walnut oil
1 small yellow onion, chopped
3 cloves garlic, minced
1 stalk of celery, chopped
4 cups vegetable broth
4 medium zucchinis, quartered and sliced
2 tablespoons fresh basil, chopped
1 teaspoon fresh parsley, chopped
1 tablespoon thyme, chopped
1 tablespoon curry powder
½ teaspoon turmeric
Sea salt to taste
1 teaspoon freshly ground black pepper

Heat the oil in a large saucepan over medium-high heat and sauté the onion, garlic, and celery until the onion is translucent.

Add the vegetable broth, zucchini, basil, parsley, thyme, curry powder, turmeric, salt, and black pepper and simmer over medium heat for 5 minutes.

Place the soup contents in a blender or food processor and purée until smooth.

Return to the saucepan and simmer for 15 minutes.

Zucchini is rich in dietary fiber, and thus controls blood sugar. Its nutritional profile, which includes vitamin C and vitamin A as well as copper make it an excellent anti-inflammatory vegetable.

"I have a lot more flexibility in my fingers now, and I don't have any pain. I also have lots of energy, and can walk for hours. My sleep is terrific, and my digestion is very good. The vegan diet has definitely improved my well-being."

– Wilma, 77-years-old arthritis sufferer

SALADS

Salads are one of the most underrated yet potentially inventive food groups in the world of vegetarian fare. Today, there are numerous options for salad greens to delight even the most adventuresome health seekers. From baby greens like kale, Swiss chard and spinach, to sprouted seeds like alfalfa, clover and broccoli, to micro-greens, a mixture of delicate, nutrition-filled powerhouses of phytonutrients, you will delight in creating the low-calorie, nutrient-dense possibilities of this important category in the vegetarian lifestyle. I invite you to visit the salad section of your local health food store and to go "green" with your diet. Not only will the extra pounds fly off your body, but you will feel more amazing by the day.

– Gary

Aduki Bean Salad

Yield: 2 servings

Aduki beans are very high in B-vitamins and trace minerals such as copper, zinc, manganese, and molybdenum, which is very helpful in liver detoxification.

Dressing:
2 tablespoons sesame oil
1 tablespoon lemon juice
1 clove garlic, pressed
Sea salt to taste
½ teaspoon freshly ground
   black pepper
Pinch cayenne

Salad:
1 cup aduki beans, cooked
1 medium onion, diced
1 tomato, chopped
1 green bell pepper, chopped
½ cup slivered almonds,
1 tablespoon fresh tarragon,
   chopped
3 tablespoons fresh basil,
   chopped
3 tablespoons fresh parsley,
   chopped
1 radish, sliced, for garnish

Whisk oil, lemon juice, garlic, salt, pepper, and cayenne together in a small bowl.

Place aduki beans, onion, tomato, bell pepper, almonds, tarragon, basil, and parsley in a salad bowl and toss with the dressing.

Garnish with sliced radish.

Apple, Walnut, and Tofu Salad

Yield: 2 servings

Dressing:
2 tablespoons walnut oil
1 tablespoon lemon juice
1 clove garlic, pressed
Sea salt to taste
½ teaspoon freshly ground
    black pepper
Pinch cayenne

Salad:
½ cup yellow onion, diced
1 stalk celery, sliced
¼ teaspoon ground cumin
1 Granny Smith apple, diced
1 package firm tofu, diced
½ cup walnuts
½ cup chives, for garnish

Whisk oil, lemon juice, garlic, salt, pepper, and cayenne together in a small bowl.

Place onion, celery, cumin, apple, tofu, and walnuts in a salad bowl and toss with the dressing.

Garnish with chives.

Apples are a terrific source of vegetarian omega-3s. Plus, apples are helpful in the eradication and prevention of all chronic disease. Of all the apple varieties, Granny Smith and Red Delicious have the highest amount of antioxidants. *Make sure to purchase organic apples only; apples, in general, are a highly sprayed crop in America.*

Artichoke and Chickpea Salad

Yield: 2 servings

Dressing:
2 tablespoons extra virgin olive oil
1 tablespoon fresh lemon juice
2 cloves garlic, minced
1 teaspoon fresh ginger, minced
Sea salt to taste
½ teaspoon freshly ground black pepper
Pinch cayenne

Salad:
1 cup brown rice, cooked
1 cup chickpeas, cooked
1 cup (approx. 2 • 6-oz. jars) marinated artichoke hearts, quartered
½ cup broccoli, steamed
½ cup fresh parsley, chopped
2 tablespoons fresh mint, chopped
2 scallions, sliced
1 tomato, chopped
½ cup fresh dill, for garnish

Whisk oil, lemon juice, garlic, ginger, salt, pepper, and cayenne together in a small bowl.

Place brown rice, chickpeas, artichoke hearts, broccoli, parsley, mint, scallions, and tomato in a salad bowl and toss with the dressing.

Garnish with dill.

Artichokes are an integral part of the Mediterranean diet, which has been shown highly favorable in the prevention of chronic disease. Artichokes are an incredibly healthy food that contain powerful components for lowering cholesterol, supporting the liver in ridding the body of harmful toxins, and improving heart health.

Arugula Orange Pepper Salad

Yield: 2 servings

Arugula is a nutritious leafy green vegetable of Mediterranean origin that has a peppery flavor, making it a wonderful complement for fruit-based dressings. It is a powerhouse of vitamins and nutrients, and a good source of omega-3 essential fatty acids.

Dressing:
1 tablespoon Dijon mustard
¼ cup lemon juice
⅓ cup extra virgin olive oil
½ shallot, minced
1 clove garlic, pressed
Sea salt to taste
½ teaspoon freshly ground black pepper
Pinch cayenne
1 tablespoon fresh Italian parsley, chopped

Salad:
1 cup mixed red, yellow and orange bell peppers, sliced into long, thin strips
½ red onion, sliced
1 cup sunflower sprouts
1 cup arugula
1 cup beets, cooked and diced
1 cup carrots, julienned
½ cup yellow cherry tomatoes, halved
½ cup red cherry tomatoes, halved
1 orange separated into segments

Whisk mustard and lemon juice together in a small bowl until smooth. Add oil, shallot, garlic, salt, pepper, cayenne, and parsley and blend well.

Stack all the vegetables artistically on individual serving dishes and cover with the dressing.

Alternative Serving Option: place peppers, sprouts, arugula, beets, carrots, and tomatoes in a salad bowl and toss the salad with the dressing.

Beet Salad

Yield: 2 servings

When choosing an apple cider vinegar, choose raw and unfiltered. Not only is it high in potassium, but it is the only commonly used vinegar that is alkalizing as well as antiviral, antibacterial and antifungal.

Dressing:
1 teaspoon raw, unfiltered apple cider vinegar
2 tablespoons walnut oil
1 clove garlic, pressed
Sea salt to taste
Freshly ground black pepper to taste

Salad:
¼ cup red onion, diced
1 apple, cored and sliced; reserve a few slices for garnish.
2 cups beets, chopped
¼ cup walnut pieces, toasted, for garnish

Whisk vinegar, oil, garlic, salt and pepper together in a small bowl to blend.

Place onion, apple, and beets in a salad bowl and toss with the dressing.

Garnish with apple slices and walnuts.

Bitters Sweet

Yield: 2 servings

Dressing:
2 tablespoons extra-virgin
 olive oil
1 tablespoon balsamic vinegar
1 clove garlic, pressed
Sea salt to taste
½ teaspoon freshly ground
 black pepper

Salad:
½ butternut squash, cut in half,
 seeds and pulp removed
½ cup arugula, chopped
¼ cup currants
2 tablespoons fresh dill, chopped
2 tablespoons fresh parsley,
 chopped
½ cup alfalfa sprouts, for garnish

Preheat oven to 350°.

Place the butternut squash on a baking sheet sprayed with non-stick olive oil and bake for 30 minutes. When squash is cool, peel and cut into pieces.

For dressing: Whisk oil, vinegar, garlic, salt, and pepper together in a small bowl.

Place squash, arugula, currants, dill, and parsley in a salad bowl and toss with the dressing

Garnish with alfalfa sprouts.

Balsamic vinegar, although not as healthful as apple cider vinegar, is helpful for reducing weight, assisting in digestion (for some), and has been used as a natural pain reliever and topical antiseptic and antibacterial for centuries.

California Marinade

Yield: 2 servings

Dressing:
2 tablespoons walnut oil
1 tablespoon raw, unfiltered apple cider vinegar
1 teaspoon soy sauce
½ teaspoon freshly ground black pepper

Salad:
1 cup cauliflower florets, steamed
1 cup bulgur, cooked
½ cup sunflower seeds
2 shallots, chopped
½ cup coconut, shredded
1 tablespoon fresh tarragon, chopped
2 tablespoons fresh basil, chopped
½ avocado, sliced, for garnish
Dill, for garnish

Whisk oil, vinegar, soy sauce, and pepper together in a small bowl until smooth.

Place cauliflower, bulgur, sunflower seeds, shallots, coconut, tarragon, and basil in a salad bowl and toss with the dressing.

Garnish with avocado slices and dill.

Bulgur is a whole wheat grain, but a less processed one, so it retains a greater percentage of its nutritional value. Traditionally used in Mediterranean dishes such as Tabbouleh salad, bulgur is an excellent source of fiber, as well as B-vitamins, folate and a whole host of minerals. It's also a terrific source of vegetarian protein.

This is a great picnic or potluck salad, offering tremendous eye appeal, nutritional benefit and taste. Packed with over 20 vitamins and minerals, and a multitude of antioxidants, the pecans add a special touch. Their nutty flavor adds to the richness of this already amazing salad.

Chopped Veggie Bean Salad

Yield: 2 servings

Dressing:
1 teaspoon Dijon mustard
1 tablespoon lemon juice
2 tablespoons walnut oil
1 clove garlic, minced
Sea salt to taste
Freshly ground black pepper
   to taste
⅛ teaspoon cayenne

Salad:
1 cup black-eyed peas, cook[
1 cup couscous, cooked
1 stalk celery, chopped
1 carrot, chopped
¾ cup pecans, chopped;
   reserve ½-cup whole peca
   for garnish
½ onion, diced
1 teaspoon fresh parsley,
   chopped
½ teaspoon marjoram

Whisk mustard and lemon juice together in a small bowl until smooth. Add oil, garlic, salt, pepper, and cayenne and blend w

Place black-eyed peas, couscous, celery, carrot, chopped pecans, onion, parsley, and marjoram in a salad bowl and tos with the dressing.

Garnish with whole pecans.

Cold German Leek Salad

Yield: 2 servings

Dressing:
2 tablespoons prepared mustard
½ cup extra virgin olive oil
1 tablespoon fresh lemon juice
2 tablespoons fresh parsley, chopped
2 tablespoons fresh dill, chopped
Sea salt to taste
½ teaspoon freshly ground black pepper

Salad:
½ cup beets, peeled, sliced, and steamed
1 cup carrots, sliced and steamed
2 cups leeks, sliced and steamed

In a small bowl, whisk together mustard, olive oil, lemon juice, parsley, dill, salt and pepper.

Place the beets, carrots, and leeks in a salad bowl and toss with the dressing.

Chill for one hour before serving.

This is a new twist on an age-old salad! Enjoy the colorful variety of vegetables and herbs that make this a lunch or dinner favorite. Serve it on a bed of greens to complete the presentation.

Cool Garden Noodles

Yield: 2 servings

Dressing:
2 tablespoons walnut oil
1 tablespoon raw, unfiltered apple cider vinegar
1 clove garlic, pressed
1 teaspoon fresh ginger, minced
Sea salt to taste
½ teaspoon freshly ground black pepper
Pinch cayenne

Salad:
1 cup brown rice, cooked
½ package buckwheat noodles, cooked
1 jar (6 oz.) marinated artichoke hearts, quartered
2 tablespoons fresh parsley, chopped
2 tablespoons fresh basil, chopped
½ avocado, sliced, for garnish

Whisk oil, vinegar, garlic, ginger, salt, pepper, and cayenne together in a small bowl.

Place brown rice, noodles, artichoke hearts, parsley, and basil in a salad bowl and toss with the dressing.

Garnish with avocado slices.

Walnut oil – as well as other oils – has a limited shelf life, about six to 12 months. After opening, keep them in a cool place out of the light, or refrigerated to prevent them from becoming rancid.

Eggplant Salad

Yield: 2-3 servings

Dressing:
2 tablespoons olive oil
1 tablespoon lemon juice
1 clove garlic, pressed
Sea salt to taste
½ teaspoon freshly ground black pepper
Pinch cayenne

Whisk oil, lemon juice, garlic, salt, pepper, and cayenne together in a small bowl.

Eggplant:
2 large eggplants
½ teaspoon cumin
Sea salt to taste
½ teaspoon freshly ground black pepper
1 small red onion, finely chopped
3 tablespoons fresh parsley, chopped; reserve 1 tablespoon
   for garnish
¼ teaspoon ground marjoram
1 teaspoon fresh thyme
½ cup cherry tomatoes, halved, for garnish
½ cup yellow cherry tomatoes, halved, for garnish

Preheat oven to 350°.

Cut the eggplants in half and place on a baking sheet sprayed with non-stick olive oil.

Season the eggplants with cumin, salt, and pepper and bake for 15-20 minutes.

When the eggplants are cool enough to handle, scrape the pulp from the skin and mash the pulp in a salad bowl.

Add the red onion, parsley, marjoram, and thyme; mix well and then toss the salad with the dressing.

Garnish with parsley and the tomatoes.

Eggplant is another nightshade vegetable, but one that packs a powerful punch. Not only is it high in omega-3s, but it is known to contain numerous vitamins and minerals. So choose this dish when you want a little bit of everything!

Enticing Endive with Berries and Seeds

Yield: 2 servings

Dressing:
1 tablespoon Dijon mustard
1 tablespoon raw, unfiltered apple cider vinegar
2 tablespoons olive oil
1 clove garlic, pressed
Sea salt to taste
½ teaspoon freshly ground black pepper
Pinch cayenne

Salad:
1 cup endive leaves
2 tablespoons lemon juice
½ head Bibb lettuce, torn into pieces
½ cup fresh basil leaves; reserve a few leaves for garnish
½ cup sunflower sprouts
½ cup red cherry tomatoes, halved
½ cup yellow cherry tomatoes, halved
½ cup carrots, shredded
¼ cup blueberries; reserve some for garnish
½ cup sunflower seeds

Whisk mustard and vinegar together in a small bowl until smooth. Add oil, garlic, salt, pepper, and cayenne and blend well.

Sprinkle the endive with lemon juice to avoid wilting.

Place the Bibb lettuce in a large salad bowl and cover with the endive leaves.

Combine basil, sprouts, tomatoes, carrots, blueberries, and sunflower seeds in a bowl and toss with the dressing.

Place the tossed salad on top of the endive and Bibb lettuce.

Garnish with blueberries and basil.

Endive is commonly known as escarole, and is packed with numerous plant nutrients such as vitamin C, vitamin A, vitamin B, beta carotene and folic acid. Like other green leafy vegetables, it is an excellent source of omega-3s.

Both endive and radicchio are in the same family – making this a powerful and gutsy, omega-3-rich, anti-inflammatory salad. Pistachios add to the punch; they are incredibly rich in vitamin B6, which is essential for making hemoglobin, the protein responsible for carrying oxygen through the blood stream to cells and increasing the amount of oxygen carried too.

Endive Salad

Yield: 4 servings

Dressing:
1 tablespoon fresh lemon juice
2 tablespoons walnut oil
1 clove garlic, pressed
Sea salt to taste
½ teaspoon freshly ground black pepper

Salad:
4 endives, chopped
1 radicchio, chopped
1 Granny Smith apple, diced
1 cup cooked beets, diced
2 scallions, chopped
1 cup button mushrooms, sliced
¼ cup pistachio nuts, chopped, for garnish
2 tablespoons fresh parsley, chopped, for garnish

Whisk lemon juice, oil, garlic, salt and pepper together in a small bowl.

Place endive, radicchio, apples, beets, scallions, mushrooms in a salad bowl and toss the salad with the dressing.

Garnish with pistachio nuts and parsley.

Fennel and Pecan Salad with Peaches

Yield: 2 servings

Dressing:
¼ cup orange juice, fresh squeezed if possible
2 tablespoons balsamic vinegar
1 teaspoon maple syrup
Sea salt to taste
½ teaspoon freshly ground black pepper
Pinch cayenne

Salad:
1 cup fennel root, sliced
½ cup dandelion greens, chopped
½ cup Italian parsley, chopped
½ cup fresh peaches, sliced; reserve a few slices for garnish
¼ cup pecans, chopped, for garnish
½ cup pomegranate seeds, for garnish

Whisk orange juice, vinegar, maple syrup, salt, pepper, and cayenne together in a small bowl.

Place fennel, dandelion greens, and parsley in a salad bowl and toss with the dressing.

Garnish with peaches, pecans and pomegranate seeds.

Fennel is one of my favorite vegetables. Eating it both raw and cooked offers wonderful benefits. Not only has fennel's phytonutrient anethole been shown to reduce inflammation, it has also been recognized for its anti-cancer capacity.

Forbidden Rice Salad

Yield: 2 servings

Dressing:
2 tablespoons olive oil
1 tablespoon fresh lemon juice
1 teaspoon fresh garlic, minced
Sea salt to taste
½ teaspoon freshly ground black pepper
Pinch cayenne

Salad:
3 cups forbidden rice, cooked
½ cup carrots, sliced
½ cup broccoli florets, steamed
½ cup chopped fresh parsley
1 teaspoon chopped fresh dill
1 radish, minced, for garnish
½ cup zucchini, sliced, for garnish

Whisk oil, lemon juice, garlic, salt, pepper, and cayenne together in a small bowl.

Place forbidden rice, carrots, broccoli, parsley, and dill in a salad bowl and toss with the dressing.

Garnish with sliced radish and zucchini.

Forbidden rice – known also as black or purple rice – is a type of sticky rice. It is a great source of protein, minerals and vitamins, and is delicious. Enjoy!

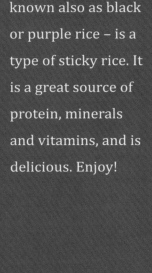

French Watercress Salad

Yield: 2 servings

Dressing:
1 teaspoon Dijon mustard
1 tablespoon apple cider vinegar
2 tablespoons olive oil
1 clove garlic, pressed
Sea salt to taste
½ teaspoon freshly ground black pepper
Pinch cayenne

Salad:
1 cup watercress
3 spears asparagus, steamed and sliced
½ cup red cherry tomatoes, halved
½ cup yellow cherry tomatoes, halved
1 scallion, sliced
½ cup carrots, steamed and chopped
2 tablespoons fresh basil, chopped; reserve a few leaves
    for garnish
2 tablespoons fresh parsley, chopped
1 tablespoon fresh tarragon, chopped

Whisk mustard and vinegar together in a small bowl until smooth.
Add oil, garlic, salt, pepper, and cayenne and blend well.

Place watercress, asparagus, tomatoes, scallion, carrots, basil,
parsley, and tarragon in a salad bowl and toss with the dressing.

Garnish with basil leaves.

Watercress is a member of the cruciferous family, making it – right off the bat – a terrific green for preventing and reversing chronic disease, including arthritis and cancer. It is also credited for aiding in vision and eye health.

Fresh Corn Salad

Yield: 2 servings

Corn has a whole host of antioxidant phyto-nutrients that make it more of a healthy food then we have previously believed... and yes, it has a high ratio of insoluble to soluble fiber! But try eating it raw, right off the cob, and chewing it well; you will be surprised how good it tastes, and how well your body uses it.

Dressing:
2 tablespoons extra virgin olive oil
1 tablespoon apple cider vinegar
1 clove garlic, pressed
¼ teaspoon salt
½ teaspoon freshly ground black pepper
½ teaspoon cayenne pepper
½ shallot, minced
1 tablespoon fresh parsley, chopped

Salad:
3 cups corn kernels (corn from about 8 cobs), steamed 10 minutes
1 cup red bell pepper, chopped
1 cup fennel (bulb), chopped and steamed 5-7 minutes
Sea salt to taste

Whisk oil, vinegar, garlic, salt, black and cayenne pepper together in a small bowl.

Add shallot and parsley, and blend well.

Place corn, red bell pepper, and fennel in a salad bowl and toss with the dressing; add sea salt to taste.

Tip: You can make this entire salad raw for added taste and health benefits.

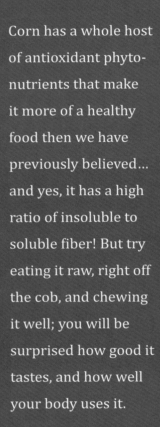

Golden Broccoli Supreme

Yield: 2 servings

Dressing:
2 tablespoons olive oil
1 tablespoon Balsamic vinegar
1 clove garlic, pressed
Sea salt to taste
½ teaspoon freshly ground
    black pepper
Pinch cayenne

Salad:
2 cups broccoli florets, steamed
1 orange, peeled and
    sectioned
¼ cup black olives, sliced
¼ cup green olives, sliced

Whisk olive oil and vinegar together in a small bowl until smooth.

Add garlic, salt, pepper, and cayenne and blend well.

Place broccoli, orange slices, and olives on a serving dish and toss with the dressing.

Garnish with orange zest.

Olives, which are technically classified as a fruit, have powerful phytonutrients that are associated with reducing the risk of bone loss and cancer.

Grecian Olive and Rice Salad

Yield: 2 servings

Greek olives are harvested from October to January. The greenest olives are harvested in October, the red or pink in November, and the black in December.

Dressing:
2 tablespoons extra-virgin olive oil
1 tablespoon fresh lemon juice
1 clove garlic, pressed
Sea salt to taste
½ teaspoon freshly ground black pepper
Pinch cayenne

Salad:
½ package (8 oz.) fresh spinach leaves
1 cup basmati rice, cooked
1 teaspoon fresh oregano, chopped
1 tablespoon Italian parsley, chopped
1 tablespoon hazelnuts, finely chopped
5 or 6 Greek olives, green and black, pitted and chopped
¼ cup crumbled tempeh
Parsley, for garnish

Whisk oil, lemon juice, garlic, salt, pepper, and cayenne together in a small bowl.

Place spinach, rice, oregano, parsley, hazelnuts, olives, and tempeh in a salad bowl and toss with the dressing.

Garnish with parsley.

Indonesian Sprout Salad

Yield: 4 servings

Dressing:
2 tablespoons walnut oil
1 tablespoon lemon juice
1 tablespoon chives, minced
Sea salt to taste
½ teaspoon freshly ground black pepper
Pinch of cayenne

Salad:
1 cup sunflower sprouts
1 cup bean sprouts
½ cup toasted walnuts, chopped
1 cup red cabbage, sliced
½ cup raw carrots, diced
¼ cup toasted sesame seeds

Whisk oil, lemon juice, chives, salt, pepper, and cayenne together in a small bowl.

Place the sprouts, walnuts, red cabbage, carrots, and sesame seeds in a salad bowl and toss with the dressing.

Sunflower sprouts are one of the few "complete" proteins in the vegetarian world, offering all eight essential amino acids.

Insalata Siciliana

Yield: 2 servings

Dressing:
2 tablespoons extra-virgin olive oil
1 tablespoon balsamic vinegar
1 teaspoon lemon juice
1 clove garlic, pressed
Sea salt to taste
½ teaspoon freshly ground black pepper

Salad:
1 cup cannellini beans, cooked
½ cup arugula, chopped
½ cup cherry tomatoes, halved
½ red bell pepper, diced
½ yellow bell pepper, diced
1 cup (approx. 2 • 6-oz. jars), artichoke hearts, chopped
½ pound mushrooms, sliced
¼ cup gherkins, sliced
8 green and black pitted olives
½ cup peas
1 teaspoon fresh oregano
2 tablespoons capers
2 scallions, chopped
½ cup broccoli florets, steamed

Whisk oil, vinegar, lemon juice, garlic, salt, and pepper together in a small bowl.

Place cannellini beans, arugula, tomatoes, red and yellow pepper, artichoke hearts, mushrooms, gherkins, olives, peas, oregano, capers, and scallions in a salad bowl and toss with the dressing.

Serve on a bed of steamed broccoli.

This fun and rich salad offers an abundance of phytonutrient, antioxidant-rich vegetables. Oh, and don't forget the gherkins; they are the novelty, and provide healthy levels of water and fiber that can help with skin inflammations.

Italian Mushroom and Potato Salad

Yield: 2 servings

1 tablespoon olive oil
1 yellow onion, diced
2 scallions, chopped; reserve ½ cup for garnish
2 cloves garlic, minced
½ cup mushrooms, sliced
½ yellow bell pepper, diced
½ red bell pepper, diced
1 potato, peeled, cooked, and diced
½ cup okra, steamed and sliced
½ cup cherry tomatoes, halved
2 tablespoons fresh basil, chopped
1 tablespoon fresh oregano, chopped
Sea salt to taste
½ teaspoon freshly ground black pepper
Pinch cayenne

Heat the oil in a skillet over medium heat and sauté the onion, scallions, garlic, and mushrooms until the onion is translucent.

Add the yellow and red bell pepper, potato, okra, cherry tomatoes, basil, oregano, salt, pepper, and cayenne and sauté for 15 minutes.

Serve warm.

Okra is a highly medicinal food, helping to eliminate toxins and assist in the effectiveness of probiotics, which promote good digestive and intestinal health.

Japanese Buckwheat Salad

Yield: 2 servings

Tamari is a premium Japanese soy sauce made from soybeans and wheat – so it is NOT gluten-free. But it is used regularly as a salt alternative in Asian cooking.

Dressing:
2 tablespoons sesame oil
3 tablespoons tamari
1 tablespoon fresh lemon juice
1 clove garlic, minced
Sea salt to taste
½ teaspoon freshly ground
   black pepper
Pinch cayenne

Salad:
3 cups cooked buckwheat
   noodles
2 scallions, sliced
2 tablespoons raisins
2 tablespoons sunflower seeds
1 cup broccoli florets, steamed
1 cup carrots, steamed and
   sliced
¼ cup gomasio, for garnish

Whisk oil, tamari, lemon juice, garlic, salt, pepper, and cayenne together in a small bowl.

Place noodles, scallions, raisins, sunflower seeds, broccoli, and carrots in a salad bowl and toss with the dressing.

Garnish with gomasio.

Mellow Rice Salad

Yield: 2 servings

Dressing:
2 tablespoons walnut oil
1 tablespoon raw, unfiltered apple cider vinegar
1 clove garlic, pressed
Sea salt to taste
½ teaspoon freshly ground black pepper
Pinch cayenne

Salad:
1 cup brown rice, cooked
½ cup pecans, chopped
2 tablespoons fresh dill, chopped
1 yellow bell pepper, diced
1 cup cherry tomatoes, halved
1 scallion, chopped finely

Whisk oil, vinegar, garlic, salt, pepper, and cayenne together in a small bowl.

Place brown rice, pecans, dill, yellow bell pepper, tomato and scallion in a salad bowl and toss the salad with the dressing.

Cherry tomatoes are a rich source of vitamin C, vitamin A, and vitamin K...and they are fun and super easy to grow, even in pots on a terrace garden.

Mykonos Bean Salad

Yield: 2 servings

Though some say that basil originated in India, it is native to central and tropical Asia and Africa. This herb from the mint family...is an important ingredient today in many cultures, with an estimated 150 varieties worldwide.

Dressing:
2 tablespoons olive oil
1 tablespoon fresh lime juice
1 clove garlic, pressed
Sea salt to taste
½ teaspoon freshly ground
   black pepper
Pinch cayenne

Salad:
½ cup steamed okra, sliced
1 cup aduki beans, cooked
1 scallion, chopped
½ green bell pepper, chopped
1 tablespoon fresh thyme, chopped
1 tablespoon fresh sage, chopped
1 teaspoon fresh dill, chopped
½ cup fresh basil leaves, for garnish
¼ lime, cut lengthwise, for garnish

Whisk oil, lime juice, garlic, salt, pepper and cayenne together in a small bowl.

Place okra, aduki beans, scallion, bell pepper, thyme, sage, dill and basil in a salad bowl and toss with the dressing.

Garnish with basil and lime.

Navy Salad

Yield: 4 servings

Dressing:
1 teaspoon Dijon mustard
1 tablespoon balsamic vinegar
2 tablespoons extra virgin olive oil
½ shallot, minced
1 clove garlic, pressed
Sea salt to taste
½ teaspoon freshly ground black pepper
Pinch cayenne
1 tablespoon fresh Italian parsley, chopped

Salad:
1 cup navy beans, cooked
½ cup beets, steamed and diced
¾ cup fennel, diced
1 tablespoon sesame seeds

Whisk mustard and balsamic vinegar together in a small bowl until smooth. Add oil, shallot, garlic, salt, pepper, cayenne, and parsley and blend well.

Place navy beans, beets, and fennel in a salad bowl and toss with the dressing.

Serve over romaine lettuce.

Romaine lettuce is a rich source of omega-3 fatty acids, is a complete protein (carrying all eight essential amino acids), and is a huge source of vitamin C!

Nice Rice Salad

Yield: 2 servings

Cayenne actually is an anti-inflammatory, and an anti-irritant. Contrary to what you might believe, it has the ability to ease stomach upset, ulcers, sore throats, and coughs.

Dressing:
2 tablespoons walnut oil
1 tablespoon lemon juice
1 clove garlic, minced
Sea salt to taste
Freshly ground black pepper to taste
$\frac{1}{8}$ teaspoon cayenne

Salad:
1 cup brown rice, cooked
$\frac{1}{2}$ cup amaranth, cooked
1 small onion, diced
1 red bell pepper, diced
1 bunch watercress, chopped; reserve $\frac{1}{2}$ cup whole leaves for garnish

Whisk oil, lemon juice, garlic, salt, pepper, and cayenne together in a small bowl.

Place the brown rice, amaranth, onion, bell pepper, and watercress in a salad bowl and toss with the dressing.

Garnish with watercress.

Quinoa and Edamame Salad

Yield: 8 servings

Dressing:
1 tablespoon spicy mustard
¼ cup fresh lime juice
1 teaspoon rice vinegar
1 clove garlic, pressed
Sea salt to taste
½ teaspoon freshly ground
   black pepper

Salad:
1 cup quinoa, cooked
1 cup edamame, cooked
½ small red onion, sliced
2 tablespoons fresh parsley,
   chopped
2 tablespoons fresh mint,
   chopped
1 green bell pepper, chopped
1 cup bean sprouts, for garnish
Sliced lime, for garnish

Whisk mustard, lime juice, and vinegar together in a small bowl; blend until smooth. Add garlic, salt and pepper and mix well.

Place quinoa, edamame, onion, parsley, mint and bell pepper in a salad bowl and toss with the dressing.

Garnish with sprouts and lime slices.

Edamame (soybean) is full of fiber, protein, vitamins and minerals. Buy them already shelled in the organic section of the produce aisles, or in the frozen section. They are a tasty treat, and a healthy addition to any dish.

Raisin and Brown Rice Salad

Yield: 2 servings

Raisins – dried grapes –
are like nature's candy.
But for as sweet as
they are, they also pack
a powerful punch: they
are known to reduce
acidity in the body,
aid in digestion, and
increase bone health.

Dressing:
2 tablespoons walnut oil
1 tablespoon raw, unfiltered apple cider vinegar
Sea salt to taste
$\frac{1}{8}$ teaspoon cayenne

Salad:
1 cup brown rice, cooked
1 stalk celery, chopped
$\frac{1}{2}$ cup raisins
$\frac{1}{2}$ cup sultanas
1 cup pineapple, cut into bite-sized pieces
2 tablespoons pineapple juice
$\frac{1}{2}$ teaspoon cinnamon
$\frac{1}{2}$ teaspoon cloves
1 tablespoon fresh parsley, chopped, for garnish

Whisk oil, vinegar, salt, and cayenne together in a small bowl.

Place the brown rice, celery, raisins, sultanas, pineapple, juice, cinnamon, and cloves in a salad bowl and toss with the dressing.

Garnish with parsley.

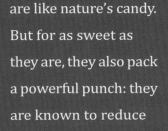

Red Salad

Yield: 2 servings

Dressing:
2 tablespoons walnut oil
1 tablespoon raw, unfiltered apple cider vinegar
1 clove garlic, pressed
1 teaspoon fresh ginger, minced
Sea salt to taste
½ teaspoon freshly ground black pepper
Pinch cayenne

Salad:
½ cup peas, cooked
½ cup white beans, cooked
1 tablespoon capers
1 yellow bell pepper, chopped
½ red bell pepper, chopped
½ cup red cherry tomatoes, halved
½ cup yellow cherry tomatoes, halved
½ cup mushrooms, sliced
½ cup olives, pitted
1 small radicchio, leaves separated
2 tablespoons fresh parsley, chopped, for garnish

Whisk oil, vinegar, garlic, ginger, salt, pepper, and cayenne together in a small bowl.

Place peas, white beans, capers, yellow bell pepper, red bell pepper, red and yellow tomatoes, mushrooms, and olives in a salad bowl and toss with the dressing.

Serve on a bed of radicchio leaves.

Garnish with parsley.

Capers help the liver break down cancer-causing chemicals that could potentially damage the cell's DNA; they share this magnificent ability with broccoli.

Sassy Bean and Quinoa Salad

Yield: 2 servings

Dressing:
2 tablespoons walnut oil
1 tablespoon raw, unfiltered apple cider vinegar
1 clove garlic, pressed
1 teaspoon fresh ginger, minced
Sea salt to taste
½ teaspoon freshly ground black pepper
Pinch cayenne

Salad:
½ cup spinach leaves, chopped
½ cup mushrooms, chopped
1 scallion, chopped
1 cup kidney beans, cooked
1 cup quinoa, cooked
1 carrot, sliced
1 tablespoon fresh oregano, chopped
2 tablespoons dill, for garnish

Whisk oil, vinegar, garlic, ginger, salt, pepper, and cayenne together in a small bowl.

Place spinach, mushrooms, scallion, kidney beans, quinoa, carrot, and oregano in a salad bowl and toss with the dressing.

Garnish with dill.

Seaweed Salad

Yield: 2 servings

1 cup dry hijiki (may also use
  arame or wakame)
1 tablespoon walnut oil
2 cloves garlic, minced
2 scallions, chopped
1 carrot, cut in long thin strips;
  reserve some for garnish
1 daikon, cut in long thin strips;
  reserve some for garnish

3 ounces amaranth, cooked
  (chilled)
½ teaspoon caraway seeds
Sea salt to taste
Freshly ground black pepper
  to taste

Soak and rinse hijiki three times (each soak should be approximately 20-minutes for a total soak time of one hour), and set aside.

(Note: if choosing replacement sea vegetable soak and rinse only once or twice for 10 minutes each soak.)

Heat the walnut oil in a skillet and lightly sauté garlic, scallions, carrots, and daikon for about 1 minute.

Combine the sautéed vegetables with the hijiki, amaranth, caraway seeds, salt and pepper in a salad bowl and mix well.

Garnish with carrot and daikon.

Hijiki is just one of many sea vegetables (seaweed) – a category of some of the most mineral-rich foods on this planet. Consume them frequently for their high levels of naturally occurring iodine, which can be very helpful in cases of hypothyroidism.

Sesame Bean Salad

Yield: 2 servings

Dressing:
2 tablespoons sesame oil
1 tablespoon fresh lemon juice
2 cloves garlic, minced
1 teaspoon fresh ginger, minced
Sea salt to taste
½ teaspoon freshly ground black pepper
Pinch cayenne

Salad:
½ cup chickpeas, cooked
½ cup black beans, cooked
½ cup kidney beans, cooked
2 scallions, sliced
2 tablespoons fresh basil, chopped
2 tablespoons fresh parsley, chopped
½ cup sesame seeds
1 orange, separated into segments, for garnish
¼ cup chives, sliced, for garnish

Whisk oil, lemon juice, garlic, ginger, salt, pepper, and cayenne together in a small bowl.

Place chickpeas, black beans, kidney beans, scallions, basil, parsley, orange slices, and sesame seeds in a salad bowl and toss with the dressing.

Garnish with orange slices and chives.

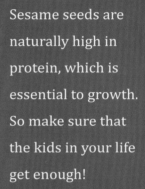

Sesame seeds are naturally high in protein, which is essential to growth. So make sure that the kids in your life get enough!

Spicy Bulgur Salad

Yield: 2 servings

Bulgur only takes 8-10 minutes to cook, so it is an excellent instant cereal or salad. If you're cooking it for a salad, consider refrigerating it before use.

Dressing:
2 tablespoons walnut oil
1 tablespoon raw, unfiltered apple cider vinegar
1 clove garlic, pressed
Sea salt to taste
½ teaspoon freshly ground black pepper
Pinch of cayenne

Salad:
1 cup bulgur, cooked
1 cup spinach, coarsely chopped
1 jar (6 oz.) marinated artichoke hearts, quartered
1 tablespoon fresh basil, chopped
½ teaspoon curry powder
½ cup alfalfa sprouts, for garnish

Whisk oil, vinegar, garlic, salt, pepper and cayenne together in a small bowl.

Place bulgur, spinach, artichoke hearts, basil, and curry powder in a salad bowl and toss the salad with the dressing.

Garnish with alfalfa sprouts.

Superior Spinach Salad

Yield: 2 servings

Dressing:
2 tablespoons walnut oil
1 tablespoon raw, unfiltered
  apple cider vinegar
1 clove garlic, pressed
Sea salt to taste
½ teaspoon freshly ground
  black pepper
Pinch cayenne

Salad:
1 package (10 oz.) fresh spinach,
  coarsely chopped
½ cup cauliflower florets
½ avocado, diced
1 jar (6 oz.) marinated artichoke
  hearts, quartered; reserve half
  for garnish
½ cup walnuts, chopped
2 shallots, minced
¼ teaspoon oregano
¼ teaspoon sage
¼ cup micro-greens, for garnish

Micro-greens are seedlings harvested when the first true leaves appear. Like sprouts, they are known for their high levels of vitamins, minerals and phyto-nutrients at this early stage of growth.

Whisk oil, vinegar, garlic, salt, pepper, and cayenne together in a small bowl.

Place spinach, cauliflower, avocado, artichoke hearts, walnuts, shallots, oregano, and sage in a salad bowl and toss with the dressing.

Garnish with micro-greens and artichoke hearts.

Steamy Summer Salad

Yield: 2 servings

Dressing:
¼ cup fresh lime juice
1 teaspoon rice vinegar
1 clove garlic, pressed
Sea salt to taste
½ teaspoon freshly ground black pepper

Salad:
½ cup peas
½ cup mushrooms, sliced
½ summer squash, diced
1 carrot, chopped
1 cup couscous, cooked
1 red onion, diced
2 tablespoons fresh parsley, chopped
1 tablespoon fresh thyme, chopped
2 tablespoons fresh basil, chopped
3 tablespoons fresh cilantro, chopped
¼ cup pine nuts
Sea salt to taste
½ teaspoon freshly ground black pepper
½ cup spinach leaves, for garnish

Whisk lime juice, vinegar, garlic, salt, and pepper together in a small bowl.

Place peas, mushrooms, squash, and carrots in a steamer and cook for 10 minutes until tender.

Place steamed vegetables, couscous, onion, parsley, thyme, basil, cilantro, pine nuts, salt, and pepper in a salad bowl and toss with the dressing.

Serve on a bed of spinach leaves.

Couscous is a North African semolina (wheat) grain that is traditionally served with vegetable or meat stew. It is a delicious base for salads and meals.

Tahini Potato Salad

Yield: 2 servings

2 tablespoons sesame oil
2 scallions, chopped
1 clove garlic, minced
½ cup mushrooms, sliced
1 potato, cooked, peeled, and diced
¼ cup sesame seeds
½ teaspoon cumin
2 tablespoons fresh basil, chopped
2 tablespoons tahini
Sea salt to taste
½ teaspoon freshly ground black pepper
2 radishes, sliced thin, for garnish

Heat the oil in a skillet over medium heat and sauté scallions, garlic, and mushrooms until tender.

Add the potato, sesame seeds, cumin, basil, tahini, salt, and pepper and sauté for 5 minutes.

Serve warm, garnished with radish slices.

Tip For Vegetarians: If you are already vegetarian, and eating a high quantity of nuts and seeds (most of which are high in omega-6), consider supplementing with DHA and EPA (beneficial omega-3 fatty acids) to balance your EFAs.

Sesame seeds (and therefore Tahini) have a higher ratio of omega-6s to omega-3s than is preferred. But they carry high levels of minerals, including copper, which is helpful to people suffering from arthritis.

Thai Style Salad

Yield: 2 servings

Dressing:
⅛ cup fresh lime juice
1 teaspoon rice vinegar
1 clove garlic, pressed
Sea salt to taste
½ teaspoon freshly ground black pepper

Salad:
1 cup bean threads
½ cup cooked chickpeas
½ cup onion, diced
1 cucumber, thinly sliced; reserve half for garnish
4 ounces firm tofu, sliced
2 red chili peppers, seeded and chopped
8 mint leaves, chopped
2 tablespoons fresh basil, chopped
3 tablespoons fresh cilantro, chopped
1 tablespoon fresh parsley, chopped
1 radish, sliced
2 scallions, chopped
¼ teaspoon allspice
¼ lime, for garnish

Cover bean threads in warm water and soak for 15 minutes; then drain and slice into 3-inch strips.

For dressing, whisk lime juice, rice vinegar, garlic, salt, and pepper together in a small bowl.

Place sliced bean threads, chickpeas, onion, cucumber, tofu, chili peppers, mint leaves, basil, cilantro, parsley, radish, scallions, and allspice in a salad bowl and toss with the dressing.

Serve on cucumber slices, garnished with lime.

Lime is another one of the citrus fruits that provides omega-3 fatty acids, and comes with a lot of beneficial antioxidants. Eat your citrus!

Thyme for Salad!

Yield: 2 servings

Thyme oil has been used since the 1500s for its antiseptic properties, as mouthwash and in topical applications for cuts and scrapes.

Dressing:
2 tablespoons walnut oil
1 tablespoon balsamic vinegar
1 clove garlic, minced
2 scallions, finely chopped
2 tablespoons fresh parsley, chopped
¼ teaspoon oregano
1 tablespoon fresh thyme, chopped
Sea salt to taste
¼ teaspoon freshly ground black pepper, or to taste

Salad:
1 cup aduki beans, cooked
¼ cup slivered almonds
½ red bell pepper, sliced
1 tomato, chopped
Several leaves of romaine lettuce

Whisk oil, vinegar, garlic, scallions, parsley, oregano, thyme, salt, and pepper together in a small bowl.

Place the beans, almonds, peppers, and tomato in a salad bowl and toss with the dressing. Serve on a bed of romaine lettuce.

Walnut and Black Bean Salad

Yield: 2 servings

Dressing:
2 tablespoons olive oil
1 tablespoon lemon juice
1 clove garlic, pressed
Sea salt to taste
½ teaspoon freshly ground black pepper
Pinch cayenne

Salad:
1 cup black beans, cooked
½ cup alfalfa sprouts
½ cup walnuts, chopped
1 tablespoon fresh tarragon, chopped
1 tablespoon fresh thyme, chopped
Sea salt to taste
½ teaspoon freshly ground black pepper

Whisk oil, lemon juice, garlic, salt, pepper, and cayenne together in a small bowl. Combine remaining ingredients in a salad bowl and toss with the dressing.

I cannot say enough about the value of walnuts; they are one of the anti-inflammatory superstars! Research abounds of their health benefits, including their ability to reduce the risk of cancer, regulate blood sugar for people with diabetes, and to help with all sorts of cardiovascular concerns.

Warm Potato and Dulse Salad

Yield: 4 servings

1 tablespoon extra virgin olive oil
1 small yellow onion, diced
1 clove garlic, minced
2 tablespoons dulse leaves, chopped
¼ cup hot water
3 large Yukon gold potatoes, peeled, quartered, and boiled
1 tablespoon ground fennel seeds

1 spicy pickle, diced
2 tablespoons fresh parsley, chopped
Sea salt to taste
½ teaspoon freshly ground black pepper
1½ tablespoons Bragg's Liquid Aminos
1 tablespoon lemon juice

Heat the oil in a large skillet over medium heat and sauté onion, garlic, and dulse until the onion is translucent.

Add the water, potatoes, fennel seeds, pickle, parsley, salt, pepper, Bragg's Liquid Aminos, and lemon juice and mix well.

Serve warm.

Dulse has a mildly spicy, salted flavor and is extremely high in vitamins B6 and B12, as well as iron, potassium and fluoride.

ENTREES

Creating amazing vegetarian entrées for you, and your family and friends, is a wonderful and amazing experience. From cajun, coconut and curry flavors, to vegan versions of traditional Italian, Greek and Russian dishes, the specialty meals in this section will delight as much as they will demonstrate the viability of a healthy vegetarian lifestyle. As extraordinarily flavorful as they are easy to prepare, these mainstays will encourage and inspire you and others on the path to a new way of living. Consider inviting friends who are making healthy changes in their life, and sharing the magic of an entire meal comprised of healthful vegetables and fruits. I guarantee you that it will spark a fever of the most wonderful kind!

– Gary

Angel Hair Pasta with Mushrooms and Peas

Yield: 2 servings

Peas are a much underrated powerhouse in the world of nutrition. More science is being conducted now to understand all of their anti-inflammation, anti-cancer properties.

2 tablespoons extra virgin olive oil
1 medium yellow onion, diced
2 cloves of garlic, minced
3 cups mushrooms, sliced
½ cup unsweetened almond milk
1 tablespoon fresh rosemary, chopped
1 teaspoon chia seeds

¼ cup pine nuts
1 cup fresh peas
Sea salt to taste
½ teaspoon freshly ground black pepper
1 cup sliced radicchio
⅔ cup grated vegan Parmesan cheese
3 cups angel hair pasta, cooked

Heat the oil in a large saucepan over medium heat and sauté the onion and garlic until the onion is translucent. Add the mushrooms and sauté for another 2 minutes.

Add the almond milk, rosemary, chia seeds, pine nuts, peas, salt, and pepper and cook for 5 minutes.

Turn off the heat and add the radicchio, allowing it to steam for a minute or two.

Toss with the vegan Parmesan cheese and pasta.

Aromatic Green Casserole

Yield: 4 servings

2 tablespoons walnut oil
1 yellow onion, diced
3 cloves garlic, minced
½ cup fennel root, chopped
1 cup vegetable broth
1 tablespoon flaxseed meal
1 tablespoon fresh dill, chopped
1 tablespoon fresh sage, chopped
Sea salt to taste
½ teaspoon freshly ground black pepper
1 tablespoon grated lemon zest
Pinch of cayenne pepper
1 cup kale, chopped
1 cup broccoli, cut into bite-sized pieces
1 cup quinoa, cooked
1 cup black beans, cooked
½ cup walnuts, chopped

Preheat oven to 375°.

Heat the oil in a large skillet over medium-high heat and sauté the onion, garlic, and fennel root until the onion is translucent.

Add the vegetable broth, flaxseed meal, dill, sage, salt, pepper, lemon zest, and cayenne and simmer for about 3 minutes, or until well blended and heated through.

Add the kale, broccoli, quinoa, black beans, and walnuts and mix thoroughly.

Transfer to a lightly greased baking dish and cook covered for 15 minutes.

Because of their mucilaginous property, flax seeds are often used in vegan baking as an egg replacer.

☆

Bammie Cakes

Yield: 2 servings

2 pounds cassava
1 tablespoon olive oil
1 yellow onion, chopped
2 cloves garlic, minced
½ red bell pepper, diced
½ yellow pepper, diced
3 teaspoons Cajun seasoning
¼ cup flaxseed meal
1 teaspoon arrowroot
½ cup walnuts, chopped
Sea salt to taste
½ teaspoon freshly ground black pepper
Olive oil for frying
Juice of one lemon, for garnish
1 small zucchini, sliced, for garnish
Red cabbage, shredded, for garnish

Note: Raw cassava juice is not safe to cook with or to drink.

Boil the cassava for 30 minutes until tender.

In a large skillet, heat olive oil over medium heat and sauté onion and garlic until the onion is translucent.

Add the peppers and sauté for another minute or two.

Peel the cassava and purée in a food processor. Add onion-garlic-pepper mixture, Cajun seasoning, flaxseed meal, arrowroot, walnuts, salt, and pepper and pulse until well-mixed.

Form the mixture into patties approximately 2 inches in diameter.

Add another tablespoon or two of oil to the skillet and fry the bammie cakes until golden brown, approximately 2 – 3 minutes.

Flip the cakes and brown the other side, another 2 – 3 minutes.

Serve warm, garnished with lemon juice, zucchini slices, and shredded red cabbage.

Cassava (also known as Yucca) is a woody shrub native to South America, but grown around the globe. Because it is high in carbohydrates, it provides a basic diet for around ½ billion people worldwide.

Broccoli and Cauliflower with Shiitake Mushrooms

Yield: 2 to 4 servings

¾ cup unsweetened almond milk
1 tablespoon gluten-free oat flour
1 tablespoon flaxseed meal
1 tablespoon grated lemon zest
1 clove garlic, minced
1 scallion, chopped
1 tablespoon fresh oregano, chopped
1 tablespoon fresh thyme, chopped
1 tablespoon fresh basil, chopped
Sea salt to taste
½ teaspoon freshly ground black pepper
¼ teaspoon cayenne
1 head broccoli, separated into florets
½ head cauliflower, separated into florets
½ cup shiitake mushrooms, chopped
1 cup extra-firm tofu, diced
½ red bell pepper, chopped
½ cup grated vegan cheese

Preheat oven to 325°.

Whisk together almond milk, flour, flaxseed meal, lemon zest, garlic, scallions, oregano, thyme, basil, salt, pepper, and cayenne in a small bowl.

Combine the broccoli, cauliflower, mushrooms, tofu, and red pepper in a mixing bowl.

Lightly grease a baking dish with olive oil, and add the broccoli-cauliflower mixture. Pour the almond milk sauce evenly over the vegetables.

Sprinkle with vegan cheese and bake until sauce thickens, approximately 25 minutes.

Shiitake mushrooms have been used medicinally in China for more than 6,000 years, and are known to promote longevity through their immune-enhancing properties.

Broccoli Au Gratin

Yield: 4 servings

½ cup unsweetened almond milk
1 tablespoon gluten-free oat flour
1 tablespoon flaxseed meal
1 sweet potato, peeled, steamed, and puréed
2 cloves garlic, minced
1 scallion, sliced
1 tablespoon fresh basil, chopped
1 tablespoon fresh thyme, chopped
Sea salt to taste
½ teaspoon freshly ground black pepper
1 bunch broccoli, chopped into bite-sized pieces
¼ cup vegan Parmesan, grated
¼ cup sesame seeds, for garnish

Preheat oven to 350°.

Mix together almond milk, flour, flaxseed meal, and puréed sweet potato in a small bowl and blend until smooth.

Add the garlic, scallion, basil, thyme, salt, and pepper and blend well.

Lightly grease a medium casserole with olive oil, and place the broccoli inside.

Pour the sauce over the broccoli, top with vegan Parmesan, and bake for 15 minutes.

Garnish with sesame seeds.

Visit your local health food store to check out the vegan cheeses made from rice, almond and soy. Their taste and melting qualities will astound you!

Broccoli Tortellini Salad

Yield: 2 servings

The frozen-food section of the health foods store offers some incredibly healthy alternatives to typical Standard American Diet fare, which is laden with unhealthy fats. Go dairy-free, and your body will thank you.

Dressing:
2 tablespoons extra-virgin olive oil
1 tablespoon fresh lemon juice
1 clove garlic, pressed
1 tablespoon fresh parsley, chopped
1 tablespoon fresh basil, chopped
Sea salt to taste
½ teaspoon freshly ground black pepper
Pinch cayenne

Salad:
2 cups vegan tortellini, cooked
½ cup broccoli florets, steamed
½ cup black olives, sliced
1 jar (6 oz.) marinated artichoke hearts, quartered; reserve a few pieces for garnish
2 red cherry peppers, halved, for garnish

Whisk oil, lemon juice, garlic, parsley, basil, salt, pepper, and cayenne together in a small bowl.

Place tortellini, broccoli, olives, and artichoke hearts in a salad bowl and toss with the dressing.

Garnish with artichoke hearts and peppers.

Red, yellow and green peppers are extremely high in vitamin C and powerful antioxidants. Red and yellow are sweeter in taste, and are generally better in terms of health and digestion because they are less acidic than green peppers. Peppers are nightshades, so make sure that you are not nightshade-sensitive. See p. 41 for more information.

Brown Rice with Peppers and Herbs

Yield: 2 servings

1 tablespoon walnut oil
1 medium yellow onion, chopped
2 cloves garlic, minced
½ green bell pepper, diced
½ red bell pepper, diced
½ yellow bell pepper, diced
1½ cups brown rice, cooked
¾ tablespoon fresh parsley, chopped

½ teaspoon fresh tarragon, chopped
Sea salt to taste
Freshly ground black pepper to taste
¼ cup arugula, for garnish
½ cup cherry tomatoes, for garnish

Heat the oil in a large saucepan over medium heat and sauté the onion and garlic until the onion is translucent.

Add the bell peppers and sauté for a minute or two.

Add the rice, parsley, tarragon, salt, and pepper and sauté for 3 – 5 minutes.

Garnish with arugula and sliced cherry tomatoes.

Brussels Sprout Creole

Yield: 4 to 6 servings

2 tablespoons olive oil
1 large yellow onion, diced
2 garlic cloves, minced
½ red bell pepper, chopped
½ orange bell pepper, chopped
1 fresh tomato, chopped
½ cup water
2 tablespoons fresh basil, chopped

2 tablespoons fresh parsley, chopped
¼ cup olives, pitted and sliced
1 tablespoon grated lemon zest
Sea salt to taste
½ teaspoon freshly ground black pepper
2 cups Brussels sprouts, steamed
½ head red leaf lettuce

Heat the oil in a medium saucepan over medium heat and sauté the onion, garlic, and bell peppers until the onion is translucent.

Add the tomato, water, basil, parsley, olives, lemon zest, salt, and pepper and let simmer for 15 minutes, stirring occasionally.

Add the Brussels sprouts and simmer for a few minutes until warm.

Serve on a bed of red leaf lettuce.

Because Brussels sprouts are in the cruciferous family, they are incredibly healthy for reducing the inflammation that leads to chronic diseases such as cancer, diabetes and arthritis.

Butternut Squash with Toasted Sesame Sauce

Yield: 2 to 3 servings

1 butternut squash, peeled and cut into ½-inch pieces
1 tablespoon toasted sesame oil
3 tablespoons tahini
1 clove garlic, minced
2 tablespoon fresh parsley, chopped; reserve half for garnish
Sea salt to taste
½ teaspoon freshly ground pepper
2 tablespoons gomasio
¼ cup sesame seeds
½ cup baby mesclun, for garnish

Steam the squash for 15 to 20 minutes until tender.

Remove from the heat and place in individual dishes.

While the squash is steaming, whisk together the oil, tahini, garlic, parsley, salt, and pepper in a small bowl.

Pour the tahini mixture over the steamed squash.

Sprinkle with gomasio, parsley, and sesame seeds.

Garnish with baby mesclun.

Butternut Tofu

Yield: 4 servings

1 butternut squash, cut in half lengthwise with seeds removed
1 tablespoon walnut oil
2 shallots, minced
2 cloves garlic, minced
1 stalk celery, chopped
½ cup vegetable broth
1 package firm tofu
2 tablespoons fresh basil, chopped
2 tablespoons fresh thyme, chopped
½ teaspoon curry powder
½ cup sunflower seeds
1 teaspoon molasses
Sea salt to taste
½ teaspoon freshly ground black pepper
1 pinch cayenne
2 tablespoons chives, minced, for garnish

Preheat oven to 350°.

Place the squash halves on a baking sheet sprayed with non-stick olive oil and bake for 30 minutes.

When cool enough to handle, peel the squash and chop into 1-inch pieces and set aside.

Heat the oil in a large saucepan over medium heat and sauté the shallots, garlic, and celery until the shallots are translucent.

Add the squash, vegetable broth, tofu, basil, thyme, curry powder, sunflower seeds, molasses, salt, pepper, and cayenne and simmer for 10 minutes.

Serve in individual serving dishes.

Garnish with chives.

Molasses, the viscous sweetener that is a by-product of the sugar-making process, is a rich source of key minerals that are extremely beneficial to your health.

Cajun Tofu

Yield: 4 servings

1 package firm tofu
½ teaspoon black pepper
1 tablespoon Cajun seasoning
1 teaspoon dried basil
1 teaspoon dried parsley
1 tablespoon olive oil
2 tablespoons fresh parsley, chopped
Several leaves of romaine lettuce, for garnish
3 collard leaves, for garnish
2 red bell peppers, sliced, for garnish
2 tomatoes, sliced, for garnish

Slice tofu into four equal pieces; set on paper towels and weigh down with a plate for 30 minutes to squeeze out excess water.

Place Cajun seasoning, dried basil, and dried parsley in a flat bowl and mix well.

Dip the tofu slices in the seasonings on both sides to coat.

Heat the oil in a large skillet over medium-high heat and sear the tofu on each side until browned, about 2 – 3 minutes a side.

Remove from pan and sprinkle with fresh parsley.

Serve on a bed of lettuce or collard greens with red peppers and tomatoes.

Serving suggestion: This dish goes well with Roasted Red Pepper Tomato Sauce, p. 267.

Carrot Kidney Bean Loaf with Mushroom Gravy

Yield: 4 servings

Mushroom Gravy:

5 tablespoons olive oil
2 cups assorted mushrooms (shiitake, white oyster, crimini, chanterelle), sliced
3 cloves garlic, minced
2 shallots, minced
½ cup whole wheat flour
2 cups vegetable stock, heated to a boil
2 tablespoons Braggs Liquid Aminos
2 tablespoons fresh rosemary, chopped
2 tablespoons fresh thyme, chopped
Sea salt to taste
½ teaspoon freshly ground black pepper

Heat two tablespoons of oil in a large skillet and sauté the mushrooms, garlic, and shallots until the mushrooms are browned, then set aside.

Add three tablespoons of oil and the flour to the skillet. Cook the flour over medium-high heat until browned but not burned (approximately 10 minutes), stirring constantly.

When flour reaches desired color, pour in hot stock and reduce heat. Stir well to mix.

Add sautéed mushrooms-garlic-shallot mixture, Bragg's Liquid Aminos, rosemary, thyme, salt, and pepper and cook until thickened, 10 – 15 minutes.

Carrot Kidney Bean Loaf

2 cups sliced carrots, steamed
2 cloves garlic, minced
2 tablespoons fresh chives, minced
2 tablespoons fresh parsley, chopped
Sea salt to taste
½ teaspoon freshly ground black pepper
2 cups kidney beans, cooked
¼ cup water
1 tablespoon chives, chopped, for garnish

Kidney beans are very high in fiber and prevent blood sugar levels from rising too rapidly after a meal; this makes these beans an especially good choice for individuals with diabetes, insulin resistance or hypoglycemia.

Carrot Kidney Bean Loaf with Mushroom Gravy

continued...

Preheat oven to 400°.

Purée the carrots in a food processor or blender until smooth.

Add half of each of the following: garlic, chives, parsley, salt, and pepper and pulse until blended; set aside.

Place the kidney beans in the food processor; add the remaining

half of garlic, chives, parsley, salt, and pepper, and purée until smooth. Add water if necessary to achieve desired consistency.

Layer the two purées in a greased loaf pan by placing half the bean mixture in first, followed by half the carrots, then repeat.

Bake for 10 minutes until thoroughly heated.

Serve with mushroom gravy and garnish with chives.

Note: This loaf has a very soft consistency. For best results, bake in individual serving dishes.

Cauliflower with Garlic Hummus Sauce

Yield: 2 servings

1 cup chickpeas, cooked
3 tablespoons tahini
2 cloves garlic, minced
1 teaspoon lemon juice
Sea salt to taste
½ teaspoon freshly ground pepper
¼ teaspoon cayenne
1 cup cauliflower florets
1 cup red bell pepper, chopped
1 small red onion, diced
3 tablespoons fresh parsley, chopped; reserve 1 tablespoon
   for garnish
¼ teaspoon turmeric
½ cup unsalted whole cashews
2 cups rice, cooked

Preheat oven to 425°.

Place chickpeas, tahini, garlic, lemon juice, salt, pepper, and cayenne in a food processor and purée until smooth.

In a mixing bowl combine the chickpea purée, cauliflower, red pepper, red onion, parsley, turmeric, and cashews and mix well.

Pour the mixture into a lightly-greased 9 x 12-inch baking dish and cover with foil.

Bake for 15 to 20 minutes, or until the cauliflower is tender.

Serve over rice. Garnish with parsley.

Because of their antioxidant and anti-inflammatory properties, which are known to reduce the risk of cancer and other diseases of inflammation, it is well advised to include cruciferous vegetables, like cauliflower, a minimum of 2-3 times per week in your diet.

Chickpea and Zucchini Curry

Yield: 4 servings

2 tablespoons olive oil
1 large yellow onion, sliced
4 cloves garlic, minced
1 teaspoon mustard seeds
1 large tomato, chopped
1 can tomato paste
½ cup water
1 tablespoon tamari
2 thin slices of fresh ginger root, minced
2 teaspoons turmeric
¼ teaspoon cayenne pepper
2 teaspoons ground cumin
2 teaspoons ground coriander
1 teaspoon ground cinnamon
½ teaspoon ground cloves
Sea salt to taste
½ teaspoon freshly ground black pepper
1 cup chickpeas, cooked
2 medium zucchinis, sliced
4-5 cups cooked brown rice
2 tablespoons fresh chives, chopped, for garnish

About 65-75% of the fiber in chickpeas is insoluble fiber, making it a dynamite food for digestive and intestinal health.

Heat the oil in a large skillet over medium heat and sauté the onion and garlic until the onion is translucent.

Add the mustard seeds and cook until they pop, stirring frequently.

Add the tomato, tomato paste, water, tamari, ginger, turmeric, cayenne, cumin, coriander, cinnamon, cloves, salt, pepper, and chickpeas and stir well.

Cover and simmer for about 15 minutes, stirring frequently.

Add the zucchini; mix well and let simmer for another 10 minutes.

Serve with brown rice. Garnish with chives.

Coconut Chickpea Burgers

Yield: 4 servings

1 cup chickpeas, cooked
2 tablespoons tahini
2 cloves garlic, minced
2 tablespoons fresh chives, minced
2 tablespoons fresh parsley, chopped
1 teaspoon curry powder

¼ cup sesame seeds
Sea salt to taste
½ teaspoon freshly ground black pepper
½ cup shredded unsweetened coconut
1 tomato, sliced
Lettuce leaves, any variety

Preheat oven to 350°.

Place the chickpeas, tahini, garlic, chives, parsley, curry powder, sesame seeds, salt, and pepper in a food processor or blender and purée until smooth. Roll the mixture into balls, then press into patties.

Dip the patties in the coconut; place on a baking sheet sprayed with non-stick olive oil and bake for 15 – 20 minutes.

Garnish with tomato and lettuce. Serve with Challah buns and veggie chips.

Spanish explorers used the word "coco," which means "monkey face," to describe these highly nutritious tree nuts. While high in fat, coconut is also rich in fiber, vitamins and minerals and considered one of the most nutritious foods on the planet.

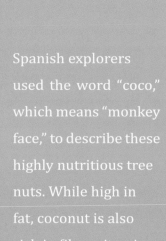

Crunchy Herbed Green Beans

Yield: 4 servings

2 tablespoons olive oil
1 small yellow onion, diced
2 cloves garlic, minced
½ cup green bell pepper
½ cup red bell pepper
½ cup yellow bell pepper
¼ cup water
1 pound green beans, trimmed
½ teaspoon marjoram
1 tablespoon fresh rosemary, chopped
Sea salt to taste
½ teaspoon freshly ground black pepper

Heat the oil in a skillet over medium heat and sauté the onion, garlic and peppers until the onions are translucent.

Add the water, green beans, marjoram, rosemary, salt, and pepper and sauté for 3 to 4 minutes until the green beans are just tender.

Green beans are rich in the mineral silicon, which is important in the health of connective tissues, as well as that of our bones. It strengthens hair and nails. Plus, they are a source of helpful omega-3 essential fatty acids.

Curried Barley
with Avocado

Yield: 2 servings

Barley is a very
versatile sweet and
nutty cereal grain.
It is known for its
cholesterol-lowering
and blood-sugar
regulating properties
and for supporting
heart health. Use it
in soups, salads,
main dishes, and
for breakfast.

2 tablespoons extra virgin olive oil
1 medium yellow onion, chopped
2 cloves garlic, minced
½ stalk celery, minced
½ red bell pepper, chopped
3 tablespoons sliced black olives
¼ cup cashews, chopped
¼ cup currants
1 tablespoon fresh parsley, chopped
1 teaspoon fresh cilantro, chopped
¼ cup chia seeds
2 cups barley, cooked
1 tablespoon curry powder
Sea salt to taste
½ teaspoon freshly ground black pepper
1 large ripe avocado, peeled and sliced
½ cup chives, cut into 2-inch pieces, for garnish

Heat the oil in a large saucepan over medium heat and sauté
the onion, garlic, and celery until the onion is translucent.

Add the red pepper, olives, cashews, currants, parsley, cilantro,
chia seeds, barley, curry powder, salt, and pepper and stir well,
and until thoroughly warmed.

Garnish with chives.

Serve with sliced avocado.

Curried Potato Masal

Yield: 2 servings

2 medium potatoes, cubed
1 tablespoon olive oil
1 large yellow onion, diced
2 cloves garlic, minced
1 teaspoon mustard seeds
½ cup vegetable broth
3 tablespoons grated fresh or dried unsweetened coconut
1 teaspoon fresh ginger, minced
½ teaspoon turmeric
¼ teaspoon cayenne
1 teaspoon cardamom
1 teaspoon anise
1 teaspoon curry powder
Sea salt to taste
½ teaspoon freshly ground black pepper
¼ cup fresh peas
3 tablespoons fresh cilantro, chopped
½ cup grated carrot, for garnish
Lettuce leaves

Boil the cubed potatoes until tender, about 15 – 20 minutes, and set aside.

Heat the oil in a skillet over medium heat and sauté the onion and garlic until the onion is translucent.

Add the mustard seeds and cook until they start to pop.

Add the vegetable broth, coconut, ginger, turmeric, cayenne, cardamom, anise, curry powder, salt, and pepper and simmer for about 5 minutes, stirring occasionally.

Add the peas, cilantro, and boiled potato cubes and simmer until the peas are cooked, about 5 minutes.

Garnish with grated carrot. Serve on a bed of lettuce.

Stomach ache? Cold or cough? Pour some hot water over anise seeds, and take a few sips; it is likely that you will feel a whole lot better. Anise has long been used as a digestive.

Dalsaag

Yield: 4 servings

Dal, a popular Indian dish, is a preparation of lentils, peas and/or beans. Dal is a ready source of protein and is typically eaten with rice and vegetables.

1¾ cups dried red or yellow lentils
3½ cups water
1 cup unsweetened almond milk
Two 10-oz. packages fresh spinach, chopped
1 yellow onion, diced
2 cloves garlic, minced
2 tablespoons fresh basil, chopped

2 tablespoons fresh cilantro, chopped
1 teaspoon curry powder
1 teaspoon ground cardamom
½ teaspoon turmeric
1 tablespoon chia seeds
1 bay leaf
Sea salt to taste
½ teaspoon freshly ground black pepper

Place the lentils, water, and almond milk in a large saucepan and bring to a boil.

Add the remaining ingredients and simmer over medium heat for 20 minutes until the lentils are done.

Serve over brown rice.

Divine Potato Casserole

Divine Potato Casserole

Yield: 4 servings

1 tablespoon walnut oil
1 red onion, diced
2 cloves garlic, minced
2 fresh tomatoes, chopped
½ cup water
2 tablespoons chopped fresh basil
2 tablespoons fresh parsley, chopped
2 tablespoons fresh oregano, chopped
½ teaspoon Hungarian paprika
½ teaspoon cayenne
Sea salt to taste
½ teaspoon freshly ground black pepper
2 cups Yukon potatoes, peeled and cubed
1 cup black beans, cooked
2 tablespoons tahini
½ cup vegan bread crumbs
2 tablespoons minced chives, for garnish

Preheat oven to 425°.

Heat the oil in a skillet over medium heat and sauté the onion and garlic until the onion is translucent.

Add the tomatoes, water, basil, parsley, oregano, paprika, cayenne, salt, and pepper, and simmer for 15 minutes.

Add the potatoes, black beans, and tahini; mix thoroughly, and place in a casserole dish.

Top with bread crumbs and bake covered for 20 minutes.

Garnish with chives.

Paprika is a spice that is made of the ground, dried fruits of either bell pepper or chili pepper varieties, or mixtures of the two. Hungarian Paprika is typically stronger in both aroma and color; however, taste may or may not vary from other types, and ranges from mild to hot.

Eggless Zucchini Pesto Quiche

Yield: 6 servings

Pesto Sauce:
1 clove garlic
¼ cup pine nuts
¼ cup fresh parsley
½ cup fresh basil
¼ cup fresh spinach
¼ teaspoon sea salt
½ teaspoon black pepper
1 pinch cayenne
2 tablespoons extra virgin olive oil

Place the garlic and pine nuts in a food processor and pulse until finely chopped.

Add the parsley, basil, spinach, salt, pepper, cayenne, and olive oil and purée until smooth.

Quiche:
2 tablespoons walnut oil
1 yellow onion, diced
2 cloves garlic, minced
1 stalk celery, chopped
½ cup button mushrooms, chopped
½ cup shiitake mushrooms, chopped
1 cup zucchini, peeled and diced
1 cup pesto sauce (see recipe above)
1 teaspoon chia seeds
1 tablespoon flaxseed meal
Sea salt to taste
½ teaspoon freshly ground black pepper
1 commercial vegan pie crust
2 button mushrooms, sliced, for garnish

Preheat oven to 375°.

Heat the oil in a skillet over medium-high heat and sauté the onion, garlic, celery, and chopped mushrooms until the onion is translucent and the mushrooms are golden brown.

Most commercial and store-bought pesto is prepared with Parmesan cheese. So check the label, or ask the preparer at a restaurant, to ensure that you are getting a vegan product.

Eggless Zucchini Pesto Quiche

continued

Place the sautéed vegetables, zucchini, pesto sauce, chia seeds, flaxseed meal, salt, and pepper in a food processor and purée until smooth.

Place the pie crust in a pie plate and fill with the purée.

Top with mushroom slices.

Bake in the oven for 20 minutes or until the top of the quiche is light brown.

Eggplant Parmesan Sesame

Yield: 4 servings

2 large eggplants, peeled and sliced
2 cups vegan breadcrumbs
1 tablespoon flaxseed meal
2 tablespoons fresh basil, chopped
1 tablespoon fresh oregano, chopped
2 tablespoons fresh parsley, chopped
1 teaspoon garlic powder
1 teaspoon onion powder
Sea salt to taste
½ teaspoon freshly ground black pepper
½ cup unsweetened almond milk
16-oz. jar vegan spaghetti sauce, divided in thirds
½ cup sesame seeds, divided in half
16-oz. container grated vegan Parmesan cheese, divided in third

Preheat oven to 375°.

In a medium bowl, mix breadcrumbs, flaxseed meal, basil, oregano, parsley, garlic powder, onion powder, salt and pepper.

Dip the eggplant slices in almond milk, and then roll in bread crumb mixture until well-coated.

Place the eggplant slices on a greased baking sheet and bake for 5 minutes on each side.

Cover the bottom of a baking dish with ¹⁄₃ of the vegan spaghetti sauce.

Place a layer of eggplant slices over the sauce, followed by a layer of the herbed bread crumbs, sesame seeds, and vegan Parmesan cheese.

Repeat the layers of spaghetti sauce, eggplant, breadcrumbs, and sesame seeds, followed by a layer of spaghetti sauce and Parmesan.

Bake for 30 minutes, or until golden brown.

The skin of eggplant contains a powerful phytonutrient called *nasunin* that has been shown to be a potent antioxidant and free-radical scavenger.

Eggplant Wraps with Roasted Red Pepper Tomato Sauce

While a Carmen pepper's elongated shape makes it appear that they would be fiery and hot, they are actually as sweet as can be!

Yield: 6 servings

2 tablespoons extra virgin olive oil
1 yellow onion, diced
2 cloves garlic, minced
1 red bell pepper, chopped
1 fresh tomato, chopped
1 cup cooked eggplant, diced
2 tablespoons fresh basil, chopped
2 tablespoons fresh parsley, chopped
1 tablespoon fresh thyme, chopped
1 tablespoon curry powder
½ cup walnuts, chopped
Sea salt to taste
½ teaspoon freshly ground black pepper
1 package Ezekiel 4:9® sprouted grain tortillas

Eggplant Wraps with Roasted Red Pepper Tomato Sauce

continued

Heat the oil in a large skillet over medium heat and sauté onion, garlic, and red pepper until the onion is translucent.

Add the tomato, eggplant, basil, parsley, thyme, curry powder, walnuts, salt, and pepper and let simmer for 10 – 15 minutes until the eggplant is tender. Add water if necessary.

Place a few tablespoons of the eggplant mixture in a tortilla and roll to create wraps.

Top with Roasted Pepper Tomato Sauce.

Roasted Pepper Tomato Sauce:
1 red Carmen or bell pepper
1 tablespoon extra virgin olive oil
1 yellow onion, diced
2 cloves garlic, minced
1 fresh tomato, chopped
3 tablespoons fresh basil
2 tablespoons fresh parsley
1 tablespoon fresh sage
Sea salt to taste
½ teaspoon black pepper

Preheat oven to 350°.

Place red pepper on a baking sheet and roast in the oven for 20 minutes, turning every 5 minutes.

Heat the oil in a skillet and sauté onion and garlic until the onion is translucent. Add the tomato, basil, parsley, sage, salt, and pepper and simmer for 15 minutes.

Place red pepper, and the onion-garlic-tomato mixture in a food processor and purée until smooth.

"Sprouted" wheat wraps are more nutritious – and typically have fewer additives – than processed wheat wraps. Sprouting does not remove the gluten though, so choose gluten-free wraps if this is important to you.

Fettuccine with Creamy Asparagus Sauce

Yield: 4 servings

1 tablespoon olive oil
1 yellow onion, diced
2 cloves garlic, minced
1 orange bell pepper, diced; reserve $1/3$ for garnish
3 cups chopped fresh tomatoes
½ cup unsweetened almond milk
2 tablespoons fresh basil, chopped
2 tablespoons fresh parsley, chopped
¼ cup green olives, sliced
2 cups asparagus, fibrous end of stalk removed, sliced into
    1½ inch pieces
Sea salt to taste
½ teaspoon freshly ground black pepper
1 box fettuccine (16 oz.), cooked

Heat the oil in a large skillet over medium heat and sauté the onion, garlic, and orange pepper until the onion is translucent.

Add the tomatoes, almond milk, basil, parsley, olives, asparagus, salt, and pepper and simmer for 15 – 20 minutes.

Toss the cooked fettuccine with the asparagus sauce until well coated.

Garnish with peppers.

Asparagus contains a unique array of anti-inflammatory nutrients that many health proponents believe have an ability to deter inflammatory as well as auto-immune conditions.

Galuska

Yield: 2 servings

Soft Noodles
1 cup buckwheat flour
⅓ cup warm water
¼ teaspoon sea salt
2 teaspoons olive oil

Sauce
2 tablespoons olive oil
1 yellow onion, diced
2 cloves garlic, minced
2 fresh tomatoes, chopped
½ green bell pepper, chopped
½ red bell pepper, chopped
2 tablespoons fresh parsley, chopped
1 tablespoon fresh thyme, chopped
1 tablespoon fresh sage, chopped
Sea salt to taste
½ teaspoon freshly ground black pepper

To prepare the noodles:

Place the flour and salt in a large mixing bowl and make a well in the center.

Add the oil and water, and mix slowly with a fork so that it blends evenly.

Once the flour appears saturated, knead by hand until the dough feels pliable, about 10 – 15 minutes. Cover the dough with a towel and let rest for half an hour.

Place the dough on a floured surface and roll out with a rolling pin to desired thickness.

Slice into pieces one inch wide and three inches long.

To cook, place the noodles in boiling water and remove when they rise to the surface, about 1 – 2 minutes.

To prepare the sauce:

Heat the oil in a skillet and sauté the onion and garlic until the onion is translucent.

Add the tomatoes, bell peppers, parsley, thyme, sage, salt, and pepper and simmer for 30 minutes.

Serve over the noodles.

Buckwheat flour is gluten-free, and comes in two forms, light and dark, with the darker flour being more nutritious.

Gary's Fat-free Sweet Potato, Black Bean and Chickpea Stew

Yield: 4 servings

1 cup vegetable broth
1 red onion, chopped
3 cloves garlic, minced
½ cup celery, chopped
1 red bell pepper, chopped
1 teaspoon jalapeño pepper, chopped
3 tablespoons fennel root, chopped
2 pounds sweet potatoes, cubed
½ cup black beans, cooked
½ cup chickpeas, cooked
¼ cup sesame seeds
½ teaspoon ground turmeric
3 tablespoons fresh parsley, chopped
Sea salt to taste
½ teaspoon freshly ground black pepper

Heat ¼ cup of the vegetable broth in a large saucepan over medium heat and sauté the onion, garlic, and celery until tender.

Add the remaining water, bell pepper, jalapeño pepper, fennel, sweet potatoes, black beans, chickpeas, sesame seeds, turmeric, parsley, salt, and pepper and simmer covered for about 20 minutes or until the sweet potatoes are tender.

Turmeric, used for more than 2500 years in India, is one of nature's most powerful healers. Hailing from the ginger family, turmeric is one of the most potent anti-inflammatories available today. It has been shown helpful in the prevention and remediation of numerous health conditions from cancer to Alzheimer's to arthritis.

Gary's Favorite Casserole

Yield: 4 servings

/₄ cup water
/₂ cup gluten-free oat flour
1 tablespoon flaxseed meal
/₂ cup split peas, cooked
1 tomato, chopped
2 cloves garlic, minced
/₂ teaspoon curry powder
1 tablespoon fresh oregano, chopped
1 tablespoon fresh parsley, chopped
1 small yellow onion, chopped
/₄ teaspoon cayenne
Sea salt to taste
/₂ teaspoon freshly ground black pepper
1 cup kale, coarsely chopped
1 cup broccoli, chopped into pieces
1 cup brown rice, cooked
/₂ cup quinoa, cooked
/₂ cup gluten-free, vegan breadcrumbs
/₄ cup bean sprouts, for garnish
/₂ cup cherry tomatoes, for garnish
/₂ avocado, sliced or cubed, for garnish

Preheat oven to 375°.

Combine water, oat flour, flaxseed meal, split peas, tomato, garlic, curry powder, oregano, parsley, onion, cayenne, salt, and pepper in a blender or food processor and purée until smooth.

In a separate bowl, combine kale, broccoli, brown rice, and quinoa.

Add the split pea mixture; mix well and place in a lightly greased 4 x 8-inch baking pan. Cover with breadcrumbs.

Bake for 15 minutes or until the breadcrumbs are golden brown.

Garnish with bean sprouts, cherry tomatoes, and avocado slices.

This is one of my favorite dishes to share with people. It is so packed with both flavor and nutritional benefit that it leaves people wondering why they don't eat vegan food every day.

Goulash

Yield: 4 servings

Bragg's Liquid Aminos is a certified NON-GMO, gluten-free liquid protein concentrate and salt alternative, derived from healthy soybeans. It contains both essential and non-essential amino acids. Find it in your local health food stores. Note: if you don't have Bragg's you can always substitute tamari – but if you are gluten sensitive remember that tamari is not gluten free.

1 tablespoon olive oil
1 medium yellow onion, chopped
2 shallots, minced
2 cloves garlic, minced
1 stalk celery, chopped
1 large tomato, chopped
1 cup vegetable broth
1 package firm tofu, diced
1 cup asparagus, sliced
½ cup chickpeas, cooked
¼ teaspoon caraway seeds
½ teaspoon Hungarian paprika
Sea salt to taste
½ teaspoon freshly ground
    black pepper
1 tablespoon Bragg's Liquid
    Aminos
¼ cup tahini

Heat the oil in a large saucepan over medium heat and sauté onion, shallots, garlic and celery until the onion is translucent.

Add tomato and vegetable broth and simmer for 15 minutes.

Add tofu, asparagus, chickpeas, caraway seeds, paprika, salt, and pepper and simmer for 10 minutes.

Add the Bragg's Liquid Aminos and stir well.

Serve with tahini.

Green Pea Millet "Couscous"

Yield: 2 servings

2 tablespoons walnut oil
2 shallots, minced
2 cloves garlic, minced
1½ cups vegetable broth
¾ cup millet
1 tablespoon chia seeds
½ cup fresh peas
⅓ cup fresh spearmint, chopped
1 tablespoon Bragg's Liquid Aminos, or to taste
½ cup parsley leaves, for garnish
½ teaspoon paprika, for garnish

Heat the oil in a large saucepan over medium heat and sauté shallots and garlic for 3 minutes until tender.

Add vegetable broth, millet, chia seeds, peas, and spearmint and simmer over low heat for about 15 – 20 minutes, or until water is absorbed and millet is tender.

Remove from heat and stir in Bragg's Liquid Aminos.

Garnish with parsley and paprika.

Millet is a wonderfully nutty flavored, not-so-well-known gluten-free "grain" that is not actually a grain, but seeds from a variety of grasses. It is an important crop in both India and Africa.

Hawaiian Tempeh Kebabs

Yield: 4 servings

Tempeh is a naturally gluten-free, fermented soybean product that is a rich source of protein – even more than tofu! It is also rich in calcium and iron, two important minerals.

Marinade;
2 tablespoons tamari
½ cup fresh lemon juice
2 cloves garlic, minced
¼ teaspoon ground allspice
½ teaspoon freshly ground black pepper

One 10-oz. package tempeh, cut into 12 cubes
1 cup pineapple, cubed
1 cup zucchini, thick slices cut into quarters
1 cup cherry tomatoes

In a large bowl, combine tamari, lemon juice, garlic, allspice, and pepper.

Add the tempeh, pineapple, zucchini, and tomatoes and marinate for 2 hours.

Place the marinated tempeh, pineapple, zucchini, and tomatoes on skewers and broil or grill for 10 minutes.

Hot and Spicy Bean Wraps

Yield: 4 servings

1 tablespoon olive oil
1 yellow onion, diced
2 cloves garlic, minced
1 jalapeño pepper, minced
½ cup water
1 tomato, chopped
1 orange bell pepper, chopped
1 cup navy beans, cooked
2 tablespoons fresh basil, chopped

1 cup basmati rice, cooked
1 tablespoon fresh ginger, minced
Sea salt to taste
½ teaspoon freshly ground black pepper
¼ teaspoon cayenne
1 jar chili sauce
Tortillas of your choice

Heat the oil in a large saucepan over medium heat and sauté the onion, garlic, and jalapeño pepper until the onion is translucent.

Add water, tomato, orange pepper, navy beans, basil, rice, ginger, salt, pepper, and cayenne and simmer for 15 – 20 minutes.

Place a few tablespoons of mixture on a tortilla and roll up to form wrap.

Serve with chili sauce.

Tortillas come in gluten-free options. Studies have shown an increase in the inflammatory response with processed wheat products. If you want to reduce your chances of chronic diseases, it would be wise to eliminate processed wheat products. See my book *Reverse Arthritis & Pain Naturally* for more information.

Indian Ratatouille

Yield: 4 servings

2 tablespoons walnut oil
1 yellow onion, diced
2 cloves garlic, minced
2-3 cups vegetable broth
2 tablespoons tomato paste
2 tomatoes, chopped
2 Yukon potatoes cut into ½ inch slices
1 red bell pepper, chopped
1 yellow bell pepper, chopped
1 green chili pepper, finely chopped
1 tablespoon fennel, chopped
1 cup okra, sliced
1 cup button mushrooms, sliced
1 teaspoon fresh ginger, minced
1 teaspoon powdered cardamom
1 teaspoon ground cloves
Sea salt to taste
½ teaspoon freshly ground black pepper
1 large eggplant, diced
1 cup cauliflower florets
1 zucchini, cut into ½ inch slices and quartered
3 tablespoons fresh cilantro, chopped

Heat the oil in a saucepan and sauté the onion and garlic until the onion is translucent.

Add vegetable broth, tomato paste, tomatoes, potatoes, bell peppers, chili pepper, fennel, okra, mushrooms, ginger, cardamom, cloves, salt, and pepper; mix well and simmer for 15 minutes.

Add eggplant, cauliflower, zucchini, and cilantro and simmer covered for 10 – 15 minutes until vegetables are tender.

Indonesian Kale

Yield: 4 servings

Allspice, also known as Jamaican pepper or pimento, is a very good spice for improving digestion. Eugenol, a compound in allspice, has anesthetic and antiseptic properties, and is useful in gum and dental treatments.

½ cup extra virgin olive oil
1 yellow onion, chopped
4 cloves garlic, sliced
4 fresh tomatoes, chopped
1 cup water
4 cups fresh kale, chopped
4 red potatoes, peeled, diced, and steamed
2 tablespoons curry powder
½ teaspoon ground allspice
½ teaspoon ground ginger
½ teaspoon paprika
Sea salt to taste
½ teaspoon freshly ground black pepper

Heat the oil in a large saucepan over medium heat and sauté the onions and garlic until the onion is translucent. Add tomatoes and sauté for 15 minutes.

Add remaining ingredients and simmer for an additional 15 minutes.

Jamaican Vegetable
Root Stew

Jamaican Vegetable Root Stew

Yield: 4 servings

2 tablespoons olive oil
1 yellow onion, diced
3 cloves garlic, minced
2 stalks celery, sliced
3 cups water
2 tomatoes, chopped
1 cup okra, sliced
½ cup chayote, peeled and diced
1 cup fresh mushrooms, sliced
¼ cup wakame leaves
1 potato, peeled and diced
½ pumpkin, peeled and cut into 1-inch pieces
½ fresh chili pepper, minced
½ cup pigeon peas, cooked
Pinch of saffron
Sea salt to taste
½ teaspoon freshly ground black pepper
1 cup tomato juice
2 tablespoons fresh-squeezed lime juice
3 tablespoons fresh cilantro, chopped
1 lime, quartered, for garnish

In a large saucepan, heat oil over medium heat and sauté onion, garlic and celery until the onion is translucent.

Add water, tomatoes, okra, chayote, mushrooms, wakame, potato, pumpkin, chili pepper, pigeon peas, saffron, salt, and pepper and simmer over medium heat for 20 minutes.

Add tomato juice, lime juice, and cilantro and stir well.

Garnish with lime.

Chayote, also known as pear squash, is native of Brazil. It is mostly eaten cooked, and is a good source of amino acids (protein builders) and vitamin C.

Khaloda Algerian Eggplant

Yield: 4 servings

2 tablespoons walnut oil
2 medium yellow onions, diced
2 cloves garlic, minced
1 green bell pepper, chopped
4 cups water
4 tomatoes, chopped
1 large eggplant, sliced
1 pound okra, sliced
5 medium potatoes, quartered
1 teaspoon tarragon
1 chili pepper, chopped
1 teaspoon fresh ginger, minced
½ teaspoon turmeric
1 tablespoon chia seeds
Sea salt to taste
½ teaspoon freshly ground black pepper
½ cup black and white sesame seeds, for garnish

Heat the oil in a large skillet over medium-high heat; add the onions, garlic, and bell pepper and sauté until the onions are translucent.

Add water, tomatoes, eggplant, okra, potatoes, tarragon, chili pepper, ginger, turmeric, chia seeds, salt, and pepper and simmer for 20 – 30 minutes

Garnish with sesame seeds.

Tarragon is an herb used plentifully in French cooking. It is lauded for its phyto-nutrient content, and noted for its mineral content. It also has the ability to stimulate the appetite, and to control blood-sugar levels.

Lemon Tofu

Yield: 4 servings

1 package firm tofu, cut into strips
1 tablespoon apple cider vinegar
2 teaspoons golden miso
2 tablespoons olive oil
1 teaspoon fresh ginger, minced
2 tablespoons garlic, minced
2 scallions, sliced
1 carrot, sliced
½ red bell pepper, sliced
1 tablespoon grated lemon zest
1 tablespoon arrowroot powder
½ cup lemon juice
1 carrot, grated, for garnish
½ lemon, thinly sliced into rounds, for garnish

Drain the tofu and place on paper towels. Place a plate on top of the tofu and let sit for 30 minutes to squeeze out the moisture.

Combine cider vinegar and golden miso in a bowl; add the tofu strips and marinate 30 – 60 minutes.

Heat oil in a wok over high heat and stir-fry ginger, garlic, scallions, carrot, pepper, and lemon zest for 3 minutes.

Remove tofu from marinade and set aside.

In a blender, combine marinade and arrowroot powder until smooth.

Pour mixture into wok and heat until thickened, stirring constantly. Add tofu and sauté until warm.

Add lemon juice; stir briefly and remove from heat.

Garnish with grated carrot and lemon slices.

Arrowroot powder is the dried root from the arrowroot plant and used as a thickening agent in vegetarian cooking. It is very easy to digest, which is why it tends to be used instead of flour in infant cookies.

Lentil Burgers

Yield: 4 servings

4 carrots, steamed
1 cup cooked brown lentils
¼ cup lentil sprouts
¼ cup unsalted cashews, chopped
¼ cup unsalted almonds, chopped
1 teaspoon chia seeds
1 small yellow onion, diced
2 teaspoons curry powder
2 tablespoons fresh cilantro
½ cup whole wheat bread crumbs
¼ teaspoon cayenne
Sea salt to taste
½ teaspoon freshly ground black pepper

Preheat oven to 425°.

Purée carrots in a food processor.

Add lentils, sprouts, cashews, almonds, chia seeds, onion, curry powder, cilantro, bread crumbs, cayenne, salt, and pepper to the food processor and purée until smooth.

Shape mixture into patties and place on an ungreased baking sheet.

Bake for 10 minutes; turn over and bake an additional 10 – 15 minutes.

Serve on sesame seed buns with lettuce and tomato.

Preparation tip: Make a double batch and store extras in the freezer for a quick and healthy meal.

While broccoli has limited amounts of omega-3 fats, it contains no omega-6 fats, and can play an important role in balancing our inflammatory system activity. Two cups of broccoli supply 450 milligrams of omega-3s in the form of alpha-linolenic acid (ALA), around the same amount as in a capsule of flaxseed oil, so the benefits mount up the more you consume. Extremely rich in vitamins C and K, a host of minerals, and phytochemicals to boot, broccoli should be a regular part of your healthy diet. Eat your broccoli!

Linguini with Garden Vegetables

Yield: 4 servings

1 tablespoon olive oil
1 yellow onion, diced
2 cloves garlic minced
1 red bell pepper, chopped
2 large tomatoes, chopped
2 cups mushrooms, sliced
1 cup water
¼ cup fresh basil, chopped
1 tablespoon fresh oregano, chopped
1 tablespoon fresh thyme, chopped
Sea salt to taste
½ teaspoon freshly ground black pepper
2 cups broccoli florets
3 to 4 cups vegan linguini, cooked

Heat the oil in a large saucepan over medium heat and sauté the onion, garlic, and pepper until the onion is translucent.

Add tomatoes, mushrooms, water, basil, oregano, thyme, salt, and pepper and simmer for 20 minutes.

Add the broccoli and continue cooking until tender, about 10 – 15 minutes.

Place the linguini in a large serving bowl and toss with the garden vegetable sauce.

Millet Coriander Stir-Fry

Yield: 2 servings

3 tablespoons sesame oil
½ cup daikon, sliced
½ cup carrots, sliced
½ cup zucchini, sliced
3 cups millet, cooked
3 tablespoons tamari
½ teaspoon fresh ginger, minced
1 teaspoon sesame seeds
2 tablespoons fresh parsley, chopped
1 tablespoon fresh cilantro, chopped

Heat the oil in large saucepan and sauté the daikon, carrots, and zucchini for 5 – 8 minutes.

Add the remaining ingredients; mix well and sauté an additional 3 – 6 minutes.

Coriander, also known as cilantro, is an incredibly fragrant seed that is known for its anti-inflammatory properties, and is useful in regulating blood sugar. This phytochemical-rich herb is also known to possess antibacterial compounds that may be helpful in addressing salmonella poisoning.

Linguini with Garden Vegetables

Mushroom Bean Curry with Butternut Squash

Yield: 2 servings

1 butternut squash, cut in half
2 tablespoons walnut oil
1 yellow onion, diced
3 cloves garlic, minced
1 stalk celery, chopped
1 cup mushrooms, sliced
¼ cup vegetable broth
1 teaspoon chia seeds
1 teaspoon madras curry powder
1 pinch cayenne
¼ teaspoon turmeric
1 cup kidney beans, puréed
½ cup kale, shredded
Sea salt to taste
½ teaspoon freshly ground black pepper
¼ cup vegan breadcrumbs
2 tablespoons kale, shredded, for garnish

Preheat oven to 350°.

Place the squash halves on a baking sheet sprayed with non-stick olive oil and bake for 15 minutes.

When slightly cooled, hollow out the squash halves. Chop the removed squash into 1-inch squares and set aside.

Heat the oil in a large skillet and sauté the onion, garlic, and celery until the onion is translucent.

Add mushrooms and sauté until lightly brown.

Add vegetable broth, chia seeds, curry, cayenne, turmeric, kidney bean purée, shredded kale, squash squares, salt, and pepper and sauté for about 5 minutes.

Fill both squash halves with the mixture and top with breadcrumbs.

Put back in the oven and bake for 15 more minutes until breadcrumbs are golden brown.

Garnish with shredded kale.

This dish is a powerhouse of omega-3 fats, and anti-inflammatory properties. Cook it up and enjoy it with friends.

Mushroom-Stuffed Tomatoes

Yield: 2 servings

2 large tomatoes
2 tablespoons olive oil
1 cup button mushrooms, diced
1 yellow onion, diced
2 cloves garlic, minced
1 red bell pepper, chopped
¾ cup vegan bread crumbs
3 tablespoons fresh basil, chopped
1 tablespoon fresh oregano, chopped
1 tablespoon fresh parsley, chopped
1 tablespoon toasted sesame seeds
Sea salt to taste
½ teaspoon freshly ground black pepper

Preheat oven to 350°.

Slice tops off tomatoes and set aside. Hollow out tomatoes leaving the skin intact. Reserve the tomato pulp and seeds.

Heat the oil in a saucepan over medium heat and sauté mushrooms until brown. Set aside.

Sauté the onion, garlic, and bell pepper until the onion is translucent.

In a small mixing bowl, combine the tomato pulp, mushrooms, sautéed vegetables, bread crumbs, basil, oregano, parsley, sesame seeds, salt, and pepper.

Fill tomatoes with mushroom stuffing; cover with tomato tops and place in a greased baking dish.

Bake for 15 – 20 minutes until golden brown.

This dish contains several nightshade vegetables, which are rich in nutrients, but can be a problem for those who are sensitive. See p. 41 for more information.

Noodles Deluxe

Yield: 2 servings

1 package extra-firm tofu, sliced
4 teaspoons tamarind pulp,
   soaked in 4 tablespoons of
   hot water
2 tablespoons yellow bean sauce
2 teaspoons arrowroot powder
3 tablespoons fresh cilantro,
   chopped
2 tablespoons fresh basil,
   chopped
1 tablespoon fresh mint, chopped
½ teaspoon cumin
½ teaspoon marjoram
1 teaspoon grated lemon zest

½ teaspoon freshly ground
   black pepper
1 tablespoon walnut oil
2 cloves garlic, minced
1 yellow onion, diced
½ yellow bell pepper, cut into
   thin strips
½ Carmen pepper, cut into
   thin strips
1 package Thai rice noodles
6 cups boiling water
½ orange, sliced into thin
   rounds, for garnish

Strain and discard tamarind pulp, reserving the juice.

In a small mixing bowl, combine the tamarind juice, bean sauce, and arrowroot powder and blend until smooth.

Add the cilantro, basil, mint, cumin, marjoram, lemon zest, and black pepper and mix well.

Heat the oil in a wok over high heat; stir-fry the sliced tofu and set aside.

Stir-fry the onion, garlic, and peppers until onion is translucent.

Add the tamarind juice mixture and the tofu; simmer until slightly thickened.

Place the rice noodles in a deep mixing bowl, trying not to break them. Cover the noodles with boiling water until submerged and gently stir to loosen.

When completely limp (about 2 – 3 minutes), carefully drain into a colander and run under cool water to stop the cooking process.

Place the noodles in a serving dish and cover with the tamarind sauce.

Garnish with orange slices.

Rice noodles are an excellent gluten-free alternative to wheat noodles. Start cooking with them and you will come to love their light and enjoyable texture.

Okra Curry

Yield: 4 servings

1 tablespoon olive oil
1 yellow onion, diced
3 cloves garlic, minced
1 stalk celery, chopped
3 fresh tomatoes, chopped
2 cups water
1½ cups fresh whole okra
1½ cups (about 12 oz.) black-eyed peas, cooked
2 tablespoons curry powder
2 tablespoons fresh cilantro, chopped
Sea salt to taste
1 teaspoon freshly ground black pepper
1 bay leaf

Heat the oil in a large saucepan over medium heat and sauté the onion, garlic, and celery until the onion is translucent.

Add the remaining ingredients and simmer for 25 minutes over medium heat.

Serve with brown rice.

The mucilaginous characteristics of okra are beneficial for binding to cholesterol, which makes it an excellent detoxifier.

Peppery Pasta

Yield: 4 servings

1 package (16 oz.) quinoa rotelle
3 tablespoons tahini
1 tablespoon fresh lemon juice
½ teaspoon dry mustard
1 clove garlic, minced
2 scallions, chopped
1 red bell pepper, chopped
2 tablespoons fresh parsley, chopped
1 tablespoon fresh dill, chopped
Sea salt to taste
1 teaspoon freshly ground black pepper
¼ teaspoon cayenne
½ cup chives, sliced, for garnish

Cook the pasta according to the directions on the package; drain well and chill.

Place the tahini, lemon juice, mustard, and garlic in a food processor and purée until smooth.

Add the scallions, red pepper, parsley, dill, salt, pepper, and cayenne and pulse until well blended.

Combine the pasta and tahini sauce in a salad bowl and mix well.

Serve on a bed of lettuce and garnish with sliced chives.

Chives are the smallest species of all the edible onions, and part of the allium family, which also includes garlic, onions, scallions and leeks. This is a power-packed group of foods full of antioxidants and minerals that are both anti-cancer and anti-inflammatory. In particular, chives assist in improving the assimilation of nutrients from other foods by clearing away bacteria, yeasts and fungi from the digestive tract.

Purple Cabbage and Spaghetti Squash Stir-Fry

Yield: 2 servings

Purple cabbage
contains anthocyanin
polyphenols,
which are strong
dietary antioxidants,
possessing anti-
inflammatory
properties.

1 tablespoon olive oil
2 scallions, sliced
3 cloves garlic, minced
2 cups vegetable broth
½ spaghetti squash, diced
2 cups broccoli florets
2 cups purple cabbage, sliced
1 package firm tofu, cubed
1 teaspoon fresh ginger, minced
2 tablespoons fresh parsley, chopped
1 tablespoon fresh thyme, chopped
2 tablespoons tamari
½ teaspoon freshly ground black pepper
¼ cup sesame seeds, for garnish

Heat the oil in a large saucepan over medium heat and sauté
the scallions and garlic until tender.

Add vegetable broth, squash, broccoli, cabbage, tofu, ginger,
parsley, thyme, tamari, and pepper and simmer for 15 – 20
minutes until vegetables are tender.

Garnish with the sesame seeds.

Red Brazilian Rice

Yield: 4 servings

4 tablespoons walnut oil
1 red onion, diced
2 cloves garlic, minced
2 fresh tomatoes, chopped
½ cup water
1 green bell pepper, chopped
1 tablespoon capers
½ cup large green olives, sliced
1 bay leaf
1 tablespoon fresh thyme, chopped
Sea salt to taste
½ teaspoon freshly ground black pepper
4 cups basmati rice, cooked
2 tablespoons pumpkin seeds, for garnish

Heat the oil in a large saucepan over medium heat and sauté the onions and garlic until the onions are translucent.

Add the tomatoes, water, bell pepper, capers, olives, bay leaf, thyme, salt, and pepper and simmer for 20 minutes.

Add the rice and mix until thoroughly heated.

Garnish with pumpkin seeds and serve with salad.

Basmati Rice comes in both white and brown varieties, with the brown being the more nutritious, as in the case of all rice. Here is the difference: brown rice has the whole kernel intact, and the kernel is still surrounded by all the layers of bran. For white rice, the bran layers are milled off, as is most of the rice germ – a very nutritious part of the kernel. At this stage, the rice is considered unpolished white rice. To complete the process of creating white rice, a machine with wire brushes is then used to remove the aleurone layer that remains on the rice, which is where most of the nutrients and fats – including fat-soluble vitamin E – are located.

Rice and Lentils

Yield: 4 servings

Lentils are believed to have originated in central Asia, and are known to have been in existence for more than 8,000 years. In addition to their high levels of minerals, lentils replenish iron stores, which help people suffering from iron deficiencies.

1 tablespoon olive oil
1 yellow onion, diced
3 cloves garlic, minced
1 teaspoon cumin seeds
1 cup washed red or yellow lentils
1 cup button mushrooms, sliced
4 cups water

1 teaspoon turmeric
2 teaspoons ground coriander
1 teaspoon fresh ginger, minced
Sea salt to taste
½ teaspoon freshly ground black pepper
2 tablespoons fresh parsley, chopped, for garnish
2 cups basmati rice, cooked

Heat the oil in a small saucepan over medium heat and sauté the onion, garlic, and cumin seeds until the cumin seeds are brown.

Add the lentils, mushrooms, water, turmeric, coriander, ginger, salt, and pepper; bring to a boil and reduce the heat and simmer, covered, for 30 minutes.

Serve with rice. Garnish with parsley.

Risotto with Tomatoes and Peas

Yield: 2 servings

2 tablespoons olive oil
1 yellow onion, diced
2 cloves garlic, minced
1 cup brown or Arborio rice
3 cups vegetable broth, hot
1 fresh tomato, chopped
½ cup fresh peas
1 tablespoon fresh Italian
  parsley, chopped

2 tablespoons fresh basil,
  chopped
1 tablespoon fresh thyme,
  chopped
Sea salt to taste
½ teaspoon freshly ground
  black pepper
2 teaspoons grated vegan
  Parmesan cheese, for garnish

Heat the oil in a saucepan and sauté onion and garlic until the onion is translucent.

Add rice and stir until grains become translucent, about 7 minutes.

Add vegetable broth one ladle at a time, stirring constantly, until absorbed fully by the rice, about 20 minutes

When the rice is just tender, add the tomatoes, peas, parsley, basil, thyme, salt, and pepper and cook for 10 more minutes.

Garnish with vegan Parmesan cheese.

Arborio rice is a variety of rice that comes from Arborio in the Po Valley region of Italy. Arborio rice is gluten-free and known for being the best possible rice with which to make risotto because of its creamy texture.

Saffron Rice

Yield: 2 servings

2 tablespoons olive oil
1 medium yellow onion, diced
2 cloves garlic, minced
2 cups Arborio or basmati rice
3 cups boiling water
¼ teaspoon saffron
1 Carmen pepper or red bell pepper, chopped
½ cup fresh peas
½ yellow bell pepper, chopped
Sea salt to taste
½ teaspoon freshly ground black pepper
½ carrot, julienned, for garnish
½ cup chopped chives, for garnish

Heat the oil in a saucepan over medium heat and sauté onion and garlic until the onion is translucent.

Add rice and stir until grains become translucent, about 7 minutes.

Add water, saffron, red pepper, peas, yellow pepper, salt, and pepper, and simmer, covered, for approximately 20 – 25 minutes until rice is cooked and all the water is absorbed.

Garnish with carrot and chives.

The chemical components of saffron are known to have many therapeutic applications. Saffron also has many antioxidants and is a proven antidepressant, antiseptic and aid for digestion.

Sautéed Dandelion Greens with Red Peppers

Dandelion greens are the miracle weed! They are a rich source of calcium, iron and chock full of minerals and antioxidant. They are also a powerful detoxifier, so use them in your salad, your soups and your veggie juices.

Yield: 2 to 4 servings

1 tablespoon walnut oil
1 yellow onion
2 cloves garlic
1 Carmen pepper or red bell pepper, chopped
½ cup water
4 cups dandelion greens
2 tablespoons fresh basil, chopped

1 teaspoon fresh ginger, minced
1 tablespoon fresh mint, chopped
Sea salt to taste
½ teaspoon freshly ground black pepper
¼ teaspoon cayenne
¼ cup balsamic vinegar
Sesame seeds, for garnish

Heat the oil in a large saucepan over medium heat and sauté the onion, garlic, and red pepper until the onion is translucent.

Add the water, dandelion greens, basil, ginger, mint, salt, pepper, and cayenne and simmer for 5 – 10 minutes until the dandelion greens are wilted.

Top with balsamic vinegar and garnish with sesame seeds.

Sautéed Kale with Fava Beans

Yield: 2 servings

2 tablespoons extra virgin olive oil
1 yellow onion, diced
2 cloves garlic, minced
½ cup fennel root, chopped
½ cup water
1 cup kale, chopped
½ cup apples, diced
1 cup mushrooms, sliced
½ cup fava beans, cooked

2 tablespoons chopped fresh cilantro
2 tablespoons chopped fresh parsley
½ teaspoon ground cinnamon
½ teaspoon ground nutmeg
Sea salt to taste
½ teaspoon freshly ground black pepper

Heat the oil in a large saucepan over medium heat and sauté the onion, garlic, and fennel until the onion is translucent.

Add the water, kale, apples, mushrooms, fava beans, cilantro, parsley, cinnamon, nutmeg, salt, and pepper and simmer for 10 – 15 minutes, until the kale is tender.

Besides being an excellent source of dietary fiber, fava beans are a very good source of vitamin B1, which is essential for nervous system function and energy metabolism.

Shiitake-Stuffed Eggplants

Yield: 4 servings

2 small eggplants, sliced in half
2 tablespoons olive oil
1 yellow onion, chopped
2 cloves garlic, minced
1 stalk celery, chopped
1 cup fresh shiitake mushrooms, chopped
1 tablespoon water
1 cup pomegranate juice
1 tablespoon maple syrup, grade B
¼ cup cashews
¼ teaspoon cumin
¼ teaspoon cayenne
2 tablespoons fresh basil, chopped
½ teaspoon ground saffron
Sea salt to taste
½ teaspoon freshly ground black pepper

Preheat oven to 350°.

Hollow out the eggplant halves, being careful not to tear the skin. Dice the eggplant pulp and set aside.

Heat the oil in a large skillet over medium heat and sauté the onion, garlic, and celery until the onion is translucent.

Add the mushrooms and sauté until brown.

Add eggplant, water, pomegranate juice, maple syrup, cashews, cumin, cayenne, basil, saffron, salt, and black pepper and cook for about 5 minutes.

Fill the eggplant shells with sautéed eggplant mixture and bake in the oven for 15 – 20 minutes until the eggplant is tender.

The special combination of antioxidants makes the shiitake mushroom a great choice for those who desire to avoid the chronic diseases of inflammation, like arthritis.

Sicilian Green Beans

Yield: 4 to 5 servings

2 tablespoons olive oil
1 yellow onion, diced
4 cloves garlic, minced
1 cup button mushrooms, sliced
½ cup water
3 cups chopped fresh tomatoes
3 cups green beans, chopped
½ cup fresh basil, chopped

2 tablespoons fresh parsley, chopped
1 tablespoon fresh oregano, chopped
Sea salt to taste
½ teaspoon freshly ground black pepper
¼ teaspoon cayenne
1 cup grated vegan Parmesan cheese, for garnish

Heat the oil in a large saucepan over medium heat and sauté the onion, garlic, and mushrooms until the onion is translucent and the mushrooms are brown.

Add the water, tomatoes, green beans, basil, parsley, oregano, salt, black pepper, and cayenne and simmer for 15 – 20 minutes.

Garnish with vegan cheese.

Serve with brown rice.

Green beans contain a unique profile of carotenoid and flavonoid content that appear to give it potentially unique anti-inflammatory benefits that could be helpful in the prevention and eradication of diseases of inflammation.

Sliced Tofu with Garlic Sauce

Yield: 2 servings

1 package extra firm tofu
2 tablespoons vegetable broth
1 tablespoon arrowroot powder
1 tablespoon walnut oil
1 scallion, chopped
4 cloves garlic, minced
1 teaspoon fresh ginger, minced
1 tablespoon tamari
1 tablespoon curry powder
½ teaspoon black pepper
½ teaspoon hot chili oil
1 tablespoon Bragg's Liquid Aminos
¼ cup thinly sliced zucchini, for garnish
¼ cup tomato, minced, for garnish

In a medium saucepan, bring water to a boil. Add tofu block and cook for 20 minutes over medium heat.

Remove tofu; let cool, cut into slices, and set aside.

In a medium bowl combine vegetable broth and arrowroot powder and whisk until smooth.

Heat the walnut oil in a skillet and sauté the scallions and garlic for 2 minutes.

Add arrowroot mixture, ginger, tamari, curry powder, and black pepper and cook over medium heat until sauce starts to thicken, about 3 – 4 minutes.

Add the hot chili oil and Bragg's Liquid Aminos; stir briefly and pour over the sliced tofu.

Garnish with thin zucchini slices and minced tomato.

Hot chili oil is generally made from chili peppers soaked in oils such as olive, soybean or canola oil. When selecting chili oils, choose one that has the healthiest carrier oil possible – organic of any of the above will do.

Spaghetti Squash Italiano

Yield: 4 servings

Spaghetti squash, another of the winter squashes, contains a powerful combination of antioxidant and anti-inflammatory compounds that make it useful in the fight against cancer, diabetes, arthritis, and other inflammatory diseases.

1 spaghetti squash, halved
2 tablespoons extra virgin olive oil
1 large yellow onion, diced
2 cloves garlic, minced
1 red bell pepper, chopped
2 fresh tomatoes, chopped
½ cup water

1 tablespoon dried oregano
1 tablespoon chopped fresh basil
1 tablespoon chopped fresh parsley
½ teaspoon salt
1 teaspoon freshly ground black pepper

Steam the halved squash until done, about 15 minutes. It is done when a strand of "spaghetti" can be removed easily by scraping the squash with a spoon. Scrape out the strands, set aside, and discard the skin.

Heat the oil in a large saucepan over medium heat and sauté the onion, garlic, and bell pepper until the onion is translucent.

Add the tomatoes, water, oregano, basil, parsley, salt, and pepper and sauté for 15 minutes.

Add the squash and sauté until thoroughly warm.

Spaghetti with Eggplant Marinara

Spaghetti with Eggplant Marinara

Yield: 4 servings

2 tablespoons olive oil
1 yellow onion, diced
4 cloves garlic, pressed
½ cup water
4 fresh tomatoes, chopped
3 tablespoons fresh basil, chopped
1 tablespoon fresh oregano, chopped
2 tablespoons fresh parsley, chopped
1 tablespoon fresh rosemary, chopped
1 tablespoon chia seeds
Sea salt to taste
½ teaspoon freshly ground black pepper
1 medium-size eggplant, peeled and cubed
2 cups mushrooms, thickly sliced
1 package spaghetti, cooked
1 tablespoon fresh parsley, for garnish
A few basil leaves, for garnish

Heat the oil in a large skillet over medium heat and sauté the onion and garlic until the onion is translucent.

Add the water, tomatoes, basil, oregano, parsley, rosemary, chia seeds, salt, and pepper and simmer for 10 minutes.

Add the eggplant and mushrooms and simmer for 15 minutes, or until eggplant is tender.

Serve over cooked spaghetti.

Garnish with parsley and fresh basil leaves.

The importance of purified water: our bodies are comprised of approximately 80% water. Unfortunately, our water supply is incredibly polluted with numerous toxins. This makes it very important for us to drink purified water and use it in our cooking. See p. 16 in this book for more information on things that you can do to optimize your health.

Spaghetti with Garlic Tomato Vegetable Sauce

Yield: 2 servings

2 tablespoons olive oil
5 cloves garlic, minced
¼ teaspoon crushed red pepper
2 tomatoes, chopped
½ cup water
½ cup asparagus, sliced
½ cup zucchini, sliced
½ cup yellow squash, sliced
2 tablespoons fresh parsley, chopped
3 tablespoons fresh basil, chopped
¼ cup black olives, pitted and sliced
1 tablespoon pine nuts
Sea salt to taste
½ teaspoon freshly ground black pepper
1 package spaghetti (8 oz.), cooked

Heat the oil in a saucepan over medium heat and sauté the garlic and crushed red pepper, stirring constantly until the garlic turns brown.

Add the tomatoes, water, asparagus, zucchini, yellow squash, parsley, basil, olives, pine nuts, salt, and pepper and simmer for 15 – 20 minutes.

Serve over cooked spaghetti.

Never underestimate the power of garlic and its active sulfur component allicin. Allicin is quite a formidable antibiotic and a potent agent for inhibiting the ability of germs to grow. It's said that 1 milligram of allicin has a potency of 15 standard units of penicillin.

Health tip: If you feel a cold coming on, fast on vegetable juices that contain raw garlic juice (just run it through the juicer with the rest of the juices), and sleep as much as you can. You may be surprised to find that your cold will not appear, or have much less fortitude.

Spring Scalloped Vegetables

Yield: 4 servings

1 tablespoon olive oil
1 yellow onion, diced
2 cloves garlic, minced
1½ cups unsweetened almond milk
1 tablespoon flaxseed meal
2 tablespoons fresh basil, chopped
2 tablespoons fresh parsley, chopped
2 tablespoons fresh cilantro, chopped
1 tablespoon fresh thyme, chopped
1 teaspoon fresh rosemary, chopped
Sea salt to taste
½ teaspoon freshly ground black pepper
5 parsnips, sliced
2 Yukon Gold potatoes, peeled and quartered
1 acorn squash, peeled and cubed
1 leek, chopped
1 cup vegan bread crumbs

Preheat oven to 425°.

Heat the oil in a medium-sized skillet over medium heat and sauté the onion and garlic until onion is translucent.

Add the almond milk, flaxseed meal, basil, parsley, cilantro, thyme, rosemary, salt, and pepper and simmer for 5 minutes.

Add the parsnips, potatoes, squash, and leek and combine well with the sauce.

Transfer everything to a lightly greased baking dish; top with bread crumbs and bake for 25 minutes, or until vegetables are tender.

Parsnips are a superstar for many reasons. Their soluble fiber makes them excellent for reducing cholesterol and for managing blood sugar. They have many anti-inflammatory properties, making them a perfect addition to the anti-inflammatory diet.

Sweet and Sour Bean Stew

Yield: 2 servings

1 tablespoon olive oil
1 yellow onion, diced
2 cloves garlic, minced
2 cups water
1 cup navy beans, cooked
½ butternut squash, peeled and cubed
1 teaspoon dry mustard
¼ cup raisins

1 tablespoon fresh thyme, chopped
Sea salt to taste
½ teaspoon freshly ground black pepper
¼ teaspoon cayenne
1 cup basmati rice, cooked
1 tablespoon chia seeds, for garnish
½ cup chives, for garnish

Heat the oil in a large saucepan over medium heat and sauté the onion and garlic until the onion is translucent.

Add water, navy beans, butternut squash, mustard, raisins, thyme, salt, pepper, and cayenne and simmer for about 20 minutes, or until squash is tender.

Add the rice and stir until heated.

Garnish with chia seeds and chives.

What's great about this dish is that it gets its sweetness from raisins, a top source of boron, which is a trace mineral that is helpful for good bone health.

Sweet and Sour Tempeh

While macadamia nuts, sometimes referred to as "mac" nuts, are very high in fat, almost 80% is good fat. Still, it is best to eat these in moderation. Mac nuts are also very high in palmitoleic acid – also known as Omega-7 – which helps to lower cholesterol, decreasing the risk for heart disease.

Yield: 2 servings

1 tablespoon walnut oil
1 scallion, sliced
1 clove garlic, minced
½ cup water
1 cup broccoli florets
1 cup tempeh, cubed
½ cup peanuts
½ cup pineapple, cubed
3 tablespoons tamari
½ teaspoon freshly ground black pepper
2 tablespoons macadamia nuts, chopped, for garnish

Heat the oil in a skillet over medium heat and sauté the scallions and garlic until tender.

Add the water, broccoli, tempeh, peanuts, pineapple, tamari, and pepper and simmer for 10 – 15 minutes, stirring frequently.

Garnish with macadamia nuts.

Sweet Cabbage and Apple Casserole

Yield: 4 servings

1 tablespoon apple cider vinegar
½ cup yellow onion, chopped
1 cup celery, sliced
½ cup apple juice
1 cup sliced green cabbage
2 large Macintosh apples, peeled, cored, and diced
½ cup prunes, chopped
1 tablespoon chia seeds
1½ teaspoons caraway seeds
1 teaspoon ground allspice

Preheat the oven to 375°.

Heat the vinegar in a large saucepan over low-medium heat and sauté the onion and celery until the onion is translucent.

Add the apple juice, cabbage, apples, prunes, chia seeds, caraway seeds, and allspice and sauté over medium heat for 5 minutes.

Place in a lightly greased baking dish and bake for 30 minutes.

Prunes are actually the dried version of the European plum, and help with numerous health concerns, including what they are best known for... regularity. They also contain some powerful antioxidants, and have been shown helpful for normalizing blood sugar levels, and therefore weight control.

Sweet Loaf

Yield: 2 servings

Dough

Kernels from 2 ears of fresh corn
1 tablespoon olive oil
Sea salt to taste
½ teaspoon agave
1 cup yellow or white hominy, cooked

Place the corn, olive oil, salt, agave, and hominy in a blender; purée until smooth, and set aside.

Filling

1 tablespoon olive oil
1 yellow onion, chopped
2 cloves garlic, minced
½ cup water
1 cup chopped shiitake mushrooms
1 tablespoon fresh thyme, chopped
1 tablespoon fresh parsley, chopped
Sea salt to taste
½ teaspoon freshly ground black pepper
¼ teaspoon cayenne

Heat the oil in a large skillet over medium heat and sauté the onion and garlic until the onion is translucent.

Add the water, mushrooms, thyme, parsley, salt, pepper, and cayenne and sauté for 10 minutes.

Preheat oven to 375°.

Lightly grease a shallow baking dish and fill with one half of the dough mixture.

Add all the filling, and arrange sliced olives on top. Cover with the remaining dough, smoothing out the surface.

Bake for 25 minutes or until golden brown.

Serve with a salad.

Hominy is a grainy mixture made from kernels of corn. Not only is it high in fiber and low in saturated fats (the unhealthy kind), it is high in iron.

Swiss Chard with Red Lentils and Carrots

Swiss chard, typically sold in green and rainbow varieties, is one of the most nutritious "greens" on the planet. It is rich in phytonutrients, which is what produces its orange, red and yellow colors. It is a very good source of calcium, which supports good bone health.

Yield: 4 to 6 servings

1 tablespoon olive oil
1 medium yellow onion, diced
2 cloves garlic, minced
1 cup vegetable stock
1 cup carrots, sliced; reserve a few slices for garnish
1 cup red lentils, cooked
1 cup brown lentils, cooked
2 cups brown rice, cooked

Sea salt to taste
Freshly ground black pepper to taste
¼ teaspoon cayenne
2 cups Swiss chard, chopped and steamed
½ cup cherry tomatoes for garnish, sliced

Heat the oil in a large saucepan over medium heat and sauté the onion and garlic until the onion is translucent.

Add the vegetable stock, carrots, lentils, rice, salt, pepper, and cayenne and simmer, covered, for 10 – 15 minutes.

Place the lentil rice mixture in a mold, invert, and cover with Swiss chard.

Garnish with carrots and tomatoes.

Tempeh and Green Bean Ragout

Yield: 2 servings

1 tablespoon olive oil
1 yellow onion, diced
1 scallion, chopped
2 cloves garlic, minced
1 tablespoon green bell
  pepper, minced
2 cups water
1 tomato, diced
1 pound tempeh cut into
  1-inch cubes
1 teaspoon ground cumin

½ teaspoon curry powder
¼ teaspoon hot red chili
  powder
½ teaspoon turmeric
3 tablespoons parsley, chopped
Sea salt to taste
½ teaspoon freshly ground
  black pepper
2 cups fresh green beans cut
  into 2-inch pieces

Because tempeh is fermented, it is easy to digest and contains natural antibiotics. It's a great food to aid with intestinal disorders.

Heat the oil in a large saucepan over medium heat and sauté onion, scallion, garlic, and green pepper until the onion is translucent.

Add water, tomato, tempeh, cumin, curry powder, chili powder, turmeric, parsley, salt, and pepper and simmer for 20 minutes.

Add the green beans and cook for 10 minutes.

Tempeh Marinara with Rice Penne

Yield: 4 servings

Tempeh is often crumbled in vegan food preparation to resemble ground beef. Use crumbled tempeh in stews, like chili, and soups when you desire more protein and good fats.

2 tablespoons extra virgin olive oil
1 onion, diced
3 large cloves garlic, minced
2 tablespoons tomato paste
1 large can (28 fl. oz.) peeled plum tomatoes in juice
1 carrot, sliced
8 oz. tempeh, crumbled
2 tablespoons fresh basil, chopped
Sea salt to taste
½ teaspoon freshly ground black pepper
1 package rice penne (16 oz.), cooked

Heat the oil in a skillet over medium heat and sauté the onion and garlic until onions are translucent.

Add tomato paste, plum tomatoes with juice, carrot, tempeh, basil, salt, and pepper, and simmer for 45 minutes.

Serve over cooked penne.

Tempeh with Cacciatore Sauce

Yield: 2 servings

1 tablespoon olive oil
1 medium white onion, diced
3 cloves garlic, minced
1 large green bell pepper, sliced
1 large red bell pepper, sliced thin
1 large yellow bell pepper, sliced thin
½ cup water
3 plum tomatoes, chopped
1½ cups shiitake mushrooms, sliced
2 cups tempeh, cut into chunks
3 tablespoons fresh parsley, chopped
2 tablespoons fresh basil, chopped
1 tablespoon fresh oregano, chopped
1 tablespoon fresh thyme
1 bay leaf
Sea salt to taste
½ teaspoon black pepper
1 package spaghetti, cooked
A few basil leaves, for garnish

Heat the oil in a skillet over medium heat and sauté onion, garlic, and peppers until onion is translucent.

Add the water, tomatoes, mushrooms, tempeh, parsley, basil, oregano, thyme, bay leaf, salt, and pepper and simmer for 20 minutes.

Serve over cooked spaghetti.

Garnish with basil leaves.

Cacciatore is Italian for "hunter," and it usually refers to a sauce composed of tomatoes, onions, mushrooms and, possibly, bell peppers.

Tempeh with Noodles and Vegetables

Yield: 2 servings

Cumin seeds have a
nutty and peppery
flavor, and are
ubiquitous in the
cuisine of India as
well as Mexico.
Not only are cumin
seeds high in iron,
magnesium, calcium,
and phosphorus,
but they are known
to promote good
digestion.

1 tablespoon olive oil
1 yellow onion, diced
1 scallion, chopped
2 cloves garlic, minced
½ red bell pepper, chopped
½ green bell pepper, chopped
½ chili pepper, chopped
½ cup water
1 carrot, sliced
1 teaspoon Dijon style mustard
1 package tempeh, thinly sliced
1 tablespoon ground flax seed
1 teaspoon cumin seed, crushed
2 tablespoons fresh basil, chopped
2 tablespoons parsley, chopped
Sea salt to taste
½ teaspoon freshly ground pepper
¼ teaspoon cayenne
1 package linguini (14 oz.), cooked

Heat the oil in a large skillet over medium heat and sauté onion, scallion, garlic, bell peppers, and chili pepper until the onion is translucent.

Add water, carrot, mustard, tempeh, flax seed, cumin seed, basil, parsley, salt, pepper, and cayenne and simmer for 20 minutes.

Serve over cooked linguini.

Tofu Orleans

Yield: 4 servings

1 package firm tofu, sliced
Ground black pepper
Onion powder
Garlic powder
½ cup spelt flour
3 tablespoons olive oil
1 medium onion, chopped
4 cloves garlic, minced
1 green bell pepper, diced
1 cup button mushrooms, sliced
½ cup shiitake mushrooms, sliced
½ cup water
2 tablespoons grated lemon zest
1 tablespoon fresh parsley, chopped
1 tablespoon fresh basil, chopped
1 tablespoon fresh cilantro, chopped
¼ teaspoon cayenne pepper
Sea salt to taste
½ teaspoon freshly ground black pepper
½ cup micro-greens, for garnish

Sprinkle the tofu slices with pepper, onion powder and garlic powder on both sides, then dredge in flour.

Heat the oil in a skillet on high and sauté the tofu until browned, about 10 minutes. Set aside.

Sauté the onion, garlic, and bell pepper until the onion is translucent.

Add the mushrooms and sauté until golden brown, about 10 minutes.

Add water, lemon zest, parsley, basil, cilantro, cayenne, salt, and pepper and simmer for 10 minutes.

Serve sauce over the sliced tofu.

Garnish with micro-greens.

While spelt is in the wheat family, and therefore contains gluten, many people with mild allergies tend to do better with spelt than wheat. Spelt is rich in protein, B-vitamins, magnesium and fiber. Use it frequently as an alternative to wheat.

Tomato Chutney with Quinoa Flatbread

Yield: 2 servings

Tomato Chutney:
1 large tomato, chopped
½ cup mango, chopped
1 medium yellow onion, chopped
1 teaspoon agave
1 teaspoon black and white sesame seeds
2 tablespoons fresh cilantro, chopped
1 teaspoon fenugreek
½ teaspoon turmeric
½ teaspoon chili pepper
Sea salt to taste
½ teaspoon freshly ground black pepper

Combine all ingredients in food processor and pulse until coarsely chopped.

Quinoa Flatbread:
2 cups quinoa flour
¾ cup water
Sea salt to taste
1 teaspoon cracked black pepper
2 tablespoons walnut oil

Combine flour, water, and salt in a mixing bowl.

Knead the dough for 5 minutes, and place on a floured surface.

Divide into 4 equal portions, and roll out each to the desired thickness.

Heat the oil in a large skillet on medium heat.

Place dough in the pan until the top starts to bubble, about 1 – 2 minutes, then flip to the other side and cook until done.

Place a tablespoon or so of tomato chutney inside a piece of quinoa flatbread and roll up to form wrap.

Garnish with black and white sesame seeds and serve with sliced mango.

Vegan Chili Deluxe

Yield: 4 to 6 servings

This vegetarian classic is full of health-promoting proteins and nutrients. Enjoy it any time of the year!

2 tablespoons extra virgin olive oil
1 large yellow onion, diced
4 cloves garlic, minced
1 scallion, chopped
1 green bell pepper, chopped
1½ small red dried chili peppers, chopped
2 tomatoes, chopped
1 small can (6 oz.) tomato paste
4 cups vegetable broth
1½ cups (about 12 oz.) navy beans, cooked
1½ cups red kidney beans, cooked

½ teaspoon ginger powder
½ tablespoon sweet paprika
2 tablespoons fresh parsley, chopped
2 tablespoons fresh basil, chopped
2 tablespoons fresh cilantro, chopped
½ teaspoon freshly ground black pepper
1 tablespoon curry powder
2 teaspoons ground cumin
1 bay leaf
Sea salt to taste
¼ teaspoon cayenne

Heat the oil in a large saucepan over medium heat and sauté the onion, garlic, scallion, bell pepper, and chili peppers until the onion is translucent.

Add the tomatoes and tomato paste and sauté for 15 minutes.

Add the vegetable broth, beans, herbs, and spices and simmer for 30 minutes over medium heat.

Vegetarian Lasagna

Vegetarian Lasagna

Yield: 6 to 8 servings

1 tablespoon olive oil
1 yellow onion, diced
3 cloves garlic, minced
1 cup button mushrooms, sliced
1 can (28-29 oz.) tomato purée
2 cups water
2 tablespoons fresh basil, chopped
2 tablespoons fresh parsley, chopped
1 tablespoon fresh sage, chopped
1 tablespoon fresh oregano, chopped
Sea salt to taste
½ teaspoon freshly ground black pepper
1 package (16 oz.) semolina or whole wheat lasagna noodles
   (no-boil if preferred)
1 package (10 oz.) fresh spinach, chopped; reserve some
   for garnish
1 eggplant, peeled and sliced
1 large sweet potato, steamed and puréed
½ cup vegan Parmesan cheese

Heat the oil in a large saucepan over medium heat and sauté the onion and garlic until the onion is translucent. Add the mushrooms and sauté until golden brown, about 10 minutes.

Add the tomato purée, water, basil, parsley, sage, oregano, salt, and pepper and simmer for 45 minutes.

Preheat oven to 375°.

Place 2 or 3 tablespoons of sauce on the bottom of a 9 x 9-inch glass baking dish.

Add in layers: uncooked lasagna noodles, spinach, eggplant, puréed sweet potato, and tomato sauce. Place another layer of uncooked lasagna noodles, spinach, eggplant, puréed sweet potato, and tomato sauce.

Cover with vegan Parmesan cheese, and top with a drizzle of tomato sauce. Bake for 35 minutes.

Remove from the oven and let cool for at least 15 minutes before slicing.

Garnish with chopped spinach.

Another vegetarian classic that is full of health-promoting nutrients, including powerful phyto-nutrients that are proven to be helpful in combatting diseases of inflammation.

Yukon Mashed Potatoes with Mushroom Gravy

Yield: 4 to 6 servings

Mashed Potatoes:

4 Yukon potatoes, peeled, quartered and boiled
1 tablespoon fresh thyme, chopped
1 tablespoon fresh rosemary, chopped
½ teaspoon white pepper
¼ cup unsweetened rice milk

Place the warm potatoes, thyme, rosemary, white pepper, and rice milk in a food processor and purée until smooth. Transfer to a serving dish.

Mushroom Gravy:

5 tablespoons olive oil
3 cloves garlic, minced
2 shallots, minced
2 cups assorted mushroom (shiitake, white oyster, Portobello, crimini, chanterelle), sliced
½ cup whole wheat flour
2 cups vegetable stock, heated to a boil
1 tablespoon chives, minced
2 tablespoons fresh rosemary, chopped
2 tablespoons fresh thyme, chopped
Sea salt to taste
½ teaspoon freshly ground black pepper
2 tablespoons Braggs Liquid Aminos

Heat two tablespoons of oil in a large skillet over medium-high heat and sauté the garlic, shallots, and mushrooms, until the mushrooms are browned, then set aside.

Add three tablespoons of oil and the flour to the skillet and stir to mix over medium-high heat.

Continue cooking the flour in oil until browned but not burned, stirring constantly.

When flour reaches desired color, pour in hot stock and reduce heat. Stir well to mix.

Add sautéed mushrooms-garlic-shallots mixture, chives, rosemary, thyme, salt, and pepper and cook until thickened, 10 – 15 minutes.

Add Bragg's Liquid Aminos to the mushroom gravy and stir well.

Pour gravy over mashed potatoes.

Rosemary, along with lavender, is one of the most popular herbs for aromatic products. As a food, rosemary is a terrific source for iron and other minerals, as well as vitamin C, vitamin A and folic acid.

DESSERTS

I tell people all the time that having a healthy diet doesn't mean that you need to desert your desserts. It is natural for us to want the sweetness of life. The best way to achieve this is through fruit-based desserts, because fruits are in essence Mother Nature's confection. One of my friends told me a while back that the word desserts spelled backwards is "stressed," which is why I became inspired to create an amazing collection of delectable treats. So now you can finally de-stress about desserts, and that's a very scrumptious thing.

– Gary

Angelica Rice Lady Fingers

Yield: 6 servings

3 cups light rice flour
1 tablespoon baking powder
1 teaspoon baking soda
1 cup maple sugar
½ cup walnut oil
⅛ cup maple syrup
½ cup vanilla almond milk
1 teaspoon vanilla extract
1 teaspoon almond extract

Sift together flour, baking powder, and baking soda.

In a medium mixing bowl, beat together sugar and oil until creamy. Stir in maple syrup, almond milk, vanilla extract, and almond extract and mix well.

Slowly add to the flour mixture until well blended.

Cover the dough and refrigerate for 1 hour.

Preheat oven to 375°.

On a lightly floured surface, roll the dough into 3 x 1-inch shapes.

Place on greased baking sheet and bake for 8 – 12 minutes, or until lightly brown.

Optional Glaze:
⅔ cup confectioners' sugar
2 tablespoons fresh lemon juice
1 teaspoon grated lemon zest

In a small bowl, whisk together the sugar, lemon juice, and lemon zest.

Drizzle over the ladyfingers.

Rice flour is a gluten-free flour that comes in both brown and white rice, with brown rice flour being significantly more nutritious than white, especially in terms of mineral content.

Anise Raisin Bread

Yield: 8 to 10 servings

¼ cup maple syrup
1½ cups hot water
2 tablespoons active dry yeast
½ cup walnut oil
3 cups brown rice flour
1 tablespoon ground cinnamon
1 teaspoon ground ginger
½ teaspoon ground cloves
1 teaspoon anise seed
1 cup raisins

In a large bowl, combine the maple syrup and hot water.

When the water is lukewarm, add the yeast; stir until dissolved and let sit until foamy, about 5 minutes.

Add the walnut oil to the yeast mixture and blend.

Combine flour, cinnamon, ginger and cloves in a separate bowl.

Add the flour mixture to the yeast mixture one-half cup at a time until well blended.

Knead dough for 10 minutes, then roll into a ball and place in a lightly oiled bowl covered with a dishtowel. Place in a warm location and let the dough rise until it doubles in size, about 1 hour.

Punch down the dough and knead in the anise seeds and raisins.

Again roll the dough into a ball and place in the lightly oiled bowl, cover with a dishtowel, and let rise for 45 minutes.

Preheat oven to 350°.

Punch down the dough and turn onto a flat surface.

Divide dough in two equal portions, and place in two lightly greased loaf pans.

Let rise for 20 minutes or until doubled in bulk.

Bake for 40 – 60 minutes, or until golden brown.

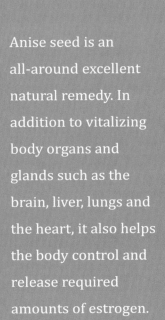

Anise seed is an all-around excellent natural remedy. In addition to vitalizing body organs and glands such as the brain, liver, lungs and the heart, it also helps the body control and release required amounts of estrogen.

Apple Banana Turnovers

Yield: 6 servings

1 banana, mashed
1 cup apples, diced
¼ cup maple sugar
1½ cups gluten-free oat flour
1 teaspoon baking powder
2 teaspoons egg replacer
1 tablespoon ground cinnamon
1 tablespoon ground ginger
1 teaspoon ground cloves
½ cup almond milk
⅓ cup maple syrup

Preheat oven to 375°.

In a medium bowl, combine the banana, apples, and maple sugar and set aside.

In another bowl, combine the flour, baking powder, egg replacer, cinnamon, ginger, and cloves.

Make a well in the flour mixture and add the almond milk and maple syrup; mix thoroughly.

Place dough on a floured surface and roll out to ¼-inch thickness with a floured rolling pin.

Cut the dough into two equal pieces.

Spread fruit filling over the first piece of dough, and very gently, lay the second piece over the filling.

Cut out triangles with a knife, and crimp the edges with a fork.

Bake on a greased baking sheet for 25 to 30 minutes until light brown.

The tiny bit of fat that bananas have is the heart healthy, omega-3, type; and, while they are very sweet, they are actually low in terms of their glycemic index, making them a perfect snack for everyone!

Banana Caramel Custard

Yield: 2 to 4 servings

1 cup almond milk
2 tablespoons arrowroot
2 teaspoons vanilla extract
½ teaspoon almond extract
2 teaspoons ground cinnamon
1 teaspoon ground ginger
½ teaspoon ground nutmeg
1 cup banana, sliced
1 cup maple sugar
1 tablespoon water

In a medium bowl, combine milk, arrowroot, vanilla extract, almond extract, cinnamon, ginger, and nutmeg and mix well.

Place the mixture in a saucepan over medium heat and simmer stirring constantly with a whisk or wooden spoon until thickened.

Once thickened, remove from heat and stir in banana slices.

In a small pan over low flame, combine the maple sugar and water and cook until golden brown.

Pour sugar mixture evenly into a large greased ramekin (or 4 individual ramekins).

Add banana mixture and refrigerate for 2 – 4 hours.

To serve, gently loosen the pudding from the sides of the dish by running a small knife around the inside of the ramekin.

Place a plate on top of the dish and invert.

It may be necessary to warm the bottom of the ramekin before inverting.

Garnish with sliced bananas and a sprinkle of maple sugar and cinnamon.

Almonds are a rich source of vitamin E and protein, containing many essential amino acids. They are also rich in fiber, B vitamins, and minerals, making them an all-around health food.

Bananas Flambé

Yield: 4 servings

Filling:
¼ cup maple sugar
2 tablespoons maple syrup
¼ cup orange juice
½ teaspoon grated orange zest
1 teaspoon ground cinnamon
1 teaspoon vanilla extract
3 ripe bananas, chopped
¼ cup golden raisins
¼ cup dark raisins

Place maple sugar, maple syrup, orange juice, orange zest, cinnamon, and vanilla extract in a small saucepan and simmer over low heat for 10 minutes.

Add the bananas and raisins, and simmer for another 5 minutes. Set aside.

Vegan Crepes:
¾ cup whole wheat pastry flour
¼ cup organic soy flour
½ teaspoon baking soda
Pinch sea salt
1 cup vanilla almond milk
1 tablespoon walnut oil
2 tablespoons maple sugar
2 or 3 tablespoons sunflower oil

Mix together flour, baking soda, and salt.

Combine almond milk, walnut oil, and maple sugar and mix well.

Make a well in the flour; add the almond milk mixture and blend until smooth.

Heat sunflower oil in a skillet over high heat.

Add ¼ cup batter to the hot skillet. Cook until bubbles appear and carefully flip to the other side. Cook until golden brown on both sides.

Place filling inside crepes and roll up.

Garnish with sliced banana.

Important: Most, if not all, of the orange juice that you get in the grocery store is pasteurized, a process of heating that removes all of the beneficial enzymes. Plus, it is very high in acid, which is a cause of inflammation. So when drinking or using orange juice, it is best to have fresh-squeezed.

Cantaloupe with Cherry Cream

Melons (watermelon, honeydew and cantaloupe) are naturally good sources of omega-3 fats. They are also the easiest and quickest of all the fruits to digest, which is why many nutritionists will recommend that you eat them alone and without other foods to maximize digestion, and nutrient utilization.

Yield: 4 servings

1 cup fresh or frozen cherries, pitted
½ teaspoon lemon extract
½ teaspoon almond extract
2 cups (approx. 16 oz.) silken tofu
1 cantaloupe

Cut the cantaloupe in quarters. Remove the fruit from the peel, slice into bite-sized pieces, and return to the peel.

Combine the cherries, lemon extract, almond extract, and tofu in a food processor or blender and purée until smooth.

Place the cherry cream in a dessert dish and serve with the sliced cantaloupe.

Garnish with sliced lemon.

Chilled Cherry Dessert Soup

Yield: 2 servings

1 cup apple juice
½ cup cherries, pitted
1 cup vanilla almond milk
1 cup coconut milk
1 cinnamon stick

Place the apple juice, cherries, almond milk, and coconut milk in a blender and purée until smooth.

Place the cherry soup mixture and the cinnamon stick in a medium-size saucepan and simmer over medium heat for 2 – 3 minutes until thickened.

Remove cinnamon stick.

Chill 1 to 2 hours.

Note: This recipe is only sugar free if you use apple juice with no added sugar.

Cherries and cherry juice are widely recognized anti-inflammatories. Consuming these products can be very helpful in avoiding and reversing diseases of inflammation. See my book *Reverse Arthritis & Pain Naturally* for more information on this and other valuable foods.

Chocolate Pudding

Yield: 4 servings

Agar flakes, also called agar-agar, are a vegan gelatin substitute used as a thickening agent for pies, custards, puddings and the like. Agar is produced from a variety of seaweed vegetation, and you can buy it at your local health food stores in both flake and powder varieties.

2 cups rice milk
2 teaspoons agar flakes
1 cup date sugar
$\frac{1}{3}$ cup cocoa powder
1 tablespoon coconut oil
2 tablespoons arrowroot dissolved in 2 tablespoons of water
1 teaspoon vanilla extract

Place rice milk and agar flakes in a small saucepan and simmer for about 5 minutes until agar is dissolved.

Add date sugar, cocoa powder, and coconut oil and simmer for two more minutes.

Remove from heat and stir in arrowroot and vanilla extract.

Place in a blender or food processor and purée until smooth. Place in dessert dishes.

Refrigerate for 1 hour, and garnish with fresh fruit.

Coconut Cherry Ice Cream

Yield: 4 servings

1 can (13.5 oz.) coconut milk
1 banana, peeled and frozen
4 tablespoons maple syrup
2 teaspoons vanilla extract
½ cup black cherries, pitted and sliced; chop and reserve some
    for garnish
¼ cup blueberries

Note: This recipe requires an ice cream maker

Combine coconut milk, banana, 3 tablespoons maple syrup, and
    teaspoon vanilla extract in a blender and blend until smooth.

Pour mixture into an ice cream maker.

When coconut mixture reaches desired consistency in the ice
    cream maker, add black cherries and blueberries.

Garnish with biscotti and chopped cherries.

Black cherries are a rich source of anthocyanins, which are antioxidants that give cherries their red color. Like other fruits, cherries are an excellent source of vitamins and minerals as well as fiber. Cherries, in particular, have high levels of potassium and vitamin C.

Coconut Custard Pie

Coconut flakes come in both sweetened and unsweetened varieties. I always use unsweetened coconut flakes. Be sure to read the package at the store for best results.

Yield: 6 servings

1 cup unsweetened coconut
2 cups vanilla almond milk
3 tablespoons egg replacer
4 tablespoons maple syrup, grade B
1 teaspoon vanilla extract
9-inch vegan pie shell, unbaked

½ cup toasted coconut, for garnish
½ lemon, sliced into rounds, for garnish
1 cup strawberries, halved, for garnish

Preheat oven to 450°.

Mix the coconut, milk, egg replacer, maple syrup, and vanilla extract together in a large bowl.

Pour into the pie shell and place in the oven.

Bake for 10 minutes at 450°, then turn oven down to 300° and bake for 30 minutes longer, or until a toothpick inserted into the custard comes out clean.

Garnish with toasted coconut, twisted lemon rounds, and strawberries.

Golden Strawberry Blueberry Crumble

Yield: 4 servings

½ cup spelt flour
½ cup rice flour
1 tablespoon arrowroot
1 cup date sugar, divided
2 tablespoons walnut oil
1 cup fresh or frozen blueberries

1 cup fresh or frozen strawberries
2 teaspoons freshly squeezed
  lemon juice
1 teaspoon ground cinnamon
1 tablespoon flaked coconut,
  fresh or packaged

Preheat oven to 300°.

In a large bowl, combine flour, arrowroot, ½ cup date sugar, and walnut oil and blend using a fork or pastry blender.

Place blueberries and strawberries in a soufflé dish and mix in lemon juice, ½ cup date sugar, cinnamon, and coconut flakes; stir until berries are well coated.

Cover berries evenly with the crumble mixture.

Place in the oven and bake for 15 – 20 minutes, or until golden brown.

Besides being a powerful anti-inflammatory and immune booster, lemons serve as a tonic to the body, helping with digestion and liver cleansing.

Holiday Gingerbread

Yield: 4 servings

¾ cup gluten-free oat flour
2 tablespoons arrowroot
1½ teaspoons baking powder
1 teaspoon ground cinnamon
1 teaspoon ground ginger
¼ teaspoon ground cloves
1 teaspoon ground nutmeg
½ cup apple butter
½ cup pure maple syrup
¼ cup almond milk
1 teaspoon orange extract
2 tablespoons walnut oil
½ cup walnuts

Preheat oven to 325º.

In a large bowl, combine flour, arrowroot, baking powder, cinnamon, ginger, cloves, and nutmeg.

In another bowl, combine apple butter, maple syrup, almond milk, orange extract, and walnut oil and beat until smooth.

Fold the batter into the flour mixture; add the walnuts and blend well.

Place in a greased loaf or baking pan and bake for 25 minutes or until a toothpick placed in the cake comes out clean.

Optional Glaze:
2 cups confectioner's sugar
2 tablespoons almond milk
1 tablespoon maple syrup
½ teaspoon vanilla extract

Combine all ingredients in a bowl or blender and mix until smooth.

Place glaze on top of the gingerbread. Garnish with sliced figs, grated carrot, or walnuts.

Figs are a member of the Mulberry family, and are a very good source of potassium, a mineral that is extremely helpful in heart health. They are also high in calcium, which promotes bone health.

Lemon Cherry Cake

Yield: 4 servings

1 2/3 cups whole wheat pastry flour
1 tablespoon baking powder
1/3 cup ground flaxseed meal
2 tablespoons grated coconut
1/2 cup pineapple juice
1/2 cup walnut oil
2 teaspoons lemon extract
1/2 cup maple syrup grade B
1 cup fresh or frozen cherries, pitted

Preheat oven to 350°.

Combine flour, baking powder, ground flaxseed meal, and grated coconut in a large bowl and mix well.

Combine the pineapple juice, oil, lemon extract, and syrup in a medium bowl and mix until smooth.

Fold the batter into the flour mixture and blend with an electric mixer until there are no lumps.

Add the cherries and mix until evenly distributed.

Place in a greased loaf pan and bake for 30 minutes.

The cake is done when a toothpick comes out clean after being inserted into the center.

Garnish with cherries.

In addition to its anti-inflammatory compound bromelain, pineapple is very high in vitamin C and vitamin A, as well as important bone-building minerals like calcium, phosphorous and potassium.

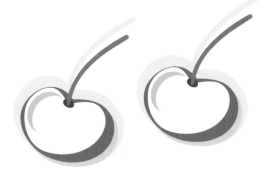

Orange-Glazed Apples

Yield: 4 servings

¼ cup maple syrup
2 tablespoons grated orange zest
¼ cup orange juice
½ tablespoon walnut oil
1 tablespoon ground cinnamon
2 large Red Delicious apples, peeled, cored, and quartered

In a saucepan, combine the maple syrup, orange zest, orange juice, oil, and cinnamon and simmer over low heat for 10 minutes.

Add the apples and simmer for 10 – 15 minutes.

Garnish with orange slices and strawberries.

Like all other citrus fruits, oranges contain a healthy amount of omega-3 fats, and are powerful immune boosters.

Peach Walnut Crisp

Yield: 4 to 6 servings

Filling:
5 cups fresh peaches, peeled and sliced
½ cup walnuts, chopped
½ cup date sugar
1 teaspoon ground cinnamon
½ teaspoon ground ginger
½ teaspoon ground nutmeg
1 tablespoon maple syrup, grade B

Combine the peaches, walnuts, date sugar, cinnamon, ginger, nutmeg, and maple syrup in a large bowl; mix well and set aside.

Topping:
1 cup date sugar
1 cup rolled oats
1 cup whole wheat flour
¼ cup walnut oil

Preheat oven to 375°.

In a large bowl, combine the date sugar, oats, whole wheat flour, and walnut oil and mix until the mixture reaches a crumbly texture.

Place half the mixture in a lightly greased 8-inch baking pan.

Spread the peaches evenly over the crumb layer.

Top with the remaining crumb mixture.

Bake for 35 – 40 minutes or until golden brown.

Date sugar is the unprocessed, unrefined sugar from the fruit of dates. It is considered a healthy sweetening agent, as it contains all the same vitamins and minerals as the fruit, which is not the case with processed cane sugar. Date sugar is also very high in potassium, iron, and wonderful rich with dietary fiber, making it a wonderful addition to the healthy lifestyle.

Pear Hazelnut Crisp

Yield: 4 servings

2 pears, cored and sliced
4 plums, peeled, pitted, and sliced
1 orange, peeled and separated into sections
1 teaspoon grated orange zest
2 tablespoons fresh lemon juice
¾ cup white grape juice
1 tablespoon lemon extract

Topping
2 tablespoons walnut oil
¾ cup maple sugar
¼ cup gluten-free oat flour
1 tablespoon ground cinnamon
1 tablespoon ground ginger
½ teaspoon ground cloves
½ cup coarsely chopped hazelnuts
½ cup coarsely chopped almonds
½ cup coarsely chopped Brazil nuts

Preheat oven to 375°.

Combine the pears, plums, orange, orange zest, lemon juice, grape juice, and lemon extract in a large bowl. Pour into a lightly greased baking dish, and set aside.

Combine the walnut oil and maple sugar in a large bowl and beat until creamy.

Add the flour, cinnamon, ginger, cloves, hazelnuts, almonds, and Brazil nuts and mix well.

Place on top of the fruit mixture and spread evenly.

Bake for 25 – 35 minutes until topping is golden brown.

Like most nuts, hazelnuts (also called filberts) are high in protein, dietary fiber and fat. In particular, hazelnuts contain oleic acid, an omega-9 fatty acid that has been shown helpful in reducing blood pressure (and therefore the risk of heart attack and stroke), and improving mental acuity.

Pears with Raisin Stuffing

Yield: 4 servings

Not only are pears an antioxidant and anti-inflammatory rich fruit, they contain a wide variety of phytonutrients that are associated with a decreased risk in chronic disease.

1 cup raisins
1 cup water
2 large Bartlett pears
½ cup maple syrup, grade B

1 tablespoon ground cinnamon
3 tablespoons orange zest, for garnish
¼ cup mint leaves, for garnish

Soak the raisins in water until they swell in size, about 10 minutes; then drain and set aside.

Cut the pears in half lengthwise and hollow out the centers, being careful not to tear the skin, and set aside.

Remove the core and seeds from the pears, and place the remaining pears in a large bowl.

Add raisins, maple syrup, cinnamon, and orange zest and stir well to mix.

Stuff the mixture into the pear shells.

Garnish with orange zest and mint.

Pecan-Maple Chia Custard

Yield: 4 servings

½ cup apple juice
2 sweet potatoes, peeled, diced, and steamed
¼ cup maple syrup, grade B, or agave
4 tablespoons vanilla extract
1 tablespoon almond extract
3 tablespoons chia seeds
1 tablespoon flaxseed meal
1 cup chopped roasted pecans, for garnish

Place the apple juice and sweet potatoes in a blender or food processor and purée until smooth.

Add the maple syrup, vanilla extract, almond extract, chia seeds, and flaxseed meal and purée until well blended.

Place in individual dessert dishes and top with chopped pecans.

Serve chilled.

This rich and creamy dessert is chock-full of valuable vitamins and minerals, along with healthy omega-3 fats. Use apple juice with no sugar added whenever possible.

Plaintain Dessert Tamale

Yield: 4 servings

4 plantains
$1/3$ cup toasted coconut flakes
1 cup whole spelt pastry flour
$1/4$ cup wheat germ
1 cup date sugar
1 teaspoon ground cinnamon
$1/2$ teaspoon ground ginger
$1/2$ tablespoon ground nutmeg
2 tablespoons vanilla extract
1 tablespoon almond extract
Pinch of sea salt
Vanilla almond milk as needed
4 large collard leaves

Preheat oven to 350°.

Cut off the ends of the plantains and cut them in half lengthwise, leaving the skin on. Place the plantains, skin side up, on a baking sheet.

Bake until soft but not falling apart, about 10 to 15 minutes.

Remove the peels when cool.

Place cooked plantains in a food processor with coconut flakes, flour, wheat germ, date sugar, cinnamon, ginger, nutmeg, vanilla extract, almond extract, and salt and purée into a smooth batter. (Add a small amount of vanilla almond milk if needed for the purée.)

Place a quarter of the mixture onto each collard leaf. Wrap each packet snugly.

Steam the packets over boiling water for 5 minutes.

Remove packets and unwrap when cool enough to handle.

Serve with raspberries or other fresh fruit.

Collard leaves make wonderful "wraps" for sweets as well as savory items. Try some of our dips with fresh veggies and sprouts rolled up in a collard for a super healthy meal.

Poached Peaches with Raspberry Sauce

Yield: 2 servings

4 peaches, peeled and halved
2 cups apple juice
1 cinnamon stick
2 cups fresh or frozen raspberries
¾ cup maple sugar
1 teaspoon lemon extract
¼ cup micro-greens or fresh mint leaves, for garnish

Place the peaches, apple juice, and cinnamon stick in a large saucepan and simmer over medium heat for 5 minutes, covered. Drain and set aside.

In a separate saucepan, combine the raspberries, maple sugar, and lemon extract and simmer for 2 minutes until the sugar is dissolved.

Remove the raspberry mixture from the heat and purée in a blender until smooth.

Place the peaches in dessert dishes and cover with raspberry sauce.

Garnish with the micro-greens or mint leaves.

Berries are a rich source of nutrients, including phytonutrients and antioxidants. Use them frequently on top of salads, breakfast cereals, and in smoothies and desserts to benefit from their powerful nutritional and anti-inflammatory offerings.

Pretty Parfait

Yield: 4 servings

Mint is perhaps one of the best-known and utilized herbs today. Well recognized for its ability to freshen breath and support good oral hygiene, mint is also an outstanding herb for soothing the digestive tract, alleviating nausea and headache, and clearing skin conditions. It has also been shown helpful in addressing respiratory concerns.

1 cup fresh pineapple, peeled, cored, and diced
1 cup papaya, cubed
½ cup raspberries
½ cup blueberries
½ cup walnuts
¼ cup fresh mint leaves, for garnish

Purée the pineapple in a blender or food processor and set aside.

Purée the papaya in a blender or food processor and set aside.

Pour the pineapple and papaya purée in clear glass parfait dishes in alternating layers.

Top with fresh raspberries, blueberries, and walnuts.

Garnish with mint leaves.

Serve chilled.

Health Tip: Give your pure drinking water a lift by infusing it with fresh herbs! Add several sprigs of peppermint and the slices from one lime to ½ gallon of water and within one hour you will have a delicious and healthful beverage. Experiment with other types of favorite herbs – like rosemary, lavender, or cilantro – and citrus like lemon, oranges and grapefruit. What a fun way to drink your water!

Raspberry Custard

Yield: 4 servings

Silken tofu is a variety of tofu that is very soft, and perfect for desserts like pudding, custard, pies and parfaits that require a creamy consistency. Plus, you get the benefit of all those healthy omega-3 fats.

1 cup silken tofu
¼ cup maple syrup, grade B
1 teaspoon vanilla extract
1 teaspoon almond extract
¾ cup raspberry jam

1 package vegan peach or apricot cookies, crushed
2 tablespoons dried coconut
½ cup raspberries, for garnish

Place the tofu, maple syrup, vanilla extract, and almond extract in a food processor or blender and purée until smooth.

Place the raspberry jam in a saucepan and melt over low heat, about 2 – 3 minutes.

Line the bottom of individual dessert dishes with a layer of crushed vegan cookies.

Cover cookies with half the melted raspberry jam, 1 tablespoon coconut, and a layer of puréed tofu.

Repeat with another layer of cookies, jam, coconut, and tofu purée.

Garnish with fresh raspberries.

RAW Banana Pineapple Dessert Soup

Yield: 4 servings

1 cup grapefruit juice
1 pineapple, peeled, cored, and cubed
2 bananas, sliced; reserve ½ for garnish
¼ cup mint leaves, for garnish

Place the pineapple, grapefruit juice, and 1 banana in a food processor or blender and purée until smooth.

Garnish with sliced banana and mint leaves.

Serve chilled.

Besides being high in vitamin C, grapefruit contains powerful omega-3 fats. It also really does curb your hunger, and like other citrus is very important in the anti-inflammatory diet.

RAW Berry Jello

Yield: 3 servings

1 cup blueberries
1 cup raspberries; reserve a few for garnish
1 banana, peeled and sliced
1 teaspoon maple syrup
1 teaspoon vanilla extract
¼ cup mint, for garnish

Place blueberries, raspberries, banana, maple syrup, and vanilla extract in a food processor and purée until smooth.

Pour into dessert dishes and chill.

Garnish with mint and raspberries.

Note: Alcohol-free vanilla is often preferred in raw-foods preparation, since it is the heating of the extract that removes the alcohol.

RAW Cinammon Papaya Pudding

Yield: 2 servings

1 papaya, peeled and seeds removed
1 Golden Delicious apple, peeled, cored, and diced
1 cup gluten-free oatmeal, cooked
1 cup apple juice
3 tablespoons maple syrup, grade B
1 tablespoon flaxseed meal
1 teaspoon ground cinnamon
½ teaspoon ground ginger
½ teaspoon ground cloves
½ cup fresh mint leaves, for garnish

Combine all ingredients in blender or food processor and purée until smooth.

Chill in refrigerator for 45 minutes.

Garnish with mint.

Papaya and mint are two digestive powerhouses, and are often found together in teas and recipes.

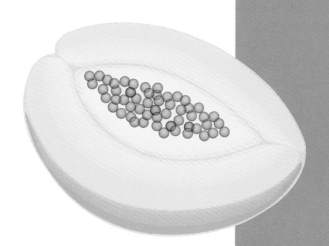

One cup of strawberries contains an incredible 140% of the Recommended Daily Allowance (RDA) of vitamin C, an extremely beneficial antioxidant that can help lower blood pressure, ensure a healthy immune system, and protect against diseases of inflammation.

RAW Strawberry Dessert Soup

Yield: 2 servings

1 pint strawberries, de-stemmed
1 cup apple-strawberry juice
Juice of 1 lemon
Fresh mint leaves, for garnish
1 tablespoon chopped strawberries, for garnish

Place the strawberries, apple-strawberry juice, and lemon juice in a food processor and purée until smooth.

Garnish with mint leaves and chopped strawberries.

Serve chilled.

Health Tip: Purchase organic strawberries whenever possible, as strawberries are one of the crops of the United States that is most exposed to toxic pesticides.

Simple Carob Cake

Yield: 6 servings

¾ cup carob chips
¼ cup walnut oil
¾ cup maple syrup, grade B,
   or agave
1 teaspoon vanilla extract
1 teaspoon almond extract

2 cups whole wheat pastry flour
½ cup flaxseed meal
1 tablespoon baking powder
1 teaspoon ground cinnamon
½ cup almond milk

Preheat oven to 375°.

Place the carob chips, walnut oil, maple syrup, vanilla extract, and almond extract in the top of a double boiler and heat until the carob chips are melted, stirring frequently.

Combine flour, flaxseed meal, baking powder, and cinnamon in a large bowl and make a well in the center.

Pour the almond milk in the center of the well and mix until coarsely blended. Add melted carob mixture and beat with an electric mixer until smooth.

Pour batter into a greased 9-inch cake pan and bake for 25 minutes, or until a toothpick placed into the center comes out clean.

Serve with fresh fruit.

Native to the Mediterranean region, carob is a caffeine-free food used as a substitute for chocolate in pies, puddings, cakes, cookies and other baked goods. Carob is very high in antioxidants as well as key minerals like calcium and phosphorous, which promotes bone health. Carob is typically sold as a powder or in the form of chips (pre- packaged or bulk), similar to chocolate chips.

Southern-Baked Pumpkin Surprise

Yield: 2 servings

1 banana, sliced
½ cup ground pumpkin
½ cup agave
1 teaspoon ground cinnamon
½ teaspoon ground nutmeg
½ cup slivered almonds

Preheat oven to 400°.

Combine the bananas and pumpkin in a small baking dish.

Mix together the agave, cinnamon, nutmeg, and almonds and pour over the fruit.

Top with slivered almonds.

Bake for 20 minutes.

Agave (pronounced ah-GAH-vay) is a sweetener that comes from the same cactus plant from where we get tequila. While it is used frequently in raw-food preparation, there is some debate about whether it is technically a raw food, or is more like maple syrup that undergoes a process of cooking to achieve the final product.

Stewed Plums

Yield: 4 servings

2 cups apple juice
½ teaspoon lemon extract
½ cup maple sugar
1 teaspoon ground cinnamon
2 cups sliced plums
½ cup chopped almonds, for garnish
Assorted vegan fruit cookies, for garnish

Mix the apple juice, lemon extract, maple sugar, and cinnamon in a small bowl until well blended.

Place the plums in a saucepan; cover with the apple juice mixture and simmer over low heat for 5 minutes.

Pour into dessert dishes, and garnish with chopped almonds and vegan cookies.

Plums, like their dried version, prunes, are a wonderful food for anyone wanting to boost their immunity and health. Plums are a rich source of antioxidants, including vitamin A and vitamin C, which have been reported to enhance the absorption of iron in the body. Plus, these fruits – like others high in antioxidants – are reported to aid in eye health and prevent Age Related Macular Degeneration (ARMD).

Sticky Sweet Rice with Papaya

Yield: 4 servings

Preparation Tip:
As an alternative, try white basmati rice for this delicious treat to mimic the traditional Thai preparation.

2 cups vanilla almond milk
1/3 cup maple syrup, grade B
1 cup quick-cooking brown basmati rice
1 teaspoon ground cinnamon
1 teaspoon ground ginger
1/2 teaspoon ground cloves

1 teaspoon vanilla extract
1 ripe papaya, seeded and cut in slices
1 tablespoon shredded mint leaves, for garnish

Place almond milk and maple syrup in a medium saucepan and bring to a boil.

Add rice, cinnamon, ginger, cloves, and vanilla extract. Reduce heat and simmer for 20 minutes.

When rice is done, place in dessert dishes and top with sliced papaya.

Garnish with shredded mint leaves.

Sweet Casava Pudding

Yield: 4 to 6 servings

1 ½ cups sweet cassava flour
¼ cup whole wheat pastry flour
¾ cup date sugar
½ teaspoon grated lemon zest
½ cup grated coconut
1 cup silken tofu

2 tablespoons walnut oil
1 teaspoon ground cinnamon
1 teaspoon ground ginger
1 teaspoon ground nutmeg
1 teaspoon vanilla extract
1 teaspoon almond extract

Preheat oven to 350°.

In a medium bowl, mix cassava flour, whole wheat flour, date sugar, lemon zest, and coconut.

Place tofu, walnut oil, cinnamon, ginger, nutmeg, vanilla extract, and almond extract in a food processor and purée until smooth.

Add the flour mixture and pulse until well blended.

Pour into a lightly greased 8-inch square glass or nonstick baking pan and bake until pudding is set, 45 – 55 minutes.

Cassava flour is a made by drying and grinding cooked cassava (a root vegetable of South American origin) into a fine powder. This gluten-free flour is used as a substitute for wheat flour. It differs from tapioca flour – which is also from the cassava vegetable – in that it is made from the ground root of the vegetable, where tapioca flour is made from the starch of the cassava plant.

Sweet Potato Pie

Yield: 4 to 6 servings

This is a wonderful vegan pie offering for Thanksgiving potlucks and gatherings. Impress your friends and family with this highly nutritious pumpkin pie alternative.

3 tablespoons walnut oil
1 cup firmly packed date sugar
   or maple sugar
1 ½ cups mashed boiled sweet
   potatoes (2 large or 3 medium)
½ cup applesauce
2 tablespoons flaxseed meal
⅓ cup almond milk
1 tablespoon fresh lemon juice

1 tablespoon freshly grated
   lemon zest
1 teaspoon vanilla extract
1 teaspoon ground cinnamon
½ teaspoon ground allspice
1 teaspoon ground nutmeg
1 prepared 9-inch vegan pie
   shell

Preheat oven to 425°.

In a food processor, blend oil and date sugar until creamy.

Mix in sweet potatoes, applesauce, flaxseed meal, almond milk, lemon juice, lemon zest, vanilla extract, cinnamon, allspice, and nutmeg and purée until smooth.

Pour the mixture into the pie shell and bake for 10 minutes at 425°.

Lower the temperature to 325° and bake for an additional 35 minutes, or until a knife inserted into the center of the pie comes out clean.

Toasted Nut Brittle

Yield: 4 to 6 servings

½ cup maple syrup, grade B
½ cup tahini
1 cup whole almonds, chopped
1 teaspoon vanilla extract
¾ cup shredded unsweetened coconut

Preheat oven to 350º.

Combine the maple syrup and tahini in a large bowl and beat until smooth.

Add the almonds, vanilla extract, and coconut and mix well.

Spread onto a greased cookie sheet and bake for 15 minutes.

Serve with fresh fruit.

Preparation tip:
Make an extra batch of this and store it in an air-tight container for a quick and healthy snack!

Truly Trifle

Yield: 2 servings

Vegan Sponge Cake:
1¼ cups whole wheat pastry flour
1 tablespoon baking powder
1 Golden Delicious apple, peeled and cored
½ cup almond milk
¼ cup maple syrup, grade B, or agave
¼ cup walnut oil
1 tablespoon vanilla extract
1 teaspoon almond extract

Custard and Fruit Jam:
1 cup silken tofu
2 tablespoons maple syrup, grade B
½ teaspoon vanilla extract
½ teaspoon almond extract
¾ cup raspberry jam
1 tablespoon date sugar
1 teaspoon ground cinnamon
½ teaspoon ground nutmeg
½ teaspoon ground cloves
1 cup strawberries, sliced; reserve a few slices for garnish
½ cup slivered almonds

Truly Trifle

Continued

Vegan Sponge Cake:
Preheat oven to 350°.

Combine the flour and baking powder in a large bowl.

Place the apple, almond milk, maple syrup, walnut oil, vanilla extract, and almond extract in a food processor and purée.

Make a well in the flour mixture; fold in the puréed ingredients and beat with an electric mixer until smooth.

Place the batter in a lightly greased square pan, and bake for 25 – 30 minutes until golden brown and a toothpick inserted in the center comes out clean.

Custard and Fruit Jam:
Place the tofu, maple syrup, vanilla extract, and almond extract in a food processor or blender and purée until smooth.

Place the raspberry jam in a saucepan with date sugar, cinnamon, nutmeg, and cloves and cook over low heat for about 2 – 3 minutes.

Place sponge cake slices in the bottom of a serving dish (can also use individual dessert dishes).

Cover cake with layers of the warm raspberry jam, strawberries, slivered almonds, and puréed tofu.

Repeat the layering process until you have used all the ingredients or the serving dish is full.

Garnish with sliced strawberries.

A food processor is an incredibly valuable piece of kitchen equipment that is very handy for vegetarian cuisine. See p. 49 for more suggestions on equipment that adds to the fun of this incredibly healthy lifestyle!

Vegan Apple Cake

Yield: 4 to 6 servings

Food preparation tip:
if you are out of
applesauce, make your
own raw, sugar-free
version by peeling and
coring 2 or 3 apples,
and placing them in
a blender or food
processor with
1 teaspoon of fresh
lemon juice, a dash
of salt and allspice,
and enough water to
blend well.

1 ½ cups whole wheat pastry flour
¼ cup flaxseed meal
1 cup sifted almond meal
1 tablespoon baking powder
Pinch salt
2 teaspoons ground cinnamon
½ teaspoon ground nutmeg
½ teaspoon ground ginger
½ teaspoon ground cloves
1 tablespoon chia seeds
1 cup unsweetened applesauce
⅓ cup maple syrup, grade B
1 cup unsweetened almond milk
1 teaspoon vanilla extract
1 teaspoon almond extract
2 tablespoons lemon zest
½ cup raisins
2 cups tart apples, sliced

Preheat oven to 350°.

In a large bowl, combine whole wheat pastry flour, flaxseed meal, almond meal, baking powder, salt, cinnamon, nutmeg, ginger, cloves, and chia seeds.

Combine applesauce, maple syrup, almond milk, vanilla extract, almond extract and lemon zest in a medium bowl and blend well.

Fold the applesauce mixture into the dry ingredients and mix thoroughly.

Add the raisins and half the apple slices.

Place batter in a lightly greased baking pan and top with remaining apples.

Bake for 50 – 60 minutes until a toothpick inserted into the center of the cake comes out clean.

Resources

Gary's Website

GaryNull.com – Gary's official website where you can listen to his radio programs and subscribe to important updates regarding your health and the health of our nation.

Gary's Publications

Reverse Arthritis & Pain Naturally:

A Proven Approach to an Anti-inflammatory, Pain-free Life

This book takes an in-depth look at the epidemic of arthritis and chronic pain sweeping our nation today, and offers a proven lifestyle protocol for easing inflammation and pain naturally.

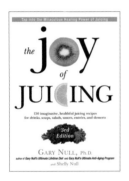

The Joy of Juicing

Get excited about juicing with the 3rd edition of this easy-to-use juice recipe book containing over 100 creative and delicious recipes for health.

The Complete Encyclopedia of Natural Healing

This unique and reliable health reference picks up where other sources leave off, offering a comprehensive listing of some of today's most common diseases and their simple, natural, inexpensive cures.

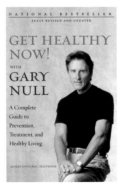

Get Healthy Now:
A Complete Guide to Prevention, Treatment, and Healthy Living

This national bestseller featured on Public Television (PBS) includes research and nutritional advice for treating allergies, diabetes, PMS, andropause, and everything in-between. From healthy skin and hair to foot and leg care, this important guide features an invaluable Alternative Practitioners Guide for helping you become healthier from top to bottom, inside to out.

Gary's DVDs

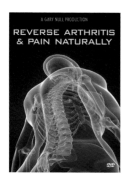

Reverse Arthritis & Pain Naturally:
A Proven Approach to an Anti-inflammatory, Pain-free Life

This DVD takes an in-depth look at the epidemic of arthritis and chronic pain sweeping our nation today, and offers a proven lifestyle protocol for easing inflammation and pain naturally.

Preventing & Reversing Diabetes Naturally – 3 DVD set

Diabetes is a health crisis reaching epidemic levels in America and, sadly, more people are succumbing to this devastating disease than ever before. In this informative DVD set, Dr. Gary Null along with the world's top medical doctors, psychiatrists and psychologists will show you the latest, most powerful natural and conventional approaches for preventing and reversing diabetes, obesity, and metabolic syndrome.

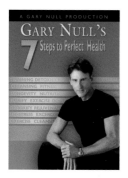

7 Steps to Perfect Health

For over three decades, Gary Null, Ph.D., has been one of the foremost advocates of alternative medicine and natural healing. Gary believes life can be lived in a manner that embraces body, mind, and spirit and that prevention is the key to healthy living. In *Seven Steps to Perfect Health,* Gary will guide you on a path toward wellness and to realizing your personal power. You will learn how to identify health-risk factors, detoxify and rebalance your system with necessary nutrients and anti-oxidants, de-stress and exercise.

Preventing & Reversing Cancer Naturally – 2 DVD set

Cancer Can't Kill You...unless you let it! In this provocative and compelling DVD set you will learn about powerful new cancer treatments that are not taught in U.S. medical schools but are saving millions of lives in more than 180 countries worldwide, including England, France, and Germany. Arm yourself with the right information, and you will have the opportunity to avoid one of the most frightening diseases, and leading causes of death today.

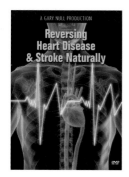

Reversing Heart Disease & Stroke Naturally

Heart disease and stroke can be prevented! There are several risk factors for both of these conditions that can be easily addressed once known. These factors can be identified with simple measurements such as waist size, and tests for C-Reactive protein, homocysteine, fibrinogen, and hemoglobin A1C levels, which can be done in your physician's office. High blood pressure, arterial and atherosclerosis, plaque and myocardial myopathy all can be reversed and prevented; learn how now!

ESSENTIAL
PUBLISHING

Reverse Arthritis & Pain Naturally:
A proven approach to an anti-inflammatory, pain-free life
by Gary Null, Ph.D.

Arthritis is the most common cause of disability in the United States today, limiting the activities of a remarkable 50 million adults. Like cancer, diabetes and heart disease, arthritis is a disease of inflammation rooted in lifestyle choices. This book takes an in-depth look at the epidemic of arthritis and chronic pain sweeping our nation today, providing an explanation for its causes while offering a proven lifestyle protocol to reverse and prevent them naturally.

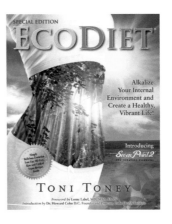

EcoDiet: Eat Clean, Go Green
by Toni Toney

Our connection to planet Earth is vaster than most of us realize. In fact, our body, like the earth, is an intricate ecosystem of interdependent organisms that depend upon one another to thrive. The balance of our ecosystem is delicate, and any disruption, such as an unsuitable food supply or a toxic overload, can damage or destroy it. In this important book, you will learn about the food choices that are creating an internal acid rain in your body – the cause of most disease – and how to restore balance and harmony.

Art & Survival in the 21st Century:
A creative response to the challenges of our time through drawing, painting & sculpture
by James Menzel Joseph

This art and social criticism book takes a profound look at the role of art in humanity's survival, and features over 200 exquisite and beautiful paintings and drawings of James Menzel Joseph, celebrated award-winning artist, author master art teacher, and activist.

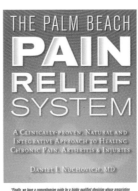

The Palm Beach Pain Relief System:
A Clinically-proven, Natural and Integrative Approach to Healing Chronic Pain, Arthritis & Injury
by Daniel Nuchovich, M.D.

This comprehensive, revolutionary, proven medical treatment program utilizes natural therapies, including the whole-food Mediterranean Diet, to overcome chronic pain. This drug-free, integrative approach is working for 90+% of patients suffering from arthritis, and other diseases of information. Avoid unnecessary surgeries and free yourself from the potentially deadly trap of unsuccessful pharmaceutical-based therapies.

www.essentialpublishing.org

ESSENTIAL PUBLISHING

Good Stress:
Living Younger Longer
by Terry Lyles, Ph.D.

Seeing stress as good is essential for achieving a youthful and vibrant life, says Dr. Terry Lyles, in this groundbreaking book inspired by years of rescue work at some the world's worst disasters: 9/11, Hurricane Katrina and the tsunami in Thailand. Dr. Lyles, known as America's Stress Doctor, implores us to see stress as a benevolent force. "If you want to live younger longer, start now by seeing stress for what it really is – a catalyst for positive growth and change.

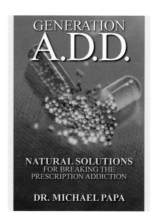

Generation A.D.D.:
Natural Solutions for
Breaking the
Prescription Addiction
by Dr. Michael Papa

Free yourself and your children from the bonds of chemical dependency! In this timely and import-ant book, Dr. Michael Papa urges us to explore and understand the symptoms and underlying causes of ADD/ADHD, and to choose natural solutions first, offering numerous approaches that have worked successfully with patients over the years.

Healthful Cuisine –
2nd Edition
by Anna Maria Clement,
Ph.D., N.M.D, L.N.C. and
Kelly Serbonich

Learn about the superior health and nutritional benefits of raw and living foods from the world's #1 medical spa, Hippocrates Health Institute. This book ontains: 150 raw and living food recipes, 40 pages illustrated raw food preparation techniques, and ore than 50 full-color photographs showing step--step instructions, plus tips from the experts. aking healthy raw foods has never been so easy.

A Families Guide to
Health & Healing:
Home Remedies from
the Heart
by Anna Maria Clement,
Ph.D., N.M.D, L.N.C.

Bring healing back into the home! In this beautifully illustrated full color book, Dr. Anna Maria Clement, co-director of the world-famous Hippocrates Health Institute, show us how easy it can be to heal naturally with herbs, natural therapies, baths, flower remedies and aromatherapy. Contains more than 40 years of time-tested, clinical experience with natural healing modalities.

Other Natural Health Resources related to food and diet

Health Care Advisors and Practitioners

Note: Nearly all natural health practitioners will be aware of the vegan vegetarian lifestyle, and will be able to help you with aspects of it; however, they will have varying degrees of expertise. Additionally, while vegetarianism is gaining in popularity, the vast majority of conventionally trained dieticians will not have the knowledge or inclination to recommend a vegetarian or even vegan diet, or be able to coach you successfully. If you are looking for support with the nutritional aspects of vegan nutrition, consider asking for referrals from naturopathic physicians, acupuncturists and chiropractors for dieticians or nutritionists who are actively working with vegan and vegetarian whole-foods nutrition. Also, your local health-food store owner would be a great source for this information, and they often distribute locally produced natural health publications that include practitioners in your area.

American Association of Acupuncture and Oriental Medicine (AAAOM) – Find an acupuncture physician in your area in the "For Patients" tab. (http://www.aaaomonline.org/)

American Association of Naturopathic Physicians – Locate a naturopathic physician who can help you on your path to recovery under the "Find a Doctor" tab. (http://www.naturopathic.org/)

American Chiropractic Association – Locate a chiropractic physician in your area who can help you with structural issues related to health. Some provide nutritional support. Click "Patient/Visitor" on the Welcome screen, and then "Find a Doctor" in the top left-hand corner of the screen. (http://www.acatoday.org/index.cfm)

National Certification Commission for Acupuncture & Oriental Medicine (NCCAOM) – Find an acupuncture physician in your area in the "Find a Practitioner" tab. (http://www.aaaomonline.org/)

*Vegetarian Nutrition, a division of the The Academy of Nutrition & Dietetics – Find a Registered dietician who is a proponent of the vegetarian lifestyle under the "Find an RD" tab at http://vegetariannutrition.net/ *Please see note above on finding a good vegetarian nutritionist.*

Other Groups and Associations

American Vegan Society – Website and newsletters for keeping abreast of the world of vegan vegetarianism. (http://www.americanvegan.org/index.htm)

IDEA Health & Fitness Association – Place where you can get more information on types of exercise and trainers in your area. (http://www.ideafit.com/)

North American Vegetarian Society (NAVS) – Great information on what is happening in the vegetarian world. Plus, they offer an annual conference. (http://www.navs-online.org/)

Organic Consumers Association – Keep up to date on important developments related to the safety of your food. (http://www.organicconsumers.org/)

The United States Department of Agriculture (USDA) – Contains information and links to resources on vegetarianism. (http://fnic.nal.usda.gov/lifecycle-nutrition/vegetarian-nutrition)

The Vegan Society – Lots of information on the vegan lifestyle, including nutritional, medical and lifestyle information. (http://www.vegansociety.com/about/)

The Vegetarian Resource Group – A terrific website for those who are interested in learning more about the vegetarian lifestyle. You will find everything from nutrition information to notices about vegetarian food festivals. Plus, they give you tips on choosing a dietician who has knowledge about the vegan lifestyle. Sign up for their email newsletter here. (http://www.vrg.org/)

Conversion Table & Lists

SIMPLE METRIC CONVERSION CHART

WHEN YOU KNOW…	MULTIPLY BY…	TO FIND…
VOLUME		
teaspoons	4.93	milliliters
tablespoons	14.97	milliliters
fluid ounces	29.57	milliliters
cups	.24	liters
pints	.47	liters
quarts	.95	liters
gallons	3.79	liters
MASS & WEIGHT		
ounces	28.35	grams
pounds	.45	kilograms
TEMPERATURE		
degrees Fahrenheit	(°F − 32) + 1.8	degrees Celsius

Other Helpful Measurements:

EASY U.S. STANDARD MEASUREMENT EQUIVALENTS

LIQUIDS

1 tablespoon = ½ fluid ounce

3 teaspoons = 1 tablespoon

1 cup = 8 ounces

EASY METRIC EQUIVALENTS LIQUID CONVERSIONS

1 tablespoon = 15 milliliters

1 teaspoon = 5 milliliters

1 cup = 250 milliliters

1 ounce = 28.35 grams

16 ounces = .47 liters

1 pound = .45 kilogram

BULK INGREDIENT APPROXIMATIONS

⅓ cup = 2 ounces

1 pound = 4 to 5 cups, packed

1 cup = 250 grams

⅓ cup to ½ cup of nuts = 50 grams

¾ cup of seeds (sesame, flax, sunflower, etc.) = 100 grams

½ cup beans (any type) = 100 grams

½ cup flour, sugar, finely ground meal = 150 to 200 grams

INDEX

A

acai berry, 37
acerola, 37
acorn squash
    Mango Squash Soup, 145
    Spring Scalloped Vegetables, 318
aduki bean(s), 47
    Aduki Bean Salad, 172
    Mykonos Bean Salad, 206
    Thyme for Salad!, 226
adzuki bean(s). *See* aduki bean(s)
agar
    Chocolate Pudding, 354
agave nectar
    Sweet Nutty Spread, 112
alcohol, 12
alfalfa seed(s), 47
alfalfa sprouts, 36, 37
    Walnut and Black Bean Salad, 227
algae
    chlorella. *See* chlorella
    spirulina. *See* spirulina
allergies, 12
    food sensitivities, 12
allspice, 47
almond butter, 47
almond extract, 47
almond milk
    Angel Hair Pasta with Mushrooms and Peas, 230
    Angelica Rice Lady Fingers, 343
    Apple Cinnamon French Toast with Bananas and
        Raspberries, 63
    Banana Caramel Custard, 348
    Bananas Flambé, 351
    Broccoli and Cauliflower with Shiitake Mushrooms, 234
    Broccoli Au Gratin, 237
    Chilled Cherry Dessert Soup, 353
    Cinnamon Pear Pancakes, 68
    Coconut Custard Pie, 356
    Cream of Broccoli Soup, 123
    Cream of Mushroom Soup, 124
    Cream of Sweet Potato Soup, 126
    Dalsaag, 260
    Eggplant Parmesan Sesame, 264
    Fettuccine with Creamy Asparagus Sauce, 269
    Quinoa Pancakes, 77
    Savory Cream of Potato Soup, 162
    Spring Scalloped Vegetables, 318
    Sticky Sweet Rice with Papaya, 382
almond(s), 36, 47
    Crunchy Granola, 70
    Fluffy Raisin Couscous, 72
    Lentil Burgers, 289
    Pear Hazelnut Crisp, 365
    Sweet Cinnamon Oatmeal, 83
    Sweet Nutty Spread, 112
    Toasted Nut Brittle, 385
aloe vera, 33

amaranth, 36, 47
    Amaranth Peach Delight, 62
    Nice Rice Salad, 208
    Seaweed Salad, 215
amino acids, 22
angel hair pasta
    Angel Hair Pasta with Mushrooms and Peas, 230
anise powder, 47
anise seed(s)
    Anise Raisin Bread, 344
anti-inflammatory, 15
antioxidants, 26
APPETIZERS AND SIDE DISHES, 87
apple juice, 47
    Chilled Cherry Dessert Soup, 353
    Sweet Cabbage and Apple Casserole, 321
apple(s), 36, 43
    Apple Banana Turnovers, 347
    Beet Salad, 178
    Sautéed Kale with Fava Beans, 309
    Triple Fruit Oatmeal Delight, 84
    Vegan Apple Cake, 388
apple(s), Gala, 37
apple(s), Golden Delicious
    Pumpkin Cream Soup, 158
    RAW Cinnamon Papaya Pudding, 377
    Truly Trifle, 386
apple(s), Granny Smith, 37
    Apple, Walnut, and Tofu Salad, 173
    Bavarian Cabbage, 90
    Endive Salad, 190
apple(s), Macintosh
    Sweet Cabbage and Apple Casserole, 321
apple(s), Red Delicious, 37
    Orange-Glazed Apples, 362
applesauce
    Apple Cinnamon French Toast with Bananas and
        Raspberries, 63
apple-strawberry juice
    RAW Strawberry Dessert Soup, 378
apricot(s), 36
    Blueberry Apricot Oatmeal, 65
apricot(s), dried
    Banana Coconut Buckwheat Cereal, 64
    Coconut Nut Rice, 69
    Sweet Cinnamon Oatmeal, 83
arame, 37
    Bavarian Cabbage, 90
    Seaweed Salad, 215
Arborio rice
    Saffron Rice, 306
arrowroot powder, 47
arthritis
    causes of, 3, 4
    disability, 5
    risk factors, 8
    types of, 5
artichoke, 37

artichoke heart(s), 37, 47
    Artichoke and Chickpea Salad, 175
    Broccoli Tortellini Salad, 238
    Cool Garden Noodles, 185
    Insalata Siciliana, 200
    Spicy Bulgur Salad, 218
    Superior Spinach Salad, 219
arugula
    Bitters Sweet, 179
    Insalata Siciliana, 200
    Italian Style Pinto Bean Soup, 137
asparagus, 37
    Fettuccine with Creamy Asparagus Sauce, 269
    French Watercress Salad, 195
    Gary's Noodle Soup, 133
    Goulash, 276
    Spaghetti with Garlic Tomato Vegetable Sauce, 316
avocado(s), 36, 37
    Curried Barley with Avocado, 256
    Spicy Raw Spinach and Avocado Soup, 164
    Superior Spinach Salad, 219

B

banana(s), 36, 37
    Apple Banana Turnovers, 347
    Apple Cinnamon French Toast with Bananas and
        Raspberries, 63
    Banana Caramel Custard, 348
    Banana Coconut Buckwheat Cereal, 64
    Blueberry Apricot Oatmeal, 65
    Coconut Cherry Ice Cream, 355
    Hawaiian Rice Cereal, 73
    Nutty Fruit Breakfast, 74
    Raspberry Blueberry Oatmeal, 78
    RAW Banana Pineapple Dessert Soup, 375
    RAW Berry Jello, 376
    Southern-Baked Pumpkin Surprise, 380
    Triple Fruit Oatmeal Delight, 84
    Two Grain Breakfast, 85
barley, 47
    Barley with Collard Greens and Leeks, 89
    Cinnamon Pear Pancakes, 68
    Curried Barley with Avocado, 256
    Nutty Fruit Breakfast, 74
    Two Grain Breakfast, 85
barley flour, 47
basil, 47
    Eggless Zucchini Pesto Quiche, 262
basmati rice
    Favorite Vegetable Soup, 130
    Grecian Olive and Rice Salad, 198
    Hot and Spicy Bean Wraps, 279
    Red Brazilian Rice, 303
    Rice and Lentils, 304
    Saffron Rice, 306
    Sweet and Sour Bean Stew, 319
basmati rice, brown
    Risotto with Tomatoes and Peas, 305
    Sticky Sweet Rice with Papaya, 382
bay leaf, 47

bean sauce, yellow
    Noodles Deluxe, 296
bean sprouts
    Indonesian Sprout Salad, 199
bean threads
    Thai Style Salad, 224
bean(s), 36
    aduki. *See* aduki bean(s)
    black. *See* black bean(s)
    fava. *See* fava bean(s)
    kidney. *See* kidney bean(s)
    mung. *See* mung bean(s)
    navy. *See* navy bean(s)
    pinto. *See* pinto bean(s)
    white. *See* white bean(s)
beet greens, 37
beet(s), 37
    Arugula Orange Pepper Salad, 176
    Beet Salad, 178
    Cold German Leek Salad, 183
    Endive Salad, 190
    Navy Salad, 207
    Thick and Hearty Borscht, 165
bell pepper(s), 37, 41, 43
    Arugula Orange Pepper Salad, 176
bell pepper(s), green
    Aduki Bean Salad, 172
    Brown Rice with Peppers and Herbs, 240
    Crunchy Herbed Green Beans, 255
    Galuska, 271
    Gazpacho, 134
    Greek Tomato Sauce, 97
    Herbed Tofu Croquettes, 104
    Khaloda Algerian Eggplant, 284
    Mykonos Bean Salad, 206
    Red Brazilian Rice, 303
    Tempeh and Green Bean Ragout, 325
    Tempeh with Cacciatore Sauce, 329
    Tempeh with Noodles and Vegetables, 330
    Tofu Orleans, 333
    Vegan Chili Deluxe, 336
    Vegetarian Chopped Liver, 114
bell pepper(s), orange
    Brussels Sprout Creole, 241
    Fettuccine with Creamy Asparagus Sauce, 269
    Hot and Spicy Bean Wraps, 279
bell pepper(s), red
    Algerian Chili, 119
    Bammie Cakes, 233
    Barley with Collard Greens and Leeks, 89
    Broccoli and Cauliflower with Shiitake Mushrooms, 234
    Brown Rice with Peppers and Herbs, 240
    Brussels Sprout Creole, 241
    Cauliflower with Garlic Hummus Sauce, 250
    Crunchy Herbed Green Beans, 255
    Curried Barley with Avocado, 256
    Eggplant Wraps with Roasted Red Pepper Tomato
        Sauce, 266
    Fresh Corn Salad, 196
    Galuska, 271

bell pepper(s), red – *continued*
 Gary's Fat-free Sweet Potato, Black Bean and Chickpea
  Stew, 272
 Heavenly Stuffed Tomatoes, 103
 Holiday Stuffed Mushrooms, 107
 Indian Ratatouille, 280
 Insalata Siciliana, 200
 Italian Mushroom and Potato Salad, 203
 Italian Style Pinto Bean Soup, 137
 Lemon Tofu, 287
 Linguini with Garden Vegetables, 290
 Miso Tofu Soup, 146
 Mushroom-Stuffed Tomatoes, 295
 Nice Rice Salad, 208
 Old Country Potato Soup, 148
 Peppery Pasta Salad, 299
 Potato Tomato Soup, 157
 RAW Cajun Squash Soup, 159
 Red salad, 213
 Saffron Rice, 306
 Sautéed Dandelion Greens with Red Peppers, 308
 Spaghetti Squash Italiano, 314
 Spicy Hummus, 109
 Tempeh with Cacciatore Sauce, 329
 Tempeh with Noodles and Vegetables, 330
 Thyme for Salad!, 226
 Vegetarian Chopped Liver, 114
bell pepper(s), yellow
 Bammie Cakes, 233
 Brown Rice with Peppers and Herbs, 240
 Crunchy Herbed Green Beans, 255
 Indian Ratatouille, 280
 Insalata Siciliana, 200
 Italian Mushroom and Potato Salad, 203
 Mellow Rice Salad, 205
 Miso Tofu Soup, 146
 Noodles Deluxe, 296
 Old Country Potato Soup, 148
 Red salad, 213
 Saffron Rice, 306
 Tempeh with Cacciatore Sauce, 329
berries, 36
bibb lettuce
 Enticing Endive with Berries and Seeds, 188
bilberry, 37
black bean(s), 37, 47
 Aromatic Green Casserole, 231
 Black Bean Sauce, 91
 Divine Potato Casserole, 261
 Gary's Fat-free Sweet Potato, Black Bean and Chickpea
  Stew, 272
 Ginger Black Bean Dip, 96
 Sesame Bean Salad, 217
 Turnip and Black Bean Soup, 167
 Walnut and Black Bean Salad, 227
black pepper, 47
blackberry/ies, 37
 Quinoa Breakfast Delight, 75
black-eyed pea(s)
 Chopped Veggie Bean Salad, 182

black-eyed pea(s) – *continued*
 New Fangled Old Timey Soup, 147
 Okra Curry, 297
bladderwrack, 37
blender. *See* equipment
blueberry/ies, 37, 43
 Blueberry Apricot Oatmeal, 65
 Blueberry Oatmeal with Soy Yogurt, 67
 Coconut Cherry Ice Cream, 355
 Enticing Endive with Berries and Seeds, 188
 Golden Strawberry Blueberry Crumble, 357
 Nutty Fruit Breakfast, 74
 Pretty Parfait, 372
 Raspberry Blueberry Oatmeal, 78
 RAW Berry Jello, 376
 Strawberry Blueberry Sunshine, 80
bok choy
 Jamaican Pepperpot Soup, 140
books, by Gary Null
 Reverse Arthritis and Pain Naturally
  A proven approach to an anti-inflammatory,
  pain-free life, 3
 The Complete Encyclopedia of Natural Healing, 390
 The Joy of Juicing, 390
boswellia, 33
bow-tie pasta
 Italian White Bean Soup with Bowtie Pasta, 139
Bragg's Liquid Aminos, 47
bran, 47
 Crunchy Granola, 70
Brazil nut(s), 36
 Pear Hazelnut Crisp, 365
 Quinoa Breakfast Delight, 75
 Sweet Nutty Spread, 112
bread crumbs, vegan, 47
BREAKFAST, 61
broccoli, 37
 Aromatic Green Casserole, 231
 Artichoke and Chickpea Salad, 175
 Broccoli and Cauliflower with Shiitake Mushrooms, 234
 Broccoli Au Gratin, 237
 Broccoli Tortellini Salad, 238
 Cream of Broccoli Soup, 123
 Forbidden Rice Salad, 192
 Gary's Favorite Casserole, 275
 Golden Broccoli Supreme, 197
 Insalata Siciliana, 200
 Japanese Buckwheat Salad, 204
 Linguini with Garden Vegetables, 290
 Old Country Potato Soup, 148
 Purple Cabbage and Spaghetti Squash, 300
 Sabzi Ka Shorba, 161
 Sweet and Sour Tempeh, 320
 Tahini-Broccoli Cream Dip, 112
 Venice Noodle Soup, 168
bromelain, 29, 73
brown rice
 Artichoke and Chickpea Salad, 175
 Brown Rice with Peppers and Herbs, 240
 Cashewy Bean Soup, 120

brown rice – *continued*
Chickpea and Zucchini Curry, 253
Coconut Nut Rice, 69
Cool Garden Noodles, 185
Favorite Vegetable Soup, 130
Gary's Favorite Casserole, 275
Hawaiian Rice Cereal, 73
Lemon Tree Soup, 144
Mellow Rice Salad, 205
New Fangled Old Timey Soup, 147
Nice Rice Salad, 208
Raisin and Brown Rice Salad, 210
Strawberry Blueberry Sunshine, 80
Swiss Chard with Red Lentils and Carrots, 324
Two Grain Breakfast, 85
brown rice flour
Anise Raisin Bread, 344
brown rice syrup, 47
Brussels sprouts, 37
Brussels Sprout Creole, 241
buckwheat, 36
buckwheat flour
Galuska, 271
buckwheat noodles
Cool Garden Noodles, 185
Gary's Noodle Soup, 133
Japanese Buckwheat Salad, 204
bulgur wheat, 47
California Marinade, 181
Spicy Bulgur Salad, 218
butter
almond. *See* almond butter
peanut. *See* peanut butter
butternut squash
Bitters Sweet, 179
Butternut Squash with Toasted Sesame Sauce, 242
Butternut Tofu, 245
Delectable Tomato Squash Soup, 129
Hearty Winter Soup, 135
Jamaican Squash Soup, 143
Mushroom Bean Curry with Butternut Squash, 292
RAW Cajun Squash Soup, 159
RAW Delectable Tomato Squash Soup, 160
Sweet and Sour Bean Stew, 319

C

cabbage, 37
cabbage, Chinese
Chinese Cabbage Soup, 121
cabbage, green
Bavarian Cabbage, 90
Sweet Cabbage and Apple Casserole, 321
Thick and Hearty Borscht, 165
cabbage, purple
Purple Cabbage and Spaghetti Squash, 300
cabbage, red
Bavarian Cabbage, 90
Favorite Vegetable Soup, 130
Indonesian Sprout Salad, 199
Thick and Hearty Borscht, 165

Cajun seasoning, 47
Cajun Tofu, 247
RAW Cajun Squash Soup, 159
camu camu, 37
cannellini bean(s)
Insalata Siciliana, 200
cantaloupe, 37
Cantaloupe with Cherry Cream, 352
capers, 47
capsaicin, 33, 96
caraway seed(s), 47
Goulash, 276
Seaweed Salad, 215
Sweet Cabbage and Apple Casserole, 321
Thick and Hearty Borscht, 165
carbohydrates, 21
cardamom, 47
Carmen pepper(s)
Cashewy Bean Soup, 120
Noodles Deluxe, 296
Saffron Rice, 306
Sautéed Dandelion Greens with Red Peppers, 308
Carmen pepper(s), red
Eggplant Wraps with Roasted Red Pepper Tomato
Sauce, 266
carob chips
Simple Carob Cake, 379
carrot(s), 37
Arugula Orange Pepper Salad, 176
Carrot Kidney Bean Loaf with Mushroom Gravy, 248
Chopped Veggie Bean Salad, 182
Cold German Leek Salad, 183
Curried Lentil Soup, 128
Enticing Endive with Berries and Seeds, 188
Forbidden Rice Salad, 192
Indonesian Sprout Salad, 199
Italian Style Pinto Bean Soup, 137
Japanese Buckwheat Salad, 204
Lemon Tofu, 287
Lentil Burgers, 289
Millet Coriander Stir-Fry, 291
New Fangled Old Timey Soup, 147
Old Country Potato Soup, 148
Penne Pasta and Kidney Bean Soup, 151
Sabzi Ka Shorba, 161
Saffron Rice, 306
Sassy Bean and Quinoa Salad, 214
Seaweed Salad, 215
Steamy Summer Salad, 220
Swiss Chard with Red Lentils and Carrots, 324
Tempeh Marinara with Rice Penne, 326
Tempeh with Noodles and Vegetables, 330
Thick and Hearty Borscht, 165
cashew(s), 47
Cashewy Bean Soup, 120
Cauliflower with Garlic Hummus Sauce, 250
Coconut Nut Rice, 69
Crunchy Granola, 70
Curried Barley with Avocado, 256
Date Spread, 94

cashew(s) – *continued*
    Herbed Tofu Croquettes, 104
    Lentil Burgers, 289
    Strawberry Blueberry Sunshine, 80
cassava
    Bammie Cakes, 233
cassava flour
    Sweet Cassava Pudding, 383
cat's claw, 33
cauliflower, 37
    Broccoli and Cauliflower with Shiitake Mushrooms, 234
    California Marinade, 181
    Cauliflower with Garlic Hummus Sauce, 250
    Hot Spinach and Bean Soup, 136
    Indian Ratatouille, 280
    Penne Pasta and Kidney Bean Soup, 151
    Sabzi Ka Shorba, 161
    Superior Spinach Salad, 219
cayenne, 33, 41, 47
    Peppery Pasta Salad, 299
celery, 37, 43
    Algerian Chili, 119
    Caponata, 92
    Chopped Veggie Bean Salad, 182
    Cucumber Mint Soup, 127
    Favorite Vegetable Soup, 130
    Goulash, 276
    Herbed Tofu Croquettes, 104
    Jamaican Vegetable Root Stew, 283
    Okra Curry, 297
    Raisin and Brown Rice Salad, 210
    Sweet Cabbage and Apple Casserole, 321
chard green(s), 37
chayote
    Jamaican Vegetable Root Stew, 283
cheese, vegan, 48
chemicals, poisonous
    foods highly sprayed, 43
cherry/ies, 37
    Cantaloupe with Cherry Cream, 352
    Chilled Cherry Dessert Soup, 353
    Coconut Cherry Ice Cream, 355
    Hawaiian Rice Cereal, 73
    Lemon Cherry Cake, 360
chestnut(s), 36
chia seed(s), 36, 47
    Amaranth Peach Delight, 62
    Blueberry Apricot Oatmeal, 65
    Blueberry Oatmeal with Soy Yogurt, 67
    Coconut Nut Rice, 69
    Curried Barley with Avocado, 256
    Dalsaag, 260
    Date Spread, 94
    Eggless Zucchini Pesto Quiche, 262
    Green Pea Millet "Couscous", 277
    Khaloda Algerian Eggplant, 284
    Lentil Burgers, 289
    Mushroom Bean Curry with Butternut Squash, 292
    Nutty Fruit Breakfast, 74
    Old Country Potato Soup, 148

chia seed(s) – *continued*
    Pecan-Maple Chia Custard, 367
    Quinoa Breakfast Delight, 75
    Raspberry Blueberry Oatmeal, 78
    Seven Grain Cereal with Peaches and Walnuts, 79
    Spaghetti with Eggplant Marinara, 315
    Sweet and Sour Bean Stew, 319
    Sweet Cabbage and Apple Casserole, 321
    Sweet Cinnamon Oatmeal, 83
    Triple Fruit Oatmeal Delight, 84
    Vegan Apple Cake, 388
chickpea(s), 47, *See also* garbanzo bean(s)
    Artichoke and Chickpea Salad, 175
    Cauliflower with Garlic Hummus Sauce, 250
    Chickpea and Zucchini Curry, 253
    Coconut Chickpea Burgers, 254
    Gary's Fat-free Sweet Potato, Black Bean and Chickpea Stew, 272
    Goulash, 276
    Sesame Bean Salad, 217
    Spicy Hummus, 109
    Thai Style Salad, 224
chili pepper(s)
    Jamaican Vegetable Root Stew, 283
    Tempeh with Noodles and Vegetables, 330
chili pepper(s), green
    Indian Ratatouille, 280
chili pepper(s), red
    Thai Style Salad, 224
chili powder, 47
chili sauce, 47
    Hot and Spicy Bean Wraps, 279
chipotle pepper(s)
    RAW Cajun Squash Soup, 159
    Spicy Hummus, 109
chlorella, 39
chondroitin sulfate, 29
cinnamon, 47
    Cinnamon Pear Pancakes, 68
    RAW Cinnamon Papaya Pudding, 377
    Sweet Cinnamon Oatmeal, 83
cleanses, 46
clover seed(s), 47
cloves, 47
coconut, 36
    Coconut Custard Pie, 356
    Crunchy Granola, 70
    flakes, 47
    Lemon Cherry Cake, 360
    Sweet Cassava Pudding, 383
coconut flakes
    Banana Coconut Buckwheat Cereal, 64
    Plantain Dessert Tamale, 368
coconut milk, 47
    Chilled Cherry Dessert Soup, 353
    Coconut Cherry Ice Cream, 355
coconut, grated
    Curried Potato Masal, 259
coconut, shredded
    California Marinade, 181

coconut, shredded – *continued*
  Coconut Chickpea Burgers, 254
  Toasted Nut Brittle, 385
collard green(s), 37, 43
  Barley with Collard Greens and Leeks, 89
  Jamaican Pepperpot Soup, 140
collard leaves
  Plantain Dessert Tamale, 368
collard(s), 37
comfrey, 33
condiments, 47
cookies, peach or apricot
  Raspberry Custard, 374
coriander, 47
corn, 37, 48
  Fresh Corn Salad, 196
  Sweet Loaf, 323
  Turnip and Black Bean Soup, 167
couscous, 47
  Chopped Veggie Bean Salad, 182
  Fluffy Raisin Couscous, 72
  Steamy Summer Salad, 220
cranberry/ies, 37
  Fluffy Raisin Couscous, 72
cranberry/ies, dried
  Crunchy Granola, 70
  Two Grain Breakfast, 85
Cream of Buckwheat
  Banana Coconut Buckwheat Cereal, 64
cucumber(s), 37
  Cucumber Mint Soup, 127
  Gazpacho, 134
  Spicy Raw Spinach and Avocado Soup, 164
  Thai Style Salad, 224
cumin, 47
curcumin, 34
currant(s), 36
  Bitters Sweet, 179
  Curried Barley with Avocado, 256
currant(s), dried
  Banana Coconut Buckwheat Cereal, 64
  Fluffy Raisin Couscous, 72
  Sweet Cinnamon Oatmeal, 83
curry, 47
  Butternut Tofu, 245
  Curried Barley with Avocado, 256
  Curried Potato Masal, 259
  Mushroom Bean Curry with Butternut Squash, 292
  Okra Curry, 297

D

daikon
  Millet Coriander Stir-Fry, 291
  Seaweed Salad, 215
dairy, 35
  dairy-free, 3
dairy products
  cause of disease, 5
dairy-free. *See also* non-dairy

dandelion green(s)
  Fennel and Pecan Salad with Peaches, 191
  Sautéed Dandelion Greens with Red Peppers, 308
dandelion(s), 37
dark leafy green(s), 37, *See also* green(s), dark leafy
date sugar, 47
  Chocolate Pudding, 354
  Crunchy Granola, 70
  Golden Strawberry Blueberry Crumble, 357
  Peach Walnut Crisp, 363
date(s), 36
decursinol, 29
DESSERTS, 341
devil's claw, 34
diabetes
  causes of, 10
diet
  anti-inflammation, 21
  vegan vegetarian, 17
Dijon mustard
  Arugula Orange Pepper Salad, 176
  Enticing Endive with Berries and Seeds, 188
  French Watercress Salad, 195
  Navy Salad, 207
  Potato Mustard Soup, 154
dill, 47
disease(s), 13
  Alzheimer's, 4
  arthritis, 4
  cancer, 4
  diabetes, 4
  heart disease, 4
  inflammation, 4
  lupus, 4
disease(s), lifestyle, 6
drug use
  cause of disease, 12
dry mustard, 47
dulse, 37

E

edamame, 48
  Quinoa and Edamame Salad, 209
egg replacer
  vegan, 47
eggplant(s), 37, 41
  Caponata, 92
  Eggplant Parmesan Sesame, 264
  Eggplant Salad, 187
  Indian Ratatouille, 280
  Khaloda Algerian Eggplant, 284
  Shiitake-Stuffed Eggplants, 310
  Spaghetti with Eggplant Marinara, 315
  Vegetarian Lasagna, 337
endive, 37
  Endive Salad, 190
  Enticing Endive with Berries and Seeds, 188
ENTREES, 229
equipment
  blender, 49

equipment – *continued*
    food processor, 49
    food savers, 50
    juicer. *See* equipment
    sprout bags, 50
    vegetable spiralizer. *See* equipment
Essential Fatty Acids, 25
exercise, 18
extract
    grape seed. *See* grape seed extract
    lemon. *See* lemon extract
    stinging nettle, 34
    vanilla. *See* vanilla extract

F

fats, 24
fatty acids, omega-3, 31
fava bean(s), 47
    Sautéed Kale with Fava Beans, 309
Federal Drug Administration, 9
fennel
    Fresh Corn Salad, 196
    Navy Salad, 207
fennel root
    Aromatic Green Casserole, 231
    Fennel and Pecan Salad with Peaches, 191
    Sautéed Kale with Fava Beans, 309
fennel seed(s), 47
fenugreek seed(s), 47
fettuccine
    Fettuccine with Creamy Asparagus Sauce, 269
fiber, 26
    sources of, 26
fig(s), 36
fig(s), dried
    Nutty Fruit Breakfast, 74
    Quinoa Breakfast Delight, 75
flax seed(s), 36, 47
    Crunchy Granola, 70
    Hawaiian Rice Cereal, 73
    Holiday Stuffed Mushrooms, 107
    Strawberry Blueberry Sunshine, 80
    Tempeh with Noodles and Vegetables, 330
flaxseed meal, 48
    Apple Cinnamon French Toast with Bananas and
        Raspberries, 63
    Aromatic Green Casserole, 231
    Banana Coconut Buckwheat Cereal, 64
    Cinnamon Pear Pancakes, 68
    Eggless Zucchini Pesto Quiche, 262
    Eggplant Parmesan Sesame, 264
    Herbed Tofu Croquettes, 104
    Lemon Cherry Cake, 360
    Lemon Tree Soup, 144
    Pecan-Maple Chia Custard, 367
    Potato Pancakes, 108
    Pumpkin Cream Soup, 158
    Quinoa Pancakes, 77
    RAW Cinnamon Papaya Pudding, 377
    Simple Carob Cake, 379

flaxsee meal – *continued*
    Tahini Oat Sauce, 112
    Vegan Apple Cake, 388
    Vegetarian Chopped Liver, 114
flour
    barley. *See* barley flour
    brown rice. *See* brown rice flour
    cassava. *See* cassava flour
    oat. *See* oat flour
    quinoa. *See* quinoa flour
    rice. *See* rice flour, *See* rice flour
    soy. *See* soy flour
flour, spelt
    Golden Strawberry Blueberry Crumble, 357
food processor. *See* equipment
food savers. *See* equipment
food sensitivities, 3, 12
food(s)
    alkaline-forming, to include, 36
    antioxidant-rich, 37
    high in omega-3 fatty acids, 36
    high-acid, 35
    highly sprayed, 43
    organic, 43
    processed and artificial, 35
    rich in folic acid, 37
    to avoid, 35
forbidden rice
    Forbidden Rice Salad, 192
free radical(s), 10, 26
fruit(s), 36, 48
    alkaline-forming, 36
    dried, 47

G

Gamma Linolenic Acid (GLA), 30
garbanzo bean(s), 37
garlic, 37, 39, 47
    Green Plantain Tostones with Garlic Mojo Sauce, 99
    Sliced Tofu with Garlic Sauce, 313
    Spaghetti with Garlic Tomato Vegetable Sauce, 316
gherkin(s)
    Insalata Siciliana, 200
ginger, 37, 47, 48
    Ginger Black Bean Dip, 96
ginger root, 39
ginseng, 34
glucosamine, 30
gluten-free, 3, 47
    Aduki Bean Salad, 172
    Algerian Chili, 119
    Amaranth Peach Delight, 62
    Angelica Rice Lady Fingers, 343
    Anise Raisin Bread, 344
    Apple Banana Turnovers, 347
    Apple, Walnut, and Tofu Salad, 173
    Aromatic Green Casserole, 231
    Artichoke and Chickpea Salad, 175
    Arugula Orange Pepper Salad, 176
    Bammie Cakes, 233

gluten-free – *continued*

Banana Caramel Custard, 348
Banana Coconut Buckwheat Cereal, 64
Bavarian Cabbage, 90
Beet Salad, 178
Bitters Sweet, 179
Black Bean Sauce, 91
Blueberry Apricot Oatmeal, 65
Blueberry Oatmeal with Soy Yogurt, 67
Broccoli and Cauliflower with Shiitake Mushrooms, 234
Broccoli Au Gratin, 237
Brown Rice with Peppers and Herbs, 240
Brussels Sprout Creole, 241
Butternut Squash with Toasted Sesame Sauce, 242
Butternut Tofu, 245
Cajun Tofu, 247
Cantaloupe with Cherry Cream, 352
Caponata, 92
Cashewy Bean Soup, 120
Cauliflower with Garlic Hummus Sauce, 250
Chilled Cherry Dessert Soup, 353
Chocolate Pudding, 354
Coconut Cherry Ice Cream, 355
Coconut Nut Rice, 69
Cold German Leek Salad, 183
Cream of Sweet Potato Soup, 126
Creamy Tofu Dip, 93
Crunchy Herbed Green Beans, 255
Cucumber Mint Soup, 127
Curried Lentil Soup, 128
Curried Potato Masal, 259
Dalsaag, 260
Date Spread, 94
Delectable Tomato Squash Soup, 129
Eggplant Salad, 187
Endive Salad, 190
Enticing Endive with Berries and Seeds, 188
Exotic Tofu Dip, 95
Favorite Vegetable Soup, 130
Forbidden Rice Salad, 192
French Watercress Salad, 195
Fresh Corn Salad, 196
Galuska, 271
Gary's Fat-free Sweet Potato, Black Bean and Chickpea Stew, 272
Gary's Favorite Casserole, 275
Gazpacho, 134
Golden Broccoli Supreme, 197
Goulash, 276
Grecian Olive and Rice Salad, 198
Greek Tomato Sauce, 97
Green Pea Millet "Couscous", 277
Green Plantain Tostones with Garlic Mojo Sauce, 99
Guilt-Free Guacamole, 100
Hawaiian Rice Cereal, 73
Heavenly Stuffed Tomatoes, 103
Holiday Gingerbread, 359
Holiday Stuffed Mushrooms, 107
Hot Spinach and Bean Soup, 136
Indian Ratatouille, 280

gluten-free – *continued*

Indonesian Kale, 282
Indonesian Sprout Salad, 199
Insalata Siciliana, 200
Italian Mushroom and Potato Salad, 203
Italian Style Pinto Bean Soup, 137
Jamaican Pepperpot Soup, 140
Jamaican Squash Soup, 143
Jamaican Vegetable Root Stew, 283
Khaloda Algerian Eggplant, 284
Lemon Tofu, 287
Lemon Tree Soup, 144
Mango Squash Soup, 145
Mellow Rice Salad, 205
Miso Tofu Soup, 146
Mykonos Bean Salad, 206
Navy Salad, 207
Nice Rice Salad, 208
Noodles Deluxe, 296
Okra Curry, 297
Old Country Potato Soup, 148
Onion Soup, 149
Orange-Glazed Apples, 362
Papaya Yam Soup, 150
Pear Hazelnut Crisp, 365
Pears with Raisin Stuffing, 366
Pecan-Maple Chia Custard, 367
Peppery Pasta Salad, 299
Poached Peaches with Raspberry Sauce, 371
Portuguese Kale and Potato Soup, 152
Potato Leek Soup, 153
Potato Mustard Soup, 154
Potato Pancakes, 108
Potato Tomato Soup, 157
Pretty Parfait, 372
Pumpkin Cream Soup, 158
Quinoa and Edamame Salad, 209
Quinoa Breakfast Delight, 75
Quinoa Pancakes, 77
Raisin and Brown Rice Salad, 210
Raspberry Blueberry Oatmeal, 78
Raspberry Custard, 374
RAW Banana Pineapple Dessert Soup, 375
RAW Berry Jello, 376
RAW Cajun Squash Soup, 159
RAW Cinnamon Papaya Pudding, 377
RAW Delectable Tomato Squash Soup, 160
RAW Strawberry Dessert Soup, 378
Red Brazilian Rice, 303
Red Salad, 213
Rice and Lentils, 304
Risotto with Tomatoes and Peas, 305
Sabzi Ka Shorba, 161
Saffron Rice, 306
Sassy Bean and Quinoa Salad, 214
Sautéed Dandelion Greens with Red Peppers, 308
Sautéed Kale with Fava Beans, 309
Savory Cream of Potato Soup, 162
Seaweed Salad, 215
Sesame Bean Salad, 217

gluten-free – *continued*
    Shiitake-Stuffed Eggplants, 310
    Sicilian Green Beans, 311
    Southern-Baked Pumpkin Surprise, 380
    Spaghetti Squash Italiano, 314
    Spicy Hummus, 109
    Spicy Peanut Sauce, 110
    Spicy Raw Spinach and Avocado Soup, 164
    Spicy Tomato Salsa, 111
    Sticky Sweet Rice with Papaya, 382
    Strawberry Blueberry Sunshine, 80
    Superior Spinach Salad, 219
    Sweet and Sour Bean Stew, 319
    Sweet Cabbage and Apple Casserole, 321
    Sweet Cinnamon Cereal, 83
    Sweet Loaf, 323
    Sweet Nutty Spread, 112
    Swiss Chard with Red Lentils and Carrots, 324
    Tahini Potato Salad, 223
    Tempeh and Green Bean Ragout, 325
    Tempeh Marinara with Rice Penne, 326
    Thai Style Salad, 224
    Thick and Hearty Borscht, 165
    Thyme for Salad!, 226
    Toasted Nut Brittle, 385
    Tomato Chutney with Quinoa Flatbread, 334
    Triple Fruit Oatmeal Delight, 84
    Turnip and Black Bean Soup, 167
    Vegan Chili Deluxe, 336
    Vegetarian Chopped Liver, 114
    Walnut and Black Bean Salad, 227
    Warm Potato and Dulse Salad, 227
    Zucchini Soup, 169
goji berry/ies, 37
    Fluffy Raisin Couscous, 72
    Sweet Cinnamon Oatmeal, 83
gomasio, 47
    Japanese Buckwheat Salad, 204
    Tahini Oat Sauce, 112
grain(s), 36
grain(s), whole, 36
grains & flours, 47
grape seed extract, 30
grape(s), 36, 37, 43
grapefruit, 36, 37
grapefruit juice
    RAW Banana Pineapple Dessert Soup, 375
green bean(s), 36
    Crunchy Herbed Green Beans, 255
    Sicilian Green Beans, 311
    Tempeh and Green Bean Ragout, 325
green tea, 39
green(s)
    dark leafy, 48
guava, 37

habanero
    Jamaican Pepperpot Soup, 140
hazelnut(s), 47
    Pear Hazelnut Crisp, 365

health
    program, 20
    support network, 20
    therapies, 20
herb(s), 52
    fresh, 48
herbs and spices
    anti-arthritis, 33
hijiki, 37
    New Fangled Old Timey Soup, 147
    Seaweed Salad, 215
hominy
    Sweet Loaf, 323
honey
    Sweet Nutty Spread, 112
horseradish, 37
how to use this book, 55
Hyaluronic Acid (HA), 30

I

illness, 13
immune system
    suppression of, 5
inflammation
    causes of, 10
    chronic, 15
    definition, 4
    effects, 4
    reduction of, 26
    results of, 9
    risk factors, 8

J

jalapeño
    Gary's Fat-free Sweet Potato, Black Bean and Chickpea
        Stew, 272
    Hot and Spicy Bean Wraps, 279
    Hot Spinach and Bean Soup, 136
    Jamaican Pepperpot Soup, 140
    Spicy Hummus, 109
juice(s), 69
    fresh, consumption of, 17
    freshly squeezed, 48
juice, grapefruit. *See* grapefruit juice
juicer. *See* equipment
juicing
    benefits of, 44

K

kale, 37, 43
    Aromatic Green Casserole, 231
    Gary's Favorite Casserole, 275
    Indonesian Kale, 282
    Italian White Bean Soup with Bowtie Pasta, 139
    Mushroom Bean Curry with Butternut Squash, 292
    Penne Pasta and Kidney Bean Soup, 151
    Portuguese Kale and Potato Soup, 152
    Sautéed Kale with Fava Beans, 309
kelp, 37
kelp flakes, 47

kelp powder, 47
kidney bean(s), 47
 Carrot Kidney Bean Loaf with Mushroom Gravy, 248
 Cashewy Bean Soup, 120
 Hearty Winter Soup, 135
 Hot Spinach and Bean Soup, 136
 Mushroom Bean Curry with Butternut Squash, 292
 Penne Pasta and Kidney Bean Soup, 151
 Sassy Bean and Quinoa Salad, 214
 Sesame Bean Salad, 217
kidney bean(s), red
 Vegan Chili Deluxe, 336
kiwi(s), 36, 37
kombu, 37
 Bavarian Cabbage, 90

L

leek(s)
 Barley with Collard Greens and Leeks, 89
 Cold German Leek Salad, 183
 Potato Leek Soup, 153
 Thick and Hearty Borscht, 165
legume(s), 36
lemon extract
 Lemon Cherry Cake, 360
lemon zest
 Lemon Tofu, 287
lemon(s), 36
 Lemon Tree Soup, 144
lentil sprouts
 Lentil Burgers, 289
lentil(s), 37
 Dalsaag, 260
 Lentil Burgers, 289
lentil(s), green, 47
 Curried Lentil Soup, 128
lentil(s), red, 47
 Hearty Winter Soup, 135
 Rice and Lentils, 304
 Swiss Chard with Red Lentils and Carrots, 324
lentil(s), yellow
 Rice and Lentils, 304
 Sabzi Ka Shorba, 161
 Swiss Chard with Red Lentils and Carrots, 324
lettuce, 37, 43, 48
lifestyle
 healthy, 16
Lima bean(s), 36
lime juice
 Thai Style Salad, 224
lime(s), 36
 Green Plantain Tostones with Garlic Mojo Sauce, 99
linguini
 Tempeh with Noodles and Vegetables, 330
linguini, vegan
 Linguini with Garden Vegetables, 290

M

macadamia nut(s), 47
 Hawaiian Rice Cereal, 73

mango(es), 36, 37
 Mango Squash Soup, 145
 Tomato Chutney with Quinoa Flatbread, 334
mango(es), dried
 Two Grain Breakfast, 85
maple sugar
 Banana Caramel Custard, 348
 Bananas Flambé, 351
maple syrup, 47
 Anise Raisin Bread, 344
 Apple Cinnamon French Toast with Bananas and
  Raspberries, 63
 Bananas Flambé, 351
 Crunchy Granola, 70
 Date Spread, 94
 Pecan-Maple Chia Custard, 367
 Raspberry Custard, 374
maqui berry/ies, 37
marjoram, 47
meal planning, 53
meat
 cause of disease, 5
melon(s), 36
Methylsulfonylmethane (MSM), 30
microwave, 50
milk, non-dairy, 47, 48
 almond. See almond milk
 coconut. See coconut milk, See coconut milk
 rice. See rice milk
millet, 36, 47
 Green Pea Millet "Couscous", 277
 Millet Coriander Stir-Fry, 291
minerals, 30
mint, fresh
 Cucumber Mint Soup, 127
miso, 48
 Lemon Tofu, 287
 Miso Tofu Soup, 146
 Spicy Raw Spinach and Avocado Soup, 164
molasses, 47
multigrain cereal (pre-packaged)
 Seven Grain Cereal with Peaches and Walnuts, 79
mung bean(s), 47
 Favorite Vegetable Soup, 130
mushroom(s), 37
 Angel Hair Pasta with Mushrooms and Peas, 230
 Barley with Collard Greens and Leeks, 89
 Carrot Kidney Bean Loaf with Mushroom Gravy, 248
 Cream of Mushroom Soup, 124
 Eggless Zucchini Pesto Quiche, 262
 Endive Salad, 190
 Herbed Tofu Croquettes, 104
 Holiday Stuffed Mushrooms, 107
 Indian Ratatouille, 280
 Insalata Siciliana, 200
 Italian Mushroom and Potato Salad, 203
 Italian Style Pinto Bean Soup, 137
 Jamaican Vegetable Root Stew, 283
 Linguini with Garden Vegetables, 290
 Mushroom Bean Curry with Butternut Squash, 292

mushroom(s) – *continued*
    Mushroom-Stuffed Tomatoes, 295
    Rice and Lentils, 304
    Sassy Bean and Quinoa Salad, 214
    Sautéed Kale with Fava Beans, 309
    Sicilian Green Beans, 311
    Spaghetti with Eggplant Marinara, 315
    Steamy Summer Salad, 220
    Tahini Potato Salad, 223
    Tofu Orleans, 333
    Vegetarian Lasagna, 337
    Venice Noodle Soup, 168
    Yukon Mashed Potatoes with Mushroom Gravy, 339
mushroom(s), shiitake
    Shiitake-Stuffed Eggplants, 310
    Sweet Loaf, 323
    Tempeh with Cacciatore Sauce, 329
    Tofu Orleans, 333
mustard
    Dijon. *See* Dijon mustard
    dry. *See* dry mustard
    prepared, 48
    spicy. *See* spicy mustard
mustard green(s), 37
mustard seed(s)
    Chickpea and Zucchini Curry, 253
mustard seed(s), black
    Sabzi Ka Shorba, 161

N
Nama Shoyu, 47
navy bean(s)
    Algerian Chili, 119
    Hot and Spicy Bean Wraps, 279
    Navy Salad, 207
    Sweet and Sour Bean Stew, 319
    Vegan Chili Deluxe, 336
nectarine(s), 36, 43
nettle, 34
niacinamide, 31
noni, 37
noodles
    buckwheat. *See* buckwheat noodles
    Venice Noodle Soup, 168
noodles, whole wheat
    Vegetarian Lasagna, 337
nori, 37
nut(s), 36, 37, 47
nutmeg, 47

oat flour, 47
    Apple Banana Turnovers, 347
    Holiday Gingerbread, 359
    Pear Hazelnut Crisp, 365
    Potato Pancakes, 108
    Tahini Oat Sauce, 112
oat(s), 37
    steel-cut, 47
    oat(s), rolled
    Blueberry Oatmeal with Soy Yogurt, 67
    Crunchy Granola, 70

oat(s), rolled – *continued*
    Peach Walnut Crisp, 363
    Quinoa Pancakes, 77
oat(s), steel-cut
    Blueberry Apricot Oatmeal, 65
    Blueberry Oatmeal with Soy Yogurt, 67
    Raspberry Blueberry Oatmeal, 78
    Sweet Cinnamon Oatmeal, 83
    Triple Fruit Oatmeal Delight, 84
oatmeal
    RAW Cinnamon Papaya Pudding, 377
    Sweet Cinnamon Oatmeal, 83
obesity
    causes of, 5, 10
oil(s), 40, 47
    avocado, 47
    flaxseed, 48
    hot chili, 47
    olive, 47, *See* olive oil
    pumpkin seed, 47
    sesame, 47, *See* sesame oil
    walnut, 47, *See* walnut oil
okra, 37
    Indian Ratatouille, 280
    Italian Mushroom and Potato Salad, 203
    Jamaican Vegetable Root Stew, 283
    Khaloda Algerian Eggplant, 284
    Mykonos Bean Salad, 206
    Okra Curry, 297
olive oil
    Artichoke and Chickpea Salad, 175
    Bitters Sweet, 179
    Broccoli Tortellini Salad, 238
    Eggplant Salad, 187
    Forbidden Rice Salad, 192
    Fresh Corn Salad, 196
    Golden Broccoli Supreme, 197
    Grecian Olive and Rice Salad, 198
    Insalata Siciliana, 200
    Mykonos Bean Salad, 206
    Walnut and Black Bean Salad, 227
olive(s), 36, 48
    Fettuccine with Creamy Asparagus Sauce, 269
    Golden Broccoli Supreme, 197
    Grecian Olive and Rice Salad, 198
    Insalata Siciliana, 200
omega-3, 25
omega-6, 25
onion(s), 37
onion(s) – *continued*
    Onion Soup, 149
orange juice
    Fennel and Pecan Salad with Peaches, 191
orange zest
    Orange-Glazed Apples, 362
orange(s), 36
    Arugula Orange Pepper Salad, 176
    Golden Broccoli Supreme, 197
    Pear Hazelnut Crisp, 365
    Sesame Bean Salad, 217

oregano, 47
oregano, fresh
Herbed Tofu Croquettes, 104

P

papaya(s), 36, 37
Papaya Yam Soup, 150
Pretty Parfait, 372
RAW Cinnamon Papaya Pudding, 377
Sticky Sweet Rice with Papaya, 382
paprika, 41, 47
Parmesan cheese, vegan
Angel Hair Pasta with Mushrooms and Peas, 230
Broccoli Au Gratin, 237
Eggplant Parmesan Sesame, 264
Heavenly Stuffed Tomatoes, 103
Vegetarian Lasagna, 337
parsley, 37, 47, 97
parsnip(s)
New Fangled Old Timey Soup, 147
Spring Scalloped Vegetables, 318
pasta
angel hair. *See* angel hair pasta
bow-tie. *See* bow-tie pasta
buckwheat, 47
linguini. *See* linguini
penne. *See* penne
rice, 47
rotelle. *See* rotelle
tortellini. *See* tortellini
pea(s), 36, 37
Green Pea Millet "Couscous", 277
Guilt-Free Guacamole, 100
Insalata Siciliana, 200
Red salad, 213
Risotto with Tomatoes and Peas, 305
Saffron Rice, 306
Steamy Summer Salad, 220
pea(s), pigeon. *See* pigeon pea(s)
peach(es), 36, 43
Fennel and Pecan Salad with Peaches, 191
Peach Walnut Crisp, 363
Poached Peaches with Raspberry Sauce, 371
Seven Grain Cereal with Peaches and Walnuts, 79
peach(es), dried
Amaranth Peach Delight, 62
peanut butter, 47
Spicy Peanut Sauce, 110
pear(s), 36
Cinnamon Pear Pancakes, 68
pear(s) – *continued*
Pear Hazelnut Crisp, 365
Triple Fruit Oatmeal Delight, 84
pear(s), Bartlett
Pears with Raisin Stuffing, 366
pecan(s), 37, 47
Amaranth Peach Delight, 62
Chopped Veggie Bean Salad, 182
Fennel and Pecan Salad with Peaches, 191
Mellow Rice Salad, 205
Pecan-Maple Chia Custard, 367

penne
Penne Pasta and Kidney Bean Soup, 151
penne, rice
Tempeh Marinara with Rice Penne, 326
pepper(s)
Carmen. *See* Carmen pepper
cayenne. *See* cayenne
chipotle. *See* chipotle pepper(s)
habanero. *See* habanero
jalapeño. *See* jalapeño
pepper(s), hot
Spicy Tomato Salsa, 111
persimmons, 36
pesto sauce
Eggless Zucchini Pesto Quiche, 262
pharmaceuticals, 12
phytochemicals. *See* phytonutrients
phytonutrients, 27
pie shell, vegan
Coconut Custard Pie, 356
Sweet Potato Pie, 384
pigeon pea(s)
Jamaican Vegetable Root Stew, 283
pimiento(s)
Gazpacho, 134
pine nut(s), 47
Caponata, 92
Eggless Zucchini Pesto Quiche, 262
pineapple, 36
Hawaiian Rice Cereal, 73
Hawaiian Tempeh Kebabs, 278
Pretty Parfait, 372
Raisin and Brown Rice Salad, 210
RAW Banana Pineapple Dessert Soup, 375
Sweet and Sour Tempeh, 320
pineapple juice
Lemon Cherry Cake, 360
pinto bean(s), 37, 47
Italian Style Pinto Bean Soup, 137
pistachio, 47
Endive Salad, 190
plantain(s)
Green Plantain Tostones with Garlic Mojo Sauce, 99
Plantain Dessert Tamale, 368
plum(s), 37
Pear Hazelnut Crisp, 365
Stewed Plums, 381
positive thinking, 16
potato(es), 37, 41, 43
Cream of Broccoli Soup, 123
Curried Potato Masal, 259
Italian Mushroom and Potato Salad, 203
Jamaican Vegetable Root Stew, 283
Khaloda Algerian Eggplant, 284
Old Country Potato Soup, 148
Potato Leek Soup, 153
Potato Tomato Soup, 157
Savory Cream of Potato Soup, 162
Tahini Potato Salad, 223
Thick and Hearty Borscht, 165

potato(es) – *continued*
　Venice Noodle Soup, 168
potato(es), red
　Indonesian Kale, 282
potato(es), Russet, 37
potato(es), Yukon Gold
　Divine Potato Casserole, 261
　Indian Ratatouille, 280
　Portuguese Kale and Potato Soup, 152
　Potato Mustard Soup, 154
　Potato Pancakes, 108
　Spring Scalloped Vegetables, 318
　Warm Potato and Dulse Salad, 227
　Yukon Mashed Potatoes with Mushroom Gravy, 339
probiotics, 31
processed foods
　cause of disease, 5
protein, 22
prune(s), 37
　Sweet Cabbage and Apple Casserole, 321
pumpkin, 37
　Jamaican Vegetable Root Stew, 283
　Pumpkin Cream Soup, 158
　Southern-Baked Pumpkin Surprise, 380
pumpkin seed(s), 47
　Quinoa Breakfast Delight, 75
　Red Brazilian Rice, 303

Q

quercetin, 31
quince, 36
quinoa, 36, 47
　Aromatic Green Casserole, 231
　Gary's Favorite Casserole, 275
　Quinoa and Edamame Salad, 209
　Quinoa Breakfast Delight, 75
　Sassy Bean and Quinoa Salad, 214
quinoa flour, 47
　Quinoa Pancakes, 77
　Tomato Chutney with Quinoa Flatbread, 334

R

adicchio
　Angel Hair Pasta with Mushrooms and Peas, 230
　Endive Salad, 190
　Red salad, 213
dish sprouts, 36
dish(es), 37
isin(s), 36
　Amaranth Peach Delight, 62
　Anise Raisin Bread, 344
　Banana Coconut Buckwheat Cereal, 64
　Crunchy Granola, 70
　Fluffy Raisin Couscous, 72
　Japanese Buckwheat Salad, 204
　Pears with Raisin Stuffing, 366
　Raisin and Brown Rice Salad, 210
　Sweet and Sour Bean Stew, 319
pberry jam
　Raspberry Custard, 374
　Truly Trifle, 386

raspberry/ies, 36, 37
　Apple Cinnamon French Toast with Bananas and
　　Raspberries, 63
　Nutty Fruit Breakfast, 74
　Poached Peaches with Raspberry Sauce, 371
　Pretty Parfait, 372
　Quinoa Pancakes, 77
　Raspberry Blueberry Oatmeal, 78
　Raspberry Custard, 374
　RAW Berry Jello, 376
raw food(s), 3, 22, 42, 53, 54, 164
　RAW Banana Pineapple Dessert Soup, 375
　RAW Berry Jello, 376
　RAW Cajun Squash Soup, 159
　RAW Cinnamon Papaya Pudding, 377
　RAW Delectable Tomato Squash Soup, 160
　RAW Strawberry Dessert Soup, 378
　the benefits of, 42
red bean(s), 37
red kidney bean(s), 37
　Date Spread, 94
red leaf lettuce
　Brussels Sprout Creole, 241
red pepper flakes, 47
rice
　Arborio. *See* Arborio rice
　basmati. *See* basmati rice
　brown. *See* brown rice
　brown basmati. *See* basmati rice, brown
　Cauliflower with Garlic Hummus Sauce, 250
　forbidden. *See* forbidden rice
rice flour, 47
　Angelica Rice Lady Fingers, 343
　Golden Strawberry Blueberry Crumble, 357
　Unfried Zucchini Fritters, 113
rice milk
　Chocolate Pudding, 354
　Yukon Mashed Potatoes with Mushroom Gravy, 339
romaine lettuce
　Thyme for Salad!, 226
rosemary, 47
rotelle, quinoa
　Peppery Pasta Salad, 299

S

S.A.D.. *See* Standard American Diet
S-Adenosylmethionine (SAMe), 31
saffron
　Saffron Rice, 306
sage, 47
SALADS, 171
saturated fats
　connection to inflammation & disease, 25
sauce
　bean. *See* bean sauce
sea palm, 37
sea salt, 47
seed(s), 36, 37, 47
　alfalfa. *See* alfalfa seed(s)
　black mustard. *See* mustard seed(s), black

INDEX

seed(s) – *continued*
  caraway. *See* caraway seed(s)
  chia. *See* chia seed(s)
  clover. *See* clover seed(s)
  fennel. *See* fennel seed(s)
  fenugreek. *See* fenugreek seed(s)
  flax. *See* flax seed(s)
  for sprouting, 47
  pumpkin. *See* pumpkin seed(s)
  sesame. *See* sesame seed(s)
  sunflower. *See* sunflower seed(s)
sesame, 36
sesame oil
  Aduki Bean Salad, 172
  Butternut Squash with Toasted Sesame Sauce, 242
  Japanese Buckwheat Salad, 204
  Sesame Bean Salad, 217
  Tahini Potato Salad, 223
sesame seed(s)
  black & white, 47
  Coconut Chickpea Burgers, 254
  Eggplant Parmesan Sesame, 264
  Gary's Fat-free Sweet Potato, Black Bean and Chickpea
      Stew, 272
  Indonesian Sprout Salad, 199
  Mushroom-Stuffed Tomatoes, 295
  Navy Salad, 207
  Sesame Bean Salad, 217
  Tahini Potato Salad, 223
  Tomato Chutney with Quinoa Flatbread, 334
shiitake mushroom(s)
  Broccoli and Cauliflower with Shiitake Mushrooms, 234
sleep, 18
Smoking
  cause of disease, 10
snack(s), 42
SOUPS, 117
soy, 37
soy flour
  Bananas Flambé, 351
soy yogurt
  Cucumber Mint Soup, 127
soybean(s), 36
spaghetti
  Spaghetti with Eggplant Marinara, 315
  Tempeh with Cacciatore Sauce, 329
spaghetti sauce, vegan, 47
spaghetti squash
  Purple Cabbage and Spaghetti Squash, 300
  Spaghetti Squash Italiano, 314
spicy mustard
  Quinoa and Edamame Salad, 209
spinach, 37, 43
  Dalsaag, 260
  Eggless Zucchini Pesto Quiche, 262
  Gary's Noodle Soup, 133
  Grecian Olive and Rice Salad, 198
  Heavenly Stuffed Tomatoes, 103
  Hot Spinach and Bean Soup, 136
  Sassy Bean and Quinoa Salad, 214

spinach – *continued*
  Spicy Bulgur Salad, 218
  Spicy Raw Spinach and Avocado Soup, 164
  Superior Spinach Salad, 219
  Vegetarian Lasagna, 337
spirulina, 39
split peas
  Gary's Favorite Casserole, 275
sprout bags. *See* equipment
sprouted bean(s), 36
sprouts, 37
squash, 37
  acorn. *See* acorn squash
  butternut. *See* butternut squash
  spaghetti. *See* spaghetti squash
  yellow. *See* yellow squash
Standard American Diet, 1, 5, 8, 9, 10, 30, 35, 53, 59
  contents, 5
strawberry/ies, 36, 37, 43
  Coconut Custard Pie, 356
  Golden Strawberry Blueberry Crumble, 357
  RAW Strawberry Dessert Soup, 378
  Strawberry Blueberry Sunshine, 80
  Truly Trifle, 386
stress, 15, 18
  physiological, 15
substitutions, 52
sugar
  date. *See* date sugar
  maple. *See* maple sugar
sugar-free desserts
  Cantaloupe with Cherry Cream, 352
  Chilled Cherry Dessert Soup, 353
  Pretty Parfait, 372
  RAW Strawberry Dessert Soup, 378
sultana(s)
  Fluffy Raisin Couscous, 72
  Raisin and Brown Rice Salad, 210
summer squash
  Steamy Summer Salad, 220
sunflower seed(s), 47
  Butternut Tofu, 245
  California Marinade, 181
  Crunchy Granola, 70
  Enticing Endive with Berries and Seeds, 188
  Herbed Tofu Croquettes, 104
  Jamaican Squash Soup, 143
sunflower seed(s) – *continued*
  Japanese Buckwheat Salad, 204
  Strawberry Blueberry Sunshine, 80
sunflower sprouts
  Arugula Orange Pepper Salad, 176
  Enticing Endive with Berries and Seeds, 188
  Indonesian Sprout Salad, 199
Superoxide Dismutase (SOD), 32
supplements
  anti-arthritis, anti-inflammation, 29
sweet potato(es)
  Broccoli Au Gratin, 237
  Cream of Sweet Potato Soup, 126

sweet potato(es) – *continued*
Gary's Fat-free Sweet Potato, Black Bean and Chickpea Stew, 272
Papaya Yam Soup, 150
Pecan-Maple Chia Custard, 367
Sweet Potato Pie, 384
Vegetarian Lasagna, 337
Swiss chard
Swiss Chard with Red Lentils and Carrots, 324
syrup
brown rice. *See* brown rice syrup
maple. *See* maple syrup

T

Tabasco, 47
tahini, 47
Cauliflower with Garlic Hummus Sauce, 250
Spicy Peanut Sauce, 110
Sweet Nutty Spread, 112
Tahini Oat Sauce, 112
Tahini Potato Salad, 223
Tahini-Broccoli Cream Dip, 112
tamari, 47
tamarind
Noodles Deluxe, 296
tangerine(s), 36
tarragon, 47
teff, 36
tempeh, 36, 48
Grecian Olive and Rice Salad, 198
Hawaiian Tempeh Kebabs, 278
Sweet and Sour Tempeh, 320
Tempeh and Green Bean Ragout, 325
Tempeh Marinara with Rice Penne, 326
Tempeh with Cacciatore Sauce, 329
Tempeh with Noodles and Vegetables, 330
Thai rice noodles
Noodles Deluxe, 296
thyme, 47
Thyme for Salad!, 226
thyme, fresh
Herbed Tofu Croquettes, 104
tofu, 36, 48
Apple, Walnut, and Tofu Salad, 173
Broccoli and Cauliflower with Shiitake Mushrooms, 234
Butternut Tofu, 245
Cajun Tofu, 247
Cantaloupe with Cherry Cream, 352
Chinese Cabbage Soup, 121
Creamy Tofu Dip, 93
Exotic Tofu Dip, 95
Goulash, 276
Heavenly Stuffed Tomatoes, 103
Herbed Tofu Croquettes, 104
Lemon Tofu, 287
Miso Tofu Soup, 146
Noodles Deluxe, 296
Pumpkin Cream Soup, 158
Purple Cabbage and Spaghetti Squash, 300
Raspberry Custard, 374

tofu – *continued*
Sliced Tofu with Garlic Sauce, 313
Tahini-Broccoli Cream Dip, 112
Thai Style Salad, 224
Tofu Orleans, 333
Truly Trifle, 386
tomato(es), 37, 41
Algerian Chili, 119
Arugula Orange Pepper Salad, 176
Barley with Collard Greens and Leeks, 89
Caponata, 92
Chickpea and Zucchini Curry, 253
Delectable Tomato Squash Soup, 129
Divine Potato Casserole, 261
Eggplant Salad, 187
Eggplant Wraps with Roasted Red Pepper Tomato Sauce, 266
Enticing Endive with Berries and Seeds, 188
Fettuccine with Creamy Asparagus Sauce, 269
Galuska, 271
Gary's Favorite Casserole, 275
Gazpacho, 134
Goulash, 276
Greek Tomato Sauce, 97
Heavenly Stuffed Tomatoes, 103
Hot and Spicy Bean Wraps, 279
Indian Ratatouille, 280
Indonesian Kale, 282
Insalata Siciliana, 200
Italian White Bean Soup with Bowtie Pasta, 139
Jamaican Vegetable Root Stew, 283
Khaloda Algerian Eggplant, 284
Linguini with Garden Vegetables, 290
Mellow Rice Salad, 205
Mushroom-Stuffed Tomatoes, 295
Okra Curry, 297
Old Country Potato Soup, 148
Penne Pasta and Kidney Bean Soup, 151
Potato Tomato Soup, 157
RAW Delectable Tomato Squash Soup, 160
Red Brazilian Rice, 303
Red salad, 213
Risotto with Tomatoes and Peas, 305
Sicilian Green Beans, 311
Spaghetti Squash Italiano, 314
Spaghetti with Eggplant Marinara, 315
Spaghetti with Garlic Tomato Vegetable Sauce, 316
Spicy Raw Spinach and Avocado Soup, 164
Spicy Tomato Salsa, 111
Tempeh and Green Bean Ragout, 325
Tempeh Marinara with Rice Penne, 326
Tempeh with Cacciatore Sauce, 329
Thyme for Salad!, 226
Tomato Chutney with Quinoa Flatbread, 334
Vegan Chili Deluxe, 336
Vegetarian Lasagna, 337
tortellini
Broccoli Tortellini Salad, 238
tortillas
Hot and Spicy Bean Wraps, 279

toxin(s)
    chemical, 13
    environmental, 20
trans-fats
    connection to inflammation & disease, 25
transitioning to vegetarian lifestyle, 53
turmeric, 34, 47
turnip(s)
    Turnip and Black Bean Soup, 167

V

vanilla extract, 47
variations, 52
vegetable broth, 47
vegetable spiralizer. *See* equipment
vegetable(s), 48
    alkaline-forming, 37
    green leafy, 36, 89
    nightshade, 37, 41
    non-green leafy, 36
    sea, 37, 47
vinegar
    apple cider, 47
    balsamic, 47
vitamin(s)
    anti-arthritis, 29
    antioxidant, 29
    B complex, 32
    K, 32

W

wakame, 37
    Jamaican Vegetable Root Stew, 283
    Seaweed Salad, 215
walnut oil
    Apple, Walnut, and Tofu Salad, 173
    Beet Salad, 178
    California Marinade, 181
    Chopped Veggie Bean Salad, 182
    Cool Garden Noodles, 185
    Endive Salad, 190
    Green Plantain Tostones with Garlic Mojo Sauce, 99
    Indonesian Sprout Salad, 199
    Mellow Rice Salad, 205
    Nice Rice Salad, 208
    Raisin and Brown Rice Salad, 210
    Red salad, 213
    Sassy Bean and Quinoa Salad, 214
    Seaweed Salad, 215
    Spicy Bulgur Salad, 218
    Superior Spinach Salad, 219
    Thyme for Salad!, 226
walnut(s), 36, 47
    Apple, Walnut, and Tofu Salad, 173
    Aromatic Green Casserole, 231
    Beet Salad, 178
    Crunchy Granola, 70
    Heavenly Stuffed Tomatoes, 103
    Holiday Gingerbread, 359
    Indonesian Sprout Salad, 199
    Nutty Fruit Breakfast, 74

walnut(s) – *continued*
    Peach Walnut Crisp, 363
    Pretty Parfait, 372
    Seven Grain Cereal with Peaches and Walnuts, 79
    Superior Spinach Salad, 219
    Vegetarian Chopped Liver, 114
    Walnut and Black Bean Salad, 227
water, purified, consumption of, 17
watercress, 37
    Cream of Sweet Potato Soup, 126
    French Watercress Salad, 195
    New Fangled Old Timey Soup, 147
watermelon, 36
wheat
    bulgur. *See* bulgur wheat
wheat germ, 47
    Herbed Tofu Croquettes, 104
wheatgrass, 37
white bean(s), 47
    Italian White Bean Soup with Bowtie Pasta, 139
    Red salad, 213
white willow bark, 34
whole wheat flour
    Bananas Flambé, 351
    Lemon Cherry Cake, 360
    Peach Walnut Crisp, 363
    Vegan Apple Cake, 388
wild green(s), 37

Y

yam(s), 37
    Jamaican Pepperpot Soup, 140
    Papaya Yam Soup, 150
yellow squash
    Spaghetti with Garlic Tomato Vegetable Sauce, 316
yogurt, soy, 48
    Blueberry Oatmeal with Soy Yogurt, 67

Z

zucchini
    Chickpea and Zucchini Curry, 253
    Eggless Zucchini Pesto Quiche, 262
    Hawaiian Tempeh Kebabs, 278
    Indian Ratatouille, 280
    Millet Coriander Stir-Fry, 291
    Spaghetti with Garlic Tomato Vegetable Sauce, 316
    Unfried Zucchini Fritters, 113
    Venice Noodle Soup, 168
    Zucchini Soup, 169